AF769192

# The Michigan State Constitution

**The Oxford Commentaries on the State Constitutions of the United States**
*G. Alan Tarr, Series Editor*

*Professor G. Alan Tarr,* Director of the Center on State Constitutional Studies at Rutgers University, serves as General Editor for this important new series which in its entirety will cover each of the 50 states. Each volume of The Oxford Commentaries on the State Constitutions of the United States contains a historical overview of the state's constitutional development, plus a section-by-section analysis of the state's current constitution. Other features included in the volumes are the text of the state's constitution, a bibliographic essay, table of cases, and index. This series provides essential reference tools for those investigating state constitutional development and constitutional law.

# The Michigan State Constitution

Susan P. Fino

THE OXFORD COMMENTARIES ON THE
STATE CONSTITUTIONS OF THE UNITED STATES
*G. Alan Tarr, Series Editor*

OXFORD
UNIVERSITY PRESS

OXFORD
UNIVERSITY PRESS

*Oxford University Press, Inc., publishes works that further Oxford University's objective of excellence in research, scholarship, and education.*

Oxford New York
Auckland Cape Town Dar es Salaam Hong Kong Karachi Kuala Lumpur Madrid Melbourne Mexico City Nairobi New Delhi Shanghai Taipei Toronto

With offices in
Argentina Austria Brazil Chile Czech Republic France Greece Guatemala Hungary Italy Japan Poland Portugal Singapore South Korea Switzerland Thailand Turkey Ukraine Vietnam

Copyright © 2011 by Susan P. Fino

Published by Oxford University Press, Inc.
198 Madison Avenue, New York, New York 10016

Oxford is a registered trademark of Oxford University Press
Oxford University Press is a registered trademark of Oxford University Press, Inc.

All rights reserved. No part of this publication may be reproduced, stored in a retrieval system, or transmitted, in any form or by any means, electronic, mechanical, photocopying, recording, or otherwise, without the prior permission of Oxford University Press, Inc.

Library of Congress Cataloging-in-Publication Data

Fino, Susan P., 1954-
The Michigan state constitution / Susan P. Fino.
p. cm. — (The Oxford commentaries on the state constitutions of the United States)
Includes bibliographical references and index.
ISBN 978-0-19-977908-6 (hardback)
1. Constitutional law—Michigan. 2. Constitutional history—Michigan. I. Title. II. Series.
KFM46011963.A6 F556 2011
342.77402—dc22 2011001730

**Note to Readers**
This publication is designed to provide accurate and authoritative information in regard to the subject matter covered. It is based upon sources believed to be accurate and reliable and is intended to be current as of the time it was written. It is sold with the understanding that the publisher is not engaged in rendering legal, accounting, or other professional services. If legal advice or other expert assistance is required, the services of a competent professional person should be sought. Also, to confirm that the information has not been affected or changed by recent developments, traditional legal research techniques should be used, including checking primary sources where appropriate.

*(Based on the Declaration of Principles jointly adopted by a Committee of the American Bar Association and a Committee of Publishers and Associations.)*

**You may order this or any other Oxford University Press publication by visiting the Oxford University Press website at www.oup.com**

For Judy
My Sister and My Best Friend

# ■ CONTENTS

# ■ SERIES FOREWORD

In 1776, following the declaration of independence from England, the former colonies began to draft their own constitutions. Their handiwork attracted widespread interest, and draft constitutions circulated up and down the Atlantic seaboard, as constitution-makers sought to benefit from the insights of their counterparts in sister states. In Europe, the new constitutions found a ready audience seeking enlightenment from the American experiments in self-government. Even the delegates to the Constitutional Convention of 1787, despite their reservations about the course of political developments in the states during the decade after independence, found much that was useful in the newly adopted constitutions. And when James Madison, fulfilling a pledge given during the ratification debates, drafted the Federal Bill of Rights, he found his model in the famous Declaration of Rights of the Virginia Constitution.

By the 1900s, however, few people would have looked to state constitutions for enlightenment. Instead, a familiar litany of complaints was heard whenever state constitutions were mentioned. State constitutions were too long and too detailed, combining basic principles with policy prescriptions and prohibitions that had no place in the fundamental law of a state. By including such provisions, it was argued, state constitutions deprived state governments of the flexibility they needed to respond effectively to changing circumstances. This—among other factors—encouraged political reformers to look to the federal government, which was not plagued by such constitutional constraints, thereby shifting the locus of political initiative away from the states. Meanwhile, civil libertarians concluded that state bills of rights, at least as interpreted by state courts, did not adequately protect rights and therefore looked to the federal courts and the federal Bill of Rights for redress. As power and responsibility shifted from the states to Washington, so too did the attention of scholars, the legal community, and the general public.

During the early 1970s, however, state constitutions were "rediscovered." The immediate impetus for this rediscovery was former President Richard Nixon's appointment of Warren Burger to succeed Earl Warren as Chief Justice of the United States Supreme Court. To civil libertarians, this appointment seemed to signal a decisive shift in the Supreme Court's jurisprudence, because Burger was expected to lead the Court away from the liberal activism that had characterized the Warren Court. They therefore sought ways to safeguard the gains they had achieved for defendants, racial minorities, and the poor during Warren's tenure from erosion by the Burger Court. In particular, they began to look to state bills of rights to secure the rights of defendants and to support other civil-liberties claims that they advanced in state courts.

This "new judicial federalism," as it came to be called, quite quickly advanced beyond its initial concern to evade the mandates of the Burger Court. Indeed, less than two decades after it originated, it has become a nationwide phenomenon. For when judges and scholars turned their attention to state constitutions, they discovered an unsuspected richness. They found not only provisions that paralleled the federal Bill of Rights but also constitutional guarantees of the right to privacy and of gender equality, for example, that had no analogue in the U.S. Constitution. Careful examination of the text and history of state guarantees revealed important differences between even those provisions that most resembled federal guarantees and their federal counterparts. Looking beyond state declarations of rights, jurists and scholars discovered affirmative constitutional mandates to state governments to address such important policy concerns as education and housing. Taken altogether, these discoveries underlined the importance for the legal community of developing a better understanding of state constitutions.

Yet the renewed interest in state constitutions has not been limited to judges and lawyers. State constitutional reformers have renewed their efforts with notable success: since 1960, ten states have adopted new constitutions and several others have undertaken major constitutional revisions. These changes have usually resulted in more streamlined constitutions and more effective state governments. Also, in recent years political activists on both the left and the right have pursued their goals through state constitutional amendments, often enacted through the initiative process, under which policy proposals can be placed directly on the ballot for voters to endorse or reject. Scholars too have begun to rediscover how state constitutional history can illuminate changes in political thought and practice, providing a basis for theories about the dynamics of political change in America.

Susan Fino's fine study of the Michigan Constitution is the latest volume in the series, The Oxford Commentaries on the State Constitutions of the United States, which reflects this renewed interest in state constitutions and will contribute to our knowledge about them. Because the constitutional tradition of each state is distinctive, the volume begins with the history and development of the Michigan Constitution. It then provides the full text of Michigan's current constitution, with each section accompanied by commentary that explains the provision and traces its origins and its interpretation by the courts and other governmental bodies. For readers with a particular interest in a specific aspect of Michigan constitutionalism, the book offers a bibliography of the most important sources dealing with the constitutional history and constitutional law of the state. Finally, the book concludes with a table of cases cited in the history and constitutional history, as well as a subject index.

*G. Alan Tarr*

# PREFACE

As a quintessential cartoon native New Yorker, I used to believe that Michigan was a frontier somewhere west of the Mississippi. I came to Michigan for a position at Wayne State University. I stayed in Michigan because I came to love it. This book on Michigan's Constitution helped me grow in my love and appreciation of this state. From its first constitution in 1835, Michigan has been a state with a strong democratic impulse married to a healthy mistrust of power. We elect all manner of public officials for short terms of office to keep them responsive to the people. At the same time, we carefully limit their authority in our fundamental law to keep them from becoming too responsive to fleeting issues or passions.

Michigan has a long tradition of vigilance for individual rights, without losing sight of the need for public good or working together for a public purpose. Our Declaration of Rights carefully sets forth the rights and freedoms of the individual, but we sometimes choose to limit our liberty and property under law to provide for public health and welfare or to conserve our natural resources. Our constitution provides for a vigorous state government with a powerful chief executive, while simultaneously maintaining one of the oldest and strongest systems of local home rule in the United States. We prize an independent judiciary, although we elect our judges to keep them subject to our will. We have a heritage of support for education that dates to the Northwest Ordinance, and we have fostered a sound system of public education. Yet, we have made the deliberate decision to make our universities independent of the legislature such that they may pursue truth in a climate of academic freedom. We do not like taxes, and we have a tendency to earmark them for particular purposes. However, we will tax ourselves and spend our resources for education, health, transportation, and the environment. We have disagreed with each other and we have made our share of mistakes, but on the whole I think we are in pretty good constitutional shape as we approach the next millennium.

I have an unusually long litany of thanks for help with this book. Al Tarr and Mim Vasan were most helpful, careful, and patient editors. Without their careful guidance and gentle prodding, I never could have seen this project to completion. Georgia Clark and her crack squad of law librarians—particularly Janice Selberg and Heather Braithwaite Simmons—tracked down obscure pamphlets and moldy tracts from the various Michigan constitutional conventions. Wayne State University has been generous with financial support. Dean Gary Heberlein of the Graduate School and Dean Sue Marx Smock of the College of Urban, Labor and Metropolitan Affairs provided grants to give me the time to do summer research. Several members of the state legislature helped me secure the latest information on constitutional amendments. Senator Jack Faxon, Representative Maxine Berman, and Representative John Freeman were all most generous with their time and attentive to my requests. Two individuals gave me invaluable technical assistance. My graduate student, Matthew Perry, entered the computer age, mastered LEXIS, and prepared the Table of Cases. Betty Walker (together with Morgan and Sara) labored long hours over the Index. To Stanley Friedelbaum, who introduced me to the intriguing world of state constitutions fifteen years ago, I owe a special debt of gratitude. My family, particularly my Mom, Dad, and Grandma (also known as Iole Aida Enis D'Ulisse Fino), provided moral support and endured more than their fair share of my mood swings and fretting. Then, of course, there are my friends: Tim Jarzembowski, Jerald Haber, Mike Wood, Harold Weiner, "Virtual" Bob Frank, and that budding young scholar, Davita Burkhead-Weiner. These are the people that stood by me and refused to roll their eyes or flee in terror when I managed to turn any reference to Michigan into an invitation to share my latest abstruse discoveries. Only they can truly understand how trying it is to suffer a discourse on the constitutional meaning of self-liquidating or revenue bonds.

PART ONE

# The History of the Michigan Constitution

# INTRODUCTION

The study of state constitutions has long been eclipsed by the study of the federal Constitution. The Supreme Court of the United States, under the leadership of Chief Justice Earl Warren, seized the Fourteenth Amendment's due process clause and used it as a vehicle to impose specific federal requirements on the states. By the end of the 1960s, almost all of the Bill of Rights, originally understood as commands to the national government, became applied to the states as a requirement of the Fourteenth Amendment's due process clause. This "incorporation" of the Bill of Rights into the Fourteenth Amendment shifted the emphasis from state to federal standards for the protection of life, liberty, and property.

Federal High Court activism does not alone account for the decline in reliance on the states, their courts and their constitutions. Some states, particularly in the South, used states' rights arguments to attempt to stop desegregation during the 1950s and 1960s. Litigants pressing constitutional equality claims came to rely almost exclusively on federal courts and the Fourteenth Amendment.

Republican dominance of the presidency for the last twenty years has gradually changed the tenor of the United States Supreme Court. Richard Nixon's four appointees to the Court arrested the expansion of the federal rights of criminal defendants. And the addition of the justices appointed by President Ronald Reagan cemented a conservative majority. This shift to the right has enhanced the importance of the states, particularly state courts and state constitutions.

The Republican politics of the past two decades emphasized the "new federalism" with its goal of returning decision-making power to the states. State governments are now required to assume a more active role in regulatory affairs and the administration of various programs. This expanded role for the states necessitates reexamination of the capacity of state government to shoulder these new responsibilities. State constitutional provisions on taxation, finance, local government, and the civil service will undoubtedly feature prominently in programs guided by the new federalism.

Civil libertarians have urged a new federalism of their own: the "new judicial federalism." Justice William Brennan of the United States Supreme Court has encouraged litigants to consider state alternatives to the conservative federal courts.[1] He has suggested that his fellow liberals rely on the protections in state constitutions to preserve and extend the legacy of the Warren Court.

Given these trends, it is critical that citizens as well as government officials study and understand the Michigan Constitution. Although the document borrows from the federal Constitution (such as a tripartite system of government and a bicameral legislature), there is much that distinguishes Michigan from the national government and other states.

In considering the Michigan Constitution, especially in areas where there are similarities between the Michigan Declaration of Rights and the federal Bill of Rights, it is important to understand the doctrine of independent and adequate state grounds. Often litigants will offer both federal and state constitutional arguments in support of the same point in the same case. Faced with both arguments, a state court has three options: It can base its decision on both grounds, the federal Constitution alone, or the state constitution alone. If the state court rules on the basis of both constitutions or the federal Constitution, the decision is open to review by a federal court, since the decision contains federal issues thereby creating federal jurisdiction. If the state court rules on the basis of the state constitution alone—without intertwining the state arguments with federal arguments—the court has ruled on independent and adequate state grounds, and the decision is shielded from federal review. A state court may wish to shield a decision from federal review if, for example, the court has interpreted the state search and seizure provision to afford a criminal defendant greater protection for his or her rights than is presently available under the federal Fourth Amendment.

---

[1] William J. Brennan, "State Constitutions and the Protection of Individual Rights," *Harvard Law Review* 90 (1977): 489–504.

State court judges must be very careful writing opinions to be sure that their decision cannot be reviewed by a federal court. In *Michigan v. Long* (1983), the United States Supreme Court set down the standards for independent and adequate state grounds. Generally, when both federal and state arguments appear in a state court's decision, a federal court can review the decision unless the state court makes a plain statement that the decision rests exclusively on state law.

Some readers may fear that the doctrine of independent and adequate state grounds could be used to provide less protection for rights and liberties than the federal Constitution as interpreted by the U.S. Supreme Court. This situation can never happen. Article VI of the federal Constitution provides that the federal Constitution, acts of Congress, and treaties are the supreme law of the land. The article specifically binds state judges to the supremacy clause, the laws of any state notwithstanding. Therefore, state courts using state law are precluded from detracting from the requirements of the federal Constitution.

## ■ THE MICHIGAN CONSTITUTION IN A COMPARATIVE PERSPECTIVE

Like all state constitutions, the four constitutions of the state of Michigan borrow fundamental elements from the federal model. There is a tripartite system of government with separate legislative, executive, and judicial branches. The provision for separation of powers and checks and balances is designed to limit government so that the threat to liberty is minimized. A Declaration of Rights further explicitly limits the government, as is the case with the federal Bill of Rights. There are important differences between the state and the federal constitutions. The federal government has functioned under only one Constitution although it has been amended 27 times. Only Massachusetts has had but one constitution; every other state has had at least two. Louisiana has written eleven constitutions and Georgia, nine. The national government is a government of enumerated (or delegated) powers; it only possesses those powers carved from the states and assigned to it by the Constitution. State governments stand on different ground: State governments possess plenary authority, which means that the power of states to govern is complete in itself and admits no qualifications or limits except those imposed by law. State constitutions generally do not assign particular powers to the state government. State governments are free to act in any area they choose so long as they do not transgress the limits imposed by the federal or the state constitutions. In other words, if an action is not prohibited, it is possible.

This statement is as true in Michigan as it is in any state. Given the enormous potential power of state governments, state constitutions often contain a level of detail not seen in the federal Constitution. The federal Constitution with its amendments contains about 7,300 words, while the constitution of Georgia, for example, contains around 48,000. Michigan's Constitution of 1963 contains approximately 20,000 words—just about the national average.[2] Daniel J. Elazar (1982) has identified a number of common state constitutional provisions designed to limit this enormous potential power and define the role of the state government. State constitutions contain: (1) an explicit declaration of rights; (2) a description of the structures of government including legislative apportionment; (3) provisions on finance including taxation, borrowing, and spending; (4) provisions detailing the state's responsibilities in areas such as education and transportation; (5) specific provisions on state land and natural resources; and (6) a description of the relationship of the state government to local government.[3] All four of Michigan constitutions have contained these typical elements.

Despite these similarities between Michigan's constitutions and those of the federal government and other states, Michigan's constitutions are unique. They have been shaped by unique forces. Michigan history, political culture, and economic development all have contributed to the evolution of the state's constitutional order.

## CONSTITUTIONAL BEGINNINGS

Michigan's political and legal history begins with the Ordinance of 1784, which was passed by the Congress of the Confederation at the urging of Thomas Jefferson. The Ordinance of 1784 decreed that ten future states would be carved from the Northwest Territories. Jefferson himself provided "fanciful" names for the future states, one of which was "Michigania." This was the first mention of Michigan as a political unit (Dunbar and May, 1980: 113). The 1784 Ordinance had a critical omission: It neglected to provide a mechanism for the orderly transition from territory to statehood. On the impetus of land speculators who held property in the territories, Congress passed the Northwest Ordinance of 1787 to govern the territories and establish a three stage progression towards statehood with increasing degrees of self-governance.[4]

---

[2] These figures are from Albert L. Sturm, "The Development of American State Constitutions," *Publius* 12 (Winter, 1982): 57–98.

[3] Daniel J. Elazar, "The Principles and Traditions Underlying State Constitutions," *Publius* 12 (Winter, 1982): 11–25.

[4] The Ordinance of 1787 was passed by the Congress of the Confederation sitting in New York City. After ratification of the Constitution, one of the first acts of the new Congress was to adopt the Ordinance and modify some of its terms to bring it into line with the structure of the new national government. See Act of Congress, August 7, 1979, 1 U.S. Stat. Chapter VII, pp. 50–53. See also James V. Campbell, *Outlines of the Political History of Michigan* (Detroit: Schober and Company, 1876), pp. 209–10.

The Northwest Ordinance of 1787 is regarded as a unique document in American legal history. James V. Campbell (1876: 207) argued that the Northwest Ordinance was "not ... properly a statute" because it was not subject to repeal or alterations in its most important provisions. These "forever unalterable" articles governed: religious toleration, the declaration of rights and liberties, the encouragement of education and the protection of the rights of Native Americans, the relationship between the territory and the Union, the creation of new states, and the prohibition of slavery (Campbell, 1876: 208–9). For Campbell, the Northwest Ordinance could be viewed from two perspectives: In one sense, it can be viewed as a kind of constitution for the territories, since it protected rights and set up a framework for government. In another sense, the Northwest Ordinance was a kind of compact between the people of the territory and the United States, because it seemed to guarantee eventual statehood as the territory grew in population.

Under the first stage of the progression towards statehood, a governor, three judges and a secretary were appointed by Congress. The governor and judges could not write new laws but were empowered to adopt any laws then in existence in any of the thirteen original states. Any law so adopted could be rejected by Congress. A territory could progress to the second stage upon demonstration that it contained 5,000 free, adult male inhabitants. At this stage, a territory could convene a general assembly to make laws provided that no law could be repugnant to any principle or article in the Ordinance of 1787. Thus, it was established early in Michigan that legislation must conform to a set of higher laws. The general assembly was to consist of an elected governor, an elected house of representatives, and a legislative council that was to be appointed by Congress from among the elected representatives. The territory now could send one delegate to Congress who could debate but not vote. Finally, when a territory contained 60,000 free, adult male inhabitants, it was to be admitted as a state.

The Northwest Ordinance contained a number of important provisions that have become part of the fabric of all subsequent Michigan constitutions. It guaranteed religious liberty, provided for due process of law, banned cruel or unusual punishment, and prohibited slavery or involuntary servitude. In fact, Thomas M. Cooley, Michigan's most noted legal scholar, praised the Northwest Ordinance for its "far-seeing statesmanship" and saw it as "the beginning of the end of American slavery" (Cooley, 1885: 127, 130). A particularly important provision held that "religion, morality, and knowledge being necessary to good government and the happiness of mankind, schools and the means of education shall forever be encouraged." Michigan's deep commitment to education that has been embodied in every constitution can be traced to the Northwest Ordinance of 1787.

At the initiative of Governor Stevens T. Mason, a census of the territory was taken in 1834. The results demonstrated that Michigan had more than enough inhabitants to qualify for statehood under the Northwest Ordinance. A state constitutional convention was called and a constitution written for the state in 1835.[5] All this was done without the benefit of an "enabling act" from Congress, the usual first step in the formal process of securing statehood.[6]

This first state constitution "was framed quickly by men of modest means" (Dunbar and May, 1980: 245). Harold M. Dorr (1940: 17) found that "with few exceptions the social position and the educational advantages enjoyed by the delegates were fairly representative of those of the people generally." Dorr found that half of the delegates were farmers; twenty came from the "less prosperous" class of businesses and worked as merchants, lumber men, and mill operators; ten were lawyers, and the remainder included "two surveyors, five doctors, an editor, an architect, and three schoolmasters." Most of the delegates were educated "outside books and classrooms" but a number of delegates held degrees from prestigious East Coast colleges and universities. A majority were Democrats who were committed to the ideals of Jacksonian democracy with its emphasis on expanded political participation.

The delegates assembled in Detroit in May 1835 to begin the work of framing Michigan's first constitution. The organizational details of the convention were worked out quickly, but "the delegates with few exceptions were at a loss . . . how to proceed to draft a constitution" (Dorr, 1940: 24). In fact, most delegates were interested only in the Bill of Rights and the suffrage provision (Dorr, 1940: 25). Ultimately, the convention created a committee of nineteen responsible for the development of an initial draft of the proposed constitution. The framers borrowed freely from extant state constitutions, particularly those of Connecticut and New York since most of the delegates came from New England and Middle Atlantic states (Dunbar and May, 1980: 245; Fuller, 1939: 245). Thus, elements of the political culture of New England came to be injected into Michigan politics and constitutional law.

The Constitution of 1835 began with a preamble that invoked the compact element of the Northwest Ordinance and declared that the territory met the qualifications that entitled it to admission to the Union. Article I, the Bill of Rights, followed, and its twenty provisions differed substantially from its federal counterpart. Article I was a mixture of elements of the Northwest Ordinance,

---

[5] Michigan adopted a state constitution in 1835 but did not formally become a state until January 26, 1837. Michigan maintained that the Ordinance of 1787 guaranteed admission to the Union after satisfying the stipulated population requirement. Congress, however, was reluctant to admit Michigan until the long-standing border dispute with Ohio was settled. Congress admitted Michigan to the Union only after the state accepted a Michigan-Ohio boundary line drawn by Congress.

[6] The enabling act allows the territory to call a constitutional convention and develop a state constitution. The proposed state constitution is then submitted to Congress for scrutiny, which allows Congress to guarantee that the people have a "republican form of government" as required by the federal Constitution.

the federal Bill of Rights, Connecticut's Bill of Rights, and some provisions unique to Michigan. The Bill of Rights began with a statement that all political power is inherent in the people and that it is the right of the people to alter or reform or abolish a form of government when required by the public good. Scrupulous attention was paid to the separation of church and state: Three different provisions addressed matters of religious liberty. Section 4 of Article I guaranteed the right of all to worship according to the dictates of conscience but also assured that no one would be compelled to attend or support any religious institution, or pay taxes to support "any minister of the gospel or teacher of religion." Section 5 prohibited the use of any state money for religious societies or seminaries, and section 6 made certain that civil and religious rights would not be affected by beliefs on matters of religion. While these religion provisions were similar to ideas embodied in the Northwest Ordinance, they represented a considerable expansion of specific protections for religious liberty.

The 1835 Bill of Rights also preserved the guarantees of due process of the Northwest Ordinance, but as is the case for religious liberty, the document elaborated on the requirements of due process. Individuals are protected against unreasonable searches and seizures, the right of trial by jury is "inviolate," accused persons must receive a speedy and public trial and the assistance of counsel, double jeopardy is proscribed and criminal trials are to proceed by grand jury indictment. And again as in the Northwest Ordinance, there can be no "cruel and unjust" punishment.

The framers of the Bill of Rights also took great pains to guarantee freedom of expression. Section 7 provided that "every person may freely speak, write, and publish his sentiments on all subjects being responsible for the abuse of that right; and no law shall be passed to restrain or abridge the liberty of speech or press." Section 20 protected the right to assemble freely, to consult for the common good, and to instruct representatives and to petition the legislature. Although the framers of the 1835 Constitution had available to them the federal Bill of Rights as a model, they chose to write a unique Michigan Bill of Rights with greater and more specific protections for the liberty of the people.

Article II on the elective franchise "excited more interest and was debated with greater zeal than any other section" (Dorr, 1940: 30). Liberal members of the convention wished to extend the franchise to resident aliens but their proposals were ultimately defeated. The franchise was extended to "every white male citizen above the age of twenty-one years having resided in the state six months." Despite the racial and gender-based restrictions on the right to vote (which occurred in every state constitution at the time), Article II may be seen as a liberal definition of the electorate because it contained no property holding qualifications for voting.

The 1835 document divided the government into three branches—legislative, executive, and judicial—and Article III required that these departments be "distinct" and that one department never exercise the powers of another. Thus, the Michigan Constitution of 1835 insisted on a much more rigorous definition of separation of powers than is found in the federal Constitution. The governor and members of the bicameral legislature were subject to short, two-year terms of office to guarantee responsiveness to the people. Supreme court justices were appointed by the governor with advice and consent of the state senate. However, lower court judges, including county, circuit, and probate judges, were to be elected—a provision that was considered ultra-democratic in its day. Michigan also adopted the New England traditions of local government, making all minor officers of the state (such as sheriffs, county treasurers, registrars of deeds, coroners, and surveyors) subject to popular choice (Fuller, 1939: 248–49). Michigan's tendency towards a large number of elected offices can be traced to the Constitution of 1835.

The concern for education that began with the Northwest Ordinance continued in the new state constitution. Article X was devoted exclusively to the responsibilities of the legislature with respect to public education. The legislature was directed to establish a perpetual fund, derived from the sale or rental of state lands, for the maintenance of schools. Section 3 required the creation of a system of common schools that would be kept up three months each year. Libraries were to be established, at least one in each township, "as soon as the circumstances of the state permit." These libraries were to be funded by fees persons would pay to be exempt from military service and by all county fines assessed for breach of penal laws. Higher education was not neglected. A land-grant university was envisioned, "with such branches as the public convenience may hereafter demand for the promotion of literature, the arts and sciences." The educational system of the state was to be overseen by a superintendent of public instructions who was to be appointed by the governor, with consent of both houses of the legislature, for a term of two years.

The education article of the Constitution of 1835 also began a tradition that would later become critical in urging constitutional reform in the 1960s—the earmarking of state revenues. The state constitution committed certain funds to certain purposes denying the governor and the legislature fiscal flexibility. In times of financial stress, such earmarking would hamstring the state government and prevent the allocation of funds to areas of dire need.

The framers of Michigan's first constitution were proud of their achievement. One delegate remarked, "The constitution is brief and contains not a solitary superfluous paragraph or even phrase. It is pronounced by all who have examined it, to be one of the most plain, finished and Republican instruments to be found in the Union" (Dorr, 1940: 29). Many scholars maintain that the 1835 Constitution was the best Michigan has written. Fuller (1939: 249) praised its "dignity and simplicity." Cooley (1885: 225) pointed out that it was carefully restricted to the fundamentals of government, and, since it did not enter the field of everyday legislation, could be regarded as a model constitution. Campbell

(1876: 464) found the broad, flexible document appropriate to the needs of a growing state.

The Constitution of 1835 was not without its weaknesses, however. Scarce attention was paid to the regulation of corporations. The only reference to corporations appears in Article XII under "Miscellaneous Provisions," which required a two-thirds vote of each house of the legislature for an act of incorporation. The legislature was "beset by an importunate and aggressive lobby" of business interests "who became intolerable nuisances and threw suspicion on the honesty of everything they favored" (Campbell, 1876: 538). Charters were granted to railroads and banks without personal liability clauses so that when these business entities failed, investors had no recourse. More importantly, the Miscellaneous Provisions required the state to encourage internal improvements. "Extravagant application" of this clause almost bankrupted the state (Bald, 1954: 198). These difficulties, coupled with the fact that other Midwestern states—Ohio, Illinois, Iowa, and Wisconsin—were engaged in constitution-making, led to a new constitutional convention in 1850.

Between 1835 and 1850, there were three amendments to the state constitution. The most important of these was the second amendment, which was proposed in 1843 and approved by the people in 1844. This amendment provided for a popular referendum on every law authorizing the borrowing of state money or the issuing of state stocks. Any such law had to be approved by a majority of people voting on the question before the law could take effect. Michigan's experiments with direct democracy began early in its constitutional history, well before the initiative, referendum, and recall became Populist reforms at the turn of the nineteenth century.[7]

## CONSTITUTIONAL REVISION: 1850

The Constitution of 1850 was framed under the continuing influence of Jacksonian democracy, "the prevailing radicalism" of the day (Cooley, 1885: 299). Of the 100 men who gathered in Lansing on June 3, 1850, almost half were farmers and 80 were Democrats. Like the convention of 1835, most of the delegates came from New York and the New England states; there was only a single native of Michigan in attendance. Unlike the earlier convention, 22 lawyers participated in the drafting of the new constitution, and one is tempted to believe that the new document's prolixity is a function of their presence. There was no real evidence of the influence of corporate wealth or railroad interests

[7] The 1835 Constitution did allow for direct democracy at the township level. The elections article was carefully written so as not to rule out the possibility of local government via a New England–style town meeting. There is no evidence that this form of government took root in Michigan despite the constitution provision.

(see, generally, Fuller, 1939: 327). There were a number of common sentiments felt at the convention. The Jacksonian impulse led the authors of the new constitution to expand the democratic framework of government and to bring "the exercise of power as near as possible to the people concerned and to make responsibility constant and direct" (Cooley, 1885: 300). Yet, the same mechanisms that rendered government so responsive to the people—frequent elections and a large number of elected officials—also made policies unpredictable and subject to change as the personnel of government changed. The desire for both accountability and consistency brought the framers to a constitutional solution: Public policy would be written into the state constitution. The Constitution of 1850 would contain much language more appropriate to a simple statute than a state constitution. Things as diverse and specific as a prohibition on state lotteries to the dedication of certain funds to education would be written into Michigan's fundamental law.

The result of the efforts of the convention was a constitution over twice the length of the 1835 one, and that "ranks as the worst state constitution" for some scholars (Dunbar and May, 1980: 368). The separate Bill of Rights disappeared, and the guarantees of individual rights and liberties were spread throughout the constitution as specific limits on particular branches of government or lumped together under the "miscellaneous provisions." Thus, important provisions on the right of petition and assembly, the exercise of eminent domain, and the prohibition of slavery or involuntary servitude were reduced to inclusion as "miscellaneous." The great guarantees of religious liberty, freedom of speech and press, and prohibitions against bills of attainder, ex post facto laws, and laws impairing the obligations of contracts were tacked onto the end of the legislative article. The judicial article concluded with the rights usually associated with civil and criminal procedure: due process of law, the protection against unreasonable searches and seizures, and coerced confessions, trial by jury, and so forth. This unusual arrangement had the effect of reducing time-honored, hard-won human freedoms to mere afterthoughts.

The Constitution of 1850 began with a definition of the territorial jurisdiction of the state and an article establishing Lansing as the seat of government.[8] Article III created a rigid system of separation of powers by dividing the government into the traditional three branches and expressly forbidding members of one branch of government from exercising the powers of another. The legislative article, Article IV, was the most detailed and engendered the most debate at the convention. The bicameral legislature consisted of a senate and a house of representatives. The 32 senators were elected for two-year terms by single district. The house of representatives was to consist of between 64 to 100 members also serving two-year terms of office. The constitution required that each representative

[8] The original state capital was Detroit. In 1847, the legislature moved the capital to Lansing.

district contain an equal number of inhabitants. The bulk of Article IV was devoted to issues of legislative procedure. The particulars of compensation, postage and mileage allowances for legislators, and the title and form of bills were all carefully set out. Hidden among the minutiae of Article IV were provisions on ethics in government that seem quite progressive for the time. A legislator was prohibited from having a direct or indirect interest in state or county contracts while sitting in the legislature and for one year after. The legislature was forbidden to increase payment to any public officer, agent, or contract after a service was provided or a contract negotiated.

As members of the legislature, the governor and lieutenant governor were elected for two-year terms of office. The governor was responsible for the faithful execution of the laws and was given the power to call out the militia, veto acts of the legislature, convene the legislature in extraordinary circumstances, and grant reprieves and pardons. The overall power of the governor, however, was decreased. The governor lost the power to appoint supreme court justices with the advice and consent of the senate. The chief executive officer could no longer remove judges and justices by joint address to the legislature. And a number of lesser executive officers such as the secretary of state, the superintendent of public instruction, the state treasurer, the commissioner of the land office, the auditor general, and the attorney general were to be chosen at biennial general elections. Popular selection of these officials meant that the governor lost direct control of offices charged with important executive functions. The lieutenant governor had a limited role in state government, which basically meant that the lieutenant governor's role was to wait for the governor to die or go away. The lieutenant governor succeeded the governor in case of death, inability, absence from the state, resignation, or impeachment and served as president of the state senate.

The Supreme Court of Michigan suffered a strange fate under the Constitution of 1850. For a period of six years after the adoption of the new constitution, there was no supreme court. Instead, the eight judges of the circuit courts formed an ad hoc tribunal that served as the state court of last resort. The legislature was empowered to create a supreme court of one chief justice and three associate justices after the passage of six years. Like all other important state officials, the justices of the new supreme court would be chosen by the people at a general election for eight-year terms of office. The work horses of the judicial system were the circuit courts. These courts, presided over by an elected judge serving a six-year term of office, heard criminal and civil cases and possessed both original jurisdiction and appellate jurisdiction over lower courts. Below the circuit courts were the probate courts of each county, and at the bottom of the judicial hierarchy were the justices of the peace, a maximum of four who could be elected in each township.

After the legislative article, the most debated issue at the Constitutional Convention of 1850 was the qualifications of voters. Fuller (1939: 330) reports two reasons for the controversy. The first and most controversial concerned suffrage for free African Americans. In Fuller's (1939: 228) words: "Difficult questions were asked, such as, for example, why an industrious taxpaying Negro should be refused a vote which was given to a recently arrived immigrant with an alien tongue. The discussion inevitably led to the subject of 'social equality' and the possibility of intermarriage between blacks and whites." Ultimately, the issue was dropped out of fear of jeopardizing ratification of the entire constitution. The issue of suffrage for free African Americans was submitted later as a separate amendment. It failed by an overwhelming majority. The second point in debate concerned the treatment of the new immigrants arriving in the United States. These new immigrants from Germany and Scandinavia were skilled farmers, miners, and lumberers. The framers of the constitution wanted to encourage settlement of these new arrivals in Michigan; therefore, few qualifications for state citizenship were included in the constitution (Dunbar and May, 1980: 329). In the end, the franchise was extended to white male citizens over the age of twenty-one and "civilized male inhabitants of Indian descent" also meeting the same age qualifications.

The new constitution also took care to remedy the defects in the 1835 document. Article XIV was devoted to finance and taxation, with an emphasis on extinguishing the state debt and balancing the state budget. The article also forbade the state from becoming involved in internal improvements, the very power that had nearly bankrupted the state under the old constitution. And, again in response to the 1835 experience, the corporations article specifically held the officers and stockholders of every corporation personally liable for all debts incurred by the corporation.

Like all constitutions, the Constitution of 1850 contained provisions for its own amendment and revision. Amendments could be proposed in either house of the legislature, and if the amendment was approved by a two-thirds majority in each house, it would be submitted to the people at the next election. Ratification required a majority vote of electors qualified to vote for members of the legislature. The new constitution included a novel provision borrowed from the ideas of Thomas Jefferson: every sixteen years (or at other times when the legislature saw the need) the question of general constitutional revision would be put to the voters. If a majority of voters voting in the election called for constitutional revision, then the legislature was obligated to call for a constitutional convention.

Despite its length, its complex statutory language, and the opinion of some historians, the Constitution of 1850 was not without merit. There were a number of progressive elements scattered throughout its articles and clauses. Women's suffrage was debated and failed. However, the article on exemptions (Article XVI) protected the property rights of a married woman, such that her real and personal estate could not be liable for the debts and obligations of her husband. Some provisions streamlined the criminal justice process and others contributed to moral reform. The old grand jury system was eliminated as "cumbrous and generally unnecessary" (Cooley, 1885: 301), and juries of less than twelve individuals could be impanelled. Prison manufacture was prohibited, and indeterminate criminal sentences were allowed through an amendment in 1902 in the interest of rehabilitation. The state was required to establish and maintain institutions for the benefit of the "deaf, dumb, blind, and insane," and libraries in each city and township. Free public primary schools were to be created by the legislature within five years of the adoption of the constitution, and schools would have a term of at least three months. Finally, the constitution directed the legislature to establish a university for instruction in agriculture and the natural sciences, the first constitution of any state to do so (Dunbar and May, 1980: 332). The constitution was ratified by a margin of 36,169 to 9,436.

The Constitution of 1850 was amended eleven times between ratification and 1867. For the most part, these amendments involved mundane measures: an alteration in compensation and mileage allowance for legislators and the time of adjournment of the legislature, changes in the banking and corporations provisions, and modification in the selection of the board of regents for the University of Michigan. And, for the most part, these constitutional issues generated little public interest. Real controversy in constitutional revision, rooted in the moral and political issues of the time, did not arise until after the Civil War.

## IN THE WAKE OF THE CIVIL WAR

The citizens of the state of Michigan took advantage of the 1850 provision allowing for general constitutional revision every sixteen years. In 1866, by a margin of 3 to 1, the people voted in favor of a new constitutional convention. Delegates convened in Lansing in May 1867, finished writing a new constitution in August, and submitted the document to the people in April 1868. It was promptly rejected by a vote of 110,582 to 71,729. There was something in the proposed constitution to displease almost anyone. The major issue was suffrage for African Americans; the convention delegates had dropped the word "white" from the list of qualifications for voters. As Fuller (1939: 409) points out, Michiganians "willingly sacrificed to save the Union, yet the majority of citizens were not ready to endorse Negro suffrage." The situation was particularly ironic since Michigan's congressional delegation had voted to impose black suffrage on the South (Dunbar and May, 1980: 446). The net result of this action was that African Americans could vote in Mississippi before they could in Michigan. It was not until 1869 that a state constitutional amendment expanding the franchise to blacks passed by a narrow margin (54,105 to 50,598), just one year before the Fifteenth Amendment to the federal Constitution would have nullified any racial restrictions on voting. Other provisions of the proposed constitution also alienated sections of the electorate: raising official salaries, prohibition, and local grants for railroad construction.

Some provisions represented relatively harmless reforms. The document proposed to elect the governor and lieutenant governor from a single slate, limit the size of the house of representatives, and increase the term of office of senators to four years. Given the bundle of controversial issues contained in the new constitution, however, it is not surprising that the document fared as poorly as it did at the polls.

The year 1873 brought another effort at general constitution revision but this time through a novel mechanism. A joint resolution of the legislature empowered the governor to create a constitutional commission. A bipartisan commission was created (although the Republicans held a 2-to-1 advantage) and a draft of a new constitution was submitted to Governor John J. Bagley. The governor called the legislature into special session to review the document, although the legislature did not make major changes in the work of the commission. Fuller (1939: 410) saw the proposed constitution as containing "nothing of a radical nature." The proposed constitution sought to: introduce the item veto on appropriations bills, increase the number of supreme court justices to five, allow the governor to appoint circuit court judges, permit the legislature to regulate railroad rates, and limit the fiscal powers of local government (Sturm, 1963: 6). The greatest single source of controversy—the extension of the franchise to women—was contained in a separate amendment submitted to the people at the same time. Both the proposed new constitution and the women's suffrage amendment met the same fate at the polls: overwhelming rejection. Unlike the 1867 proposal, there was no particular fatal error in the 1873 document that can account for its failure. Fuller (1939: 410) simply says, "the people were opposed to wholesale revision and were satisfied to leave well enough alone."

Michigan voters rejected general constitutional revision in 1882 and 1898, the dates stipulated by the sixteen-year interval requirement in the 1850 Constitution. Legislative initiatives on general constitutional revision were also spurned in 1890 and 1892. There were, however, 56 amendments proposed, of which half were ratified. As Fuller (1939: 410) put it, "The old Constitution was being kept abreast of the times, not by total revision but by amendment."

After the turn of the century, there was strong sentiment in Michigan that a nineteenth-century constitution was no longer adequate for a state in the process of transition from agriculture to industry. Politics in the state and nation had also changed. The Democratic Party that had dominated the constitutional conventions of 1835 and 1850 was in disarray, and Republicans came to control state house and White House. This period was also the age of reform—the Progressive Era—during which idealistic individuals believed that government and society could and should be changed for the better. In 1907, Governor Fred M. Warner campaigned successfully for a new constitution. Warner saw the landslide victory of Teddy Roosevelt as an indication of widespread popular support for progressive reforms (Dunbar and May, 1980: 517). On October 22, 1907, 96 delegates gathered in Lansing to write a new constitution for the Michigan of the twentieth century.

## CONSTITUTIONAL CHANGE FOR THE TWENTIETH CENTURY

The delegates to the convention reflected changes in the Michigan economy, politics, and society. All but eight delegates were Republicans (Dunbar and May, 1980: 518) and only seven could claim farming as their principal occupation. At least 60 delegates had some legal training. Most of the other participants at the convention were associated with various business interests, although representatives of organized labor were present (Fuller, 1939: 410). Conservative Republicans dominated the convention and resisted wholesale change, so that the new constitution was essentially a reworking and expansion of the 1850 document (Dunbar and May, 1980: 518). In fact, Fuller (1939: 412) believes that the greatest single accomplishment of the 1907 convention was in the organization of the constitution: the restoration of the separate Bill of Rights and the placement of the several provisions under the appropriate headings.

The Constitution of 1908, which was ratified by a vote of 244,705 to 130,783, was a ponderous code of seventeen lengthy articles riddled with much statutory language. The framers continued the trend begun in 1850 to embed policy decisions in the constitution in order to place them beyond the reach of a fickle legislature. The basic framework of government remained from the 1850 Constitution, but the new document went into much greater detail on legislative procedure and introduced the governor's item veto for appropriations. Guarantees of individual rights and liberties were collected and reestablished as a separate Declaration of Rights. The article on taxation and finance grew in length and detail as did the article on local government. The local government provisions gave greater autonomy to cities and villages. Under earlier constitutions, Michigan used special legislation to govern cities and villages. The 1908 Constitution required general laws on city government and allowed each city or village to frame a charter and pass municipal ordinances for its own purposes (Fairlie, 1908: 445). Women's suffrage was again debated and defeated, but women were allowed to vote on bond issues (Dunbar and May, 1980: 513). Progressive elements at the convention argued for inclusion of provisions to give the people a direct role in the initiation or approval of laws, and for a way for the people to oust an official before his term of office was completed. The wisdom of these mechanisms (initiative, referendum, and recall) was debated at the convention. Unhappily for the Progressives, Conservatives outnumbered them and the move to direct democracy failed. A limited form of initiative was included in the constitution. The 1908 document allowed for constitutional amendment to be proposed by voter petition as well as through the traditional way of proposing amendment through a vote of two-thirds of each house of the legislature. The new twentieth-century constitution, essentially an expansion and slight revision of the Constitution of 1850, was firmly rooted in the antebellum world.

## THE INTRODUCTION OF DIRECT DEMOCRACY

Perhaps the most important single development in Michigan constitutional history came in the form of the 1913 amendments to the Constitution of 1908. In 1912, the Republican Party split between William H. Taft and the Progressive Theodore Roosevelt, and the division brought Democrat Woodrow Wilson to the White House. Democrats and Progressives came to dominate Michigan politics, and together they sought to amend the constitution to include the provisions for direct democracy that had been debated but failed at the last constitutional convention. In 1913, the initiative, referendum, and recall were added to the state constitution.

The wisdom of direct democracy was hotly debated in Michigan and across the United States. For the most part, progressive sympathizers such as W. A. Coutts (1908) argued in favor of the reforms: *vox populi, vox dei.* Others such as Henry M. Campbell, perhaps a bit of an alarmist, saw direct democracy as "a crisis as great as any" (1912: 427) except for, perhaps, the Civil War. The arguments made by Campbell are remarkably similar to those made today by opponents of initiative, referendum, and recall. Direct democracy is not possible in political units of any considerable size; what works in a New England town meeting cannot work in a large populous state. Fleeting passions may govern the choice of an aroused electorate, or uninformed voters may decide on the basis of an attractive title to a dubious proposal. Propositions are placed before the people in a "take it or leave it" fashion, and there is no room for discussion, modification, or accommodation as in a representative legislative chamber. The good must go along with the bad.

Campbell (1912) warned the people of Michigan of the excesses of the initiative and referendum in operation in other states. In Oregon in 1908, voters were asked to deliberate on 126 pages of constitutional amendments and statutes. The next year, the issues had grown to 208 pages of laws and amendments, among them a constitutional amendment of 36 sections that had to be voted upon as a single proposition. In South Dakota in 1910, the ballot was seven feet long: one foot of candidates and six feet of initiatives and referenda. Recall was just as inadvisable an innovation: Its "natural effect" would be to place every office holder on the lookout for "every passing whim, the clamor of newspapers, the shouting of agitators" (Campbell, 1912: 432). Nevertheless, the amendments were adopted, and initiative, referendum, and recall became Michigan fundamental law in April 1913.

The framers of the direct democracy amendments were careful to include much statutory-type detail on procedure for initiative and referendum so that the provisions would be self-executing (i.e., not dependent on the legislature for implementation). Initiative, defined as the power to "propose legislative measures, resolutions and laws" (Article V, section 1), required a petition signed by the equivalent of at least 8 percent of the total vote cast for candidates for governor at the last preceding election at which a governor was elected. Referendum, or the power to "approve or reject any act passed by the legislature," required a 5 percent signature threshold. The requirement of a certain percentage of voters as signatories to a petition is referred to as an "intensity check" that assures that the ballot will not be cluttered by trivial or frivolous proposals. Laws proposed by the initiative had to be presented to the legislature for approval or rejection. Initiatives enacted by the legislature were subject to referendum at the next general election. The legislature could reject an initiated law; it could also propose another measure on the same subject. If the latter course was followed, both the original initiative and the legislative version would be presented to the electorate for a decision. To allow for the operation of the referendum, all acts passed by the legislature, except appropriations to state institutions and acts "immediately necessary for the preservation of the public peace, health or safety," could not go into effect until 90 days after passage. This time period allowed for the collection of the necessary signatures to place the act before the people at the next general election. A majority vote of the electorate was sufficient for the passage of an initiative or referendum, and no act adopted by either mechanism could be vetoed by the governor. No act passed under the initiative could be repealed or amended by the legislature: Resubmission of the issue to the people via referendum was the only constitutional method of change.

The Constitution of 1908 did place limitations on the power of initiative and referendum that remain in place today. The power of the initiative has extended only to laws that could be enacted by the legislature under the constitution. Generally, the Michigan Supreme Court has allowed measures of questionable constitutionality to be placed before the people. The court in *Hamilton v. Secretary of State* (1920) reasoned that there was a chance that the measure would be rejected by the people anyway, and, that should the initiative succeed, there would be ample opportunity for judicial review of the initiative in actual operation. The power of referendum does not extend to acts of appropriations for state institutions or to meet deficiencies in state funds. These two exceptions have been used by the legislature, with approval from the state supreme court, to place certain taxes beyond the reach of the people by referendum. To avoid the possibility of a referendum, the legislature can create a tax, place its proceeds in a special fund, and immediately appropriate the tax to a "state institution." The state supreme court in *Detroit Automobile Club v. Secretary of State* (1925) and *Moreton v. Secretary of State* (1927) upheld this practice as beyond the power of the referendum and expanded the number of exemptions by broadly construing the term "state institutions" to include "all organized departments of the State to which the legislature has delegated or should delegate the exercise of state functions."

The Constitution of 1908 contained less statutory detail on the power of recall. Under Article III, section 8, all elective offices, except judges of courts of record, were subject to recall. Signatures amounting to 25 percent of voters for governor in the last election in the appropriate electoral district were required to trigger recall. Unlike the sections on initiative and referendum that spell out the precise procedures for their operation, the procedures for recall were to be provided by the legislature.

## AMENDMENTS TO THE CONSTITUTION OF 1908

Between 1908 and 1961, there were 125 proposed amendments to the constitution; of these, 69 were adopted (Glazer, 1961). Of the 35 amendments proposed via the constitutional initiative, only nine were ratified by the voters (Glazer, 1961: 1). Amendments to the constitution began within a few years of ratification. Some amendments, such as the provisions for direct democracy, represented real changes in fundamental law appropriate for inclusion in the state constitution. Others expressed the desire of the people of Michigan to enshrine certain public policies in the constitution in order to place them beyond the reach of an inconstant legislature.

The major amendments to the constitution can be grouped under four general headings: The first, provisions for direct democracy, came soon after ratification. After introduction in 1912, there were no further amendments on the initiative, referendum, or recall. The second series of amendments involved changes to the structure and efficiency of state government. These amendments were not restricted to any particular decade.

In 1912, municipal home rule was added to the constitution. Cities and villages were given power to frame, adopt, and amend a charter as well as the authority to pass all laws and ordinances related to municipal concerns. A state civil service was established in 1940 to provide for selection of most public servants solely on the basis of merit, efficiency, and fitness. The civil service amendment was careful to guarantee that no civil servant would be removed or demoted for partisan, racial, or religious considerations. A bipartisan commission was charged with the administration of the civil service system and given the authority to classify personnel and develop a salary scale.

Two constitutional amendments affected two of the branches of state government. In 1947, an amendment required a nonpartisan primary and general election of supreme court justices, circuit court and probate judges, and all county judicial officers. What the amendment may have removed in terms of partisan advantage for a judicial candidate, the amendment replaced with a different advantage—a sitting judge was given the designation of incumbent. Given the low salience of judicial candidates and election for most voters, the incumbent designation almost guarantees reelection. After all, who would want to replace an experienced jurist with a novice? The next year in 1948, an amendment specified the line of succession after the governor. It is easy to imagine how the death in office of four-term President Franklin Delano Roosevelt prompted increased attention to the details of executive succession. The final change to state governmental structure came in 1959. Three sections were added to the education article to allow for the election of the board of trustees for Michigan State University and the board of governors for Wayne State University. These additions created a similar system of governance for Michigan State and Wayne State as the University of Michigan had enjoyed since 1850.

A third series of constitutional amendments was added in 1950. A new section creating and defining the crime of subversion was added to the Declaration of Rights. Adding to the inappropriate placement of the crime of subversion in the Declaration of Rights, language in the section held that liberty of speech and press could not be used as a defense in any trial for subversion. Section 5 of Article V on the legislative department made anyone convicted of subversion ineligible for either house of the legislature. These additions to the state constitution sadly placed Michigan in the mainstream of the growing river of anti-Communist hysteria in American law and politics.

The fourth and final series of constitutional amendments reflected Michiganians' traditional distrust of leaving public policy to a mercurial legislature. Numerous amendments were added limiting state and local indebtedness and taxes. At the same time, other amendments earmarked tax revenues for narrow specific purposes. For example, Article X, section 22 created a gasoline and motor vehicles tax and required that all proceeds from the tax be used exclusively for highways and "not diverted or appropriated for any other purpose." These amendments fettered the revenue raising ability of the state and denied government the flexibility to respond to changes in the state's development or economy. As Arthur W. Bromage put it, legislative discretion was "confined in a cast-iron, constitutionally-restricted crib."[9] Perhaps more than any other defect in the Constitution of 1908 and its amendments, these rigid restrictions with respect to taxation and spending led to calls for a new constitution towards the end of the 1950s.

## ATTEMPTS AT REVISION

The Constitution of 1908 envisioned two major avenues of constitutional reconsideration. Like the 1850 Constitution, the 1908 document embodied the Jeffersonian idea that each new generation should rethink the fundamental

[9] Arthur W. Bromage, "Restrictions on the Financial Powers of the Legislature in Michigan," *State Government* 20 (1947): 141–43.

structure of government; therefore every sixteen years the question of general constitutional revision was put to the electorate. The other avenue was a seriatim amendment via a proposal from the state legislature or through the constitutional initiative and referendum. The 1908 Constitution made it relatively easy to ratify an individual amendment. A simple majority of the voters voting on the question of amendment was sufficient for ratification. Wholesale revision was another matter. Here the constitution required that the call for a convention be ratified by a majority of voters voting in the election. This prerequisite meant that even if a majority of voters voting on the convention question favored the constitutional convention, the convention call would still fail if the number of votes in favor of the convention did not equal a majority of the total votes cast in the election. The Supreme Court of Michigan upheld this reading of the 1908 Constitution in *People v. Board of State Canvassers* (1949). There is a well-known phenomenon in voting behavior called "ballot fall-off." Voters most often vote for the high-profile offices at the beginning of a ballot but often tend to ignore the low-salience offices and questions placed towards the end. Given the placement of the constitutional convention question at the end of the ballot and ballot fall-off, the majority-voting-in-the-election requirement proved to be an insurmountable barrier to the call for a new constitution.

In 1938, Governor Frank Murphy created the Commission on Reform and the Modernization of Government. The commission was convened to lay the ground work for the next required vote on constitutional revision that would occur in 1942. Governor Murray Van Wagoner continued the interest in constitutional reform and appointed a study commission in 1941. The study commission recommended a number of significant and progressive changes to the 1908 Constitution: the allowance for nonunanimous civil juries; the prohibition of a poll tax; protection for the right of labor to organize; the elimination of a spring election; the reduction in the number of elective offices; unification of the court system; the strengthening of local government; and the revision of provisions on taxation and finance. Despite years of preparation, the question of general constitutional revision failed again in 1942. Sturm (1963: 16) attributed the failure to preoccupation with World War II and inadequate time and money to educate the public as to the wisdom of revision.

Sixteen years later, there was yet another attempt at general constitutional revision. By then, however, there was greater support for a constitutional convention. State Republicans and a number of interest groups (including the League of Women Voters, the Michigan Junior Chamber of Commerce, the American Association of University Women, the Michigan Education Association, and the Michigan Municipal League) were in favor of constitutional reform (Sturm, 1963: 19). Generally, rural groups such as the Farm Bureau and The Grange resisted any wholesale revision. Democrats and labor were not opposed to a new constitution in principle; rather, they were concerned about the selection of delegates and representation at any constitutional convention

(Sturm, 1963: 19). The breakdown of interests supporting and opposing a call for a convention reflected the potential winners and losers under a new constitution. Farm groups and rural residents had disproportionate power under the 1908 Constitution. The 1908 system of representation was essentially a carryover from 1850. The state senate consisted of 34 members chosen by single district; the house of representatives, also elected by single districts, consisted of not less than 64 nor more than 100 members. Under the 1908 Constitution, reapportionment based on the results of the federal census would take place every ten years. State constitutional requirements notwithstanding, the Michigan legislature was never apportioned according to any standard resembling the contemporary rule of one-person, one-vote. The so-called "Balanced Legislature Amendment" of 1952 was the only major change to apportionment: The house of representatives was apportioned by population—again, not close to the one-person, one-vote standard—but senatorial districts were frozen. As rural areas declined in population and the cities of southeastern Michigan grew, the malapportionment of the state legislature, particularly the senate, grew worse. A constitutional convention would undoubtedly consider the problem of legislative apportionment. Any constitutional change to make representation more equitable would dramatically change the balance of power in state politics. Michiganians would be facing the prospect of state politics controlled by the three counties of the southeastern corner of the state. Resistance from rural groups coupled with the rigorous requirements of the constitution for calling a convention seemed to guarantee the status quo.

Social and economic change in the late 1950s exacerbated the need for a new constitution. By 1960, the transition from a rural to an urban society was almost complete: Over three-quarters of the people of the state were city dwellers. Michigan's economic fate was tied to that of the automobile industry. Employment in Michigan peaked in 1953 and then began a steady decline due to automation and centralization in automobile production (Sturm, 1963: 20). State government failed to keep up with the surge and decline of the economy. In 1959, there was "a financial crisis of the first order" (Sturm, 1963: 20), which was a product of a stalemate on a tax program between the Democratic Governor G. Mennen Williams and the Republican legislature. As a result, there was a massive deficit in the state budget, and constitutionally mandated payments for public education and old age and children's programs were far behind. The numerous constitutional restrictions on revenue raising and the earmarking of taxes for narrow purposes that had accreted over the years did not make solutions easy to find.[10]

---

[10] In 1960, 65 percent of the state's $1.1 billion budget was earmarked primarily for school aid, highways, municipalities, and townships. Restrictions on state borrowing resulted in "payless paydays" in April 1959. See Andrew F. Wilson, "Citizenship vs. the Power Groups: A Review of the Citizens for Michigan," *Historical Society Chronicle* 21 (1985): 21–29.

The solution came in the form of an initiative petition to amend the constitution to facilitate calling a constitutional convention. Developed by the League of Women Voters and the Junior Chamber of Commerce and endorsed by the Citizens for Michigan, the "Gateway Amendment" had three important provisions.[11] The first required that a question on general constitutional revision be placed on the ballot in 1961 and every sixteen years thereafter. The second reduced the threshold number of votes to call a constitutional convention. Under the Gateway Amendment, a majority of voters voting on the question of constitutional revision, rather than in the election, was sufficient to call a convention. Finally, the system of representation at the constitutional convention was changed to minimize the impact of the badly apportioned state senatorial districts. Now only one delegate would be chosen from each senatorial district rather than the three allotted under the Constitution of 1908. The Gateway Amendment appeared on the ballot as Proposal 3 in November 1960, and it was ratified by a margin of over 350,000 votes. The large voter turnout on the question was due to the campaign of public education on the question as well as the intense interest in the presidential election.

April of 1961 brought the question of general constitutional revision to the people under the requirements of the Gateway Amendment. Voter interest was minimal: Less than one-third of registered voters voted in the spring election (Sturm, 1963: 28). Nevertheless, the referendum on calling a convention squeaked by with a margin of just over 23,000 votes. The constitutional convention was supported by a majority of voters in only Wayne, Oakland, Washtenaw, and Macomb counties—the counties with the most to gain and the least to lose under a new constitutional order. Michigan voters remained apathetic to the idea of a constitutional convention. Turnout for the June 25 delegate selection primary was low as is the case for most primaries. But turnout for the September 12 election of delegates was abysmal, the lowest turnout in any election since 1945 (Sturm, 1963: 45). Republicans went to the polls in greater number than the Democrats and the labor vote stayed home. The net result was a convention in which Republicans secured 99 out of 144 seats.

---

[11] Citizens for Michigan (CFM) was a "non-partisan, grass-roots citizen organization through which individuals could work for community betterment." The moving force behind the creation of Citizens for Michigan was George Romney. Although some suggested that CFM was simply the organizational alter ego of George Romney, numerous other prominent citizens such as Robert S. McNamara, Wade H. McCree, Leonard Woodcock, Richard Austin, and Edward Cushman were active participants. CFM vanished from the political scene shortly after the ratification of the 1963 Constitution. See Andrew F. Wilson, "Citizenship vs. the Power Groups: A Review of the Citizens for Michigan," *Historical Society Chronicle* 21 (1985): 21–29.

## THE 1961–1962 CONSTITUTIONAL CONVENTION

For the first time in Michigan history, women and African Americans participated in the drafting of the state constitution. Although white males still dominated the convention, eleven women and thirteen African Americans (all Wayne County Democrats) were in attendance (Sturm, 1982: 47–50). And again for the first time, a majority of delegates were Michigan natives. Like past conventions, most delegates were middle-aged and Protestant, and, as in 1908, the largest occupational group was lawyers. The convention membership was remarkable for its high level of education; only seven delegates failed to complete high school, while 71 were college graduates. One characteristic that all delegates shared was their activity in public affairs. Sturm described the delegates as "joiners and leaders in civic organizations" and found that 93 percent had some kind of political experience before coming to the constitutional convention (Sturm, 1982: 52).

Preparation for the convention began with the creation of study commissions by Governor John Swainson. These initial surveys showed that more work was needed, so Governor Swainson appointed the Constitutional Convention Preparatory Commission. The legislature balked at paying for the commission, but fortunately the Kellogg Foundation financed the effort. The commission prepared a valuable series of papers to inform the delegates, ranging from the powers of a constitutional convention to specific sections of state and local government. The commission also tended to the other, more mundane needs of a constitutional convention such as providing research staff for delegates and finding and preparing a place in Lansing for the convention to meet. Meanwhile, other groups also contributed research in anticipation of a new constitution. The Citizens Research Council independently developed a careful two-volume comparison of the 1908 Constitution.

The initial sessions of the convention were devoted to organization and procedure. Both Democratic and Republican representatives caucused to select leadership for the convention. After lengthy intramural debate, the Republicans nominated Stephen S. Nisbet as convention president, and the Democrats chose not to oppose his candidacy. The delegates agreed on three vice presidents to reflect the partisan balance in the convention. There would be two Republican vice presidents, Edward Hutchinson and George Romney, and one Democratic vice president, Tom Downs. The convention was divided into thirteen standing committees, nine of which were to cover substantive issues and four of which were devoted to operations and procedure.[12] Membership on the committees

[12] The substantive committees were: Declaration of Rights, Suffrage and Elections; Legislative Organization; Legislative Powers; Executive Branch; Judicial Branch; Finance and Taxation; Local Government; Education; and Miscellaneous Provisions and Schedule. The organizational committees were: Style and Drafting; Administration; Public Information; and Rules and Resolutions.

reflected the partisan balance of the convention, with a ratio of two Republicans to each Democrat. The procedure used in the convention was based on the rules used by the Michigan House of Representatives. Committees developed proposals, held public hearings, and reported the proposals back to the convention. Each proposal was then read and debated by the all the delegates. The bulk of the work of the convention was accomplished between October 1961 and May 1962, and the constitution was approved by the delegates on May 11 by a vote of 90 for, and 44 against.

Given the financial crisis of the late 1950s, it was inevitable that the delegates would spend much time over taxation and the earmarking of state funds. There were also a number of other areas of intense controversy. Legislative apportionment was a great concern. The Michigan legislature had been malapportioned for years, and an equitable reapportionment of the legislature would shift political control of the state to three counties in southeastern Michigan. As the convention debated apportionment, the United States Supreme Court handed down *Baker v. Carr* (1962), which held that federal courts could entertain challenges to legislative malapportionment under the federal Constitution. This decision raised the distinct possibility that federal courts would hold that malapportioned state legislatures offended the equal protection clause of the Fourteenth Amendment to the federal Constitution. The delegates to the constitutional convention were very much aware of *Baker v. Carr* and other cases pending before the U.S. Supreme Court. The convention ultimately agreed on a "balanced legislature" approach that apportioned the state house by population and the state senate by a formula based on population and land area. To assure that the legislature would be reapportioned after each federal census, the delegates created a bipartisan commission to oversee the process.[13]

The executive and judicial branches did not escape careful scrutiny at the convention. The position of the governor was strengthened, and the executive was streamlined and reorganized to facilitate administration. Michigan added a new tier of courts, an intermediate appellate tribunal called the court of appeals, and eliminated the office of justice of the peace.

The protection of the civil rights and liberties of the people of Michigan was another area of intense debate. Again, the delegates paid careful attention to decisions of the U.S. Supreme Court under the leadership of Earl Warren. The delegates added an equal protection clause to the constitution and specifically prohibited discrimination on account of religion, race, color, or national origin. A civil rights commission was created and given constitutional status so that the legislature could not interfere with its work to protect

[13] Ultimately, the entire apportionment system developed by the convention was declared unconstitutional by the Michigan Supreme Court. See Article IV, sections 2 through 6.

individual rights. The delegates recognized the increased use of legislative investigations and sought to guarantee fair treatment for those associated with these procedures. Michigan's counterpart to the Fourth Amendment's guarantee against unreasonable searches and seizures was of particular concern. Most delegates agreed that Michigan's constitutional provisions did not square with the requirements of *Mapp v. Ohio* (1961), but carried over the old language into the new constitution anyway. The delegates thought that the federal courts could sort out the problems later.

All in all, the convention drafted a document squarely within Michigan's constitutional traditions. The 1963 Constitution had clear ties to the Northwest Ordinance and each subsequent statement of fundamental law. The 1908 Constitution had been characterized as "progressively conservative," and the same could be said of this most recent constitution. The framers of the 1963 Constitution solved many of the problems that brought the delegates to Lansing to reconsider the old constitutional order. Earmarks were removed from most taxes, the governor's office strengthened, and the judiciary made more efficient. Language was clarified, obsolete provisions were deleted, and much of the statutory-type detail was eliminated. Yet the 1963 constitution—without any of its amendments—contained 19,203 words, only about 2,600 words shy of the prolix 1908 code the delegates sought to revise.

As Albert Sturm put it, the 1963 constitution "reflects the political environment in which it was written" (Sturm, 1982: 278). This environment accounts for the failure of the convention to solve the apportionment problem and the resistance to wholesale change. But the political environment of the 1960s also accounts for some unanticipated limitations inherent in the Michigan Constitution. The 1963 Constitution was framed in the shadow of the United States Supreme Court under the leadership of Earl Warren. The Court's activism in solving state problems through federal action led the delegates to make constant reference to developments in Washington. This Washington view can be seen, for example, in the debates on apportionment, searches and seizures, and equal protection.

In some cases, the efforts of the federal Court served the delegates well as a political expedient. The federal courts could reapportion the state houses, so the delegates did not have to work through this troublesome issue. Federal courts had not yet addressed the apportionment of state senates, so the delegates took a conservative approach to the apportionment of the senate. If there was a problem with Michigan's "balanced legislature," well, the federal courts could fix that too. Michigan's constitutional provisions on searches and seizures were clearly not consistent with *Mapp v. Ohio*, but who wants to limit use of "any narcotic drug, firearm, bomb, explosive or any other dangerous weapon" as evidence in a criminal trial? So, if Article I, section 11 does not square with federal law, the federal courts can supply the remedy. Expediency was not the only reason the delegates looked to Washington, however. The Warren Court's efforts on equal rights for African Americans were well known and appreciated by the delegates. Michigan's new equal protection guarantee in Article I, section 2 was a product of this appreciation. Such an inclusion of an equal rights guarantee was progressive in 1963.

The problem with the constant reference to Washington is that it created at least a Declaration of Rights firmly rooted in the federal constitutional law. Despite warnings that the delegates should reject "wholesale acceptance of the proposition that the Federal Bill of Rights and the Fourteenth Amendment are better protectors of the people" than state guarantees, the convention did hitch the fate of the Michigan rights to federal law.[14] Of course, the delegates could not have anticipated the new judicial federalism with its emphasis on the independent content of state constitutions. However, the legacy of the federal perspective is seen in the reluctance of Michigan courts to go beyond federal guarantees for the protection of individual rights, or their tendency to read federal and state legal precedents interchangeably. The federal view may have been useful in 1963, but it has caused us to neglect Michigan's rich and unique constitutional heritage.

## THE MICHIGAN CONSTITUTION OF 1963

Michigan courts adhere to certain basic rules in interpreting the Michigan Constitution. These rules are derived from Thomas Cooley, Michigan's most noted legal scholar, and are recounted in *Traverse City School District v. Attorney General* (1971):

> The primary rule is the rule of "common understanding." . . . A constitution is made for the people and by the people. The interpretation that should be given it is that which reasonable minds, the great mass of the people themselves would give it. For the Constitution does not derive its force from the convention which framed but from the people who ratified it, the intent to be arrived at is that of the people, and it is not to be supposed that they have looked for any dark or abstruse meaning in the words employed, but rather they accepted them in the sense most obvious to the common understanding, and ratified the instrument in the belief that was the sense designed to be conveyed.
>
> A second rule is that to clarify meaning, the circumstances surrounding the adoption of a constitutional provision and the purpose sought to be accomplished may be considered.
>
> A third rule is that wherever possible an interpretation that does not create constitutional invalidity is preferred to one that does.

[14] Charles Shull, "The Declaration of Rights in the Michigan Constitution," Michigan Constitutional Convention Studies, prepared for the Constitutional Convention Study Commission, September 1961, p. 12.

Throughout this constitutional commentary, the reader will note references to the *Address to the People.* The *Address to the People* was drawn up by the drafters of the 1963 Constitution to explain the new constitution to the voters. The *Address to the People* highlighted changes, additions, and deletions to the old Constitution of 1908 and provided the rationales for these changes.

# PART TWO
# The Michigan Constitution and Commentary

## PREAMBLE

> We, the people of the State of Michigan, grateful to Almighty God for the blessings of freedom, and earnestly desiring to secure these blessings undiminished to ourselves and our posterity, do ordain and establish this constitution.

The Preamble to the Michigan Constitution, like the preambles to the federal Constitution and other state constitutions, indicates the general purpose of the constitution. The preamble does not have the force of law. The language of the Preamble is identical to the language of the preamble of the 1908 Constitution. The preamble to the 1850 Constitution simply stated that the people of Michigan ordain the constitution. The 1908 Constitution added the reference to God and the purpose of the constitution as well as the statement that the constitution binds this and future generations.

# Article I

## *The Declaration of Rights*

Every state constitution contains provisions for the protection of individual rights and liberties. Each state constitution is different. Although many provisions of state constitutions express sentiments similar to the federal Bill of Rights, state constitutions differ from the federal guarantees in language, scope, and the intent of the framers. Traditionally, there has been a tendency on the part of state supreme courts to look to federal court interpretations of the Bill of Rights for guidance in interpreting state declarations of rights. Nothing, however, compels state supreme courts in interpreting state constitutions to mirror federal court construction of federal law. State constitutions can provide greater protections for individual rights and liberties. The Supreme Court of Michigan is aware that the Michigan Constitution can provide such enhanced protections for the rights and liberties of the people of Michigan. However, the Michigan court has not read the Michigan Constitution as consistently commanding greater safeguards, and often federal and state standards are so intertwined in opinions that it is difficult to tell one from the other. Michigan courts are particularly reluctant to give more expansive protections to rights under the Michigan Constitution when the Michigan and federal provisions are identically worded. In this instance, the only time a Michigan court should assign greater protection under the Michigan Constitution is when such a reading of a provision is deeply rooted in the document. The Michigan Supreme Court has stated that it will "not engraft on to the constitutional text 'more enlightened' rights than the framers intended" (*People v. Pickens*, 1994).

The Michigan Supreme Court has determined that the provisions of the Declaration of Rights restrict government conduct only. Just as is the case for the federal Bill of Rights, Michigan's Declaration of Rights cannot reach purely private conduct (*Woodland v. Michigan's Citizens Lobby*, 1985).

## SECTION 1

**Political power.** All political power is inherent in the people. Government is instituted for their equal benefit, security and protection.

Section 1 of the 1963 Declaration of Rights is identical to section 1 in the Constitution of 1908. This section can trace its origins to Michigan's first constitution. Parallels to the Declaration of Independence are clear: Governments are instituted to secure rights and to ensure governments derive their just powers from the consent of the people. Unlike the Declaration of Independence and the Constitution of 1835, the current constitution omits reference to the right of the people to alter or abolish one form of government when the public good requires it.

Before inclusion in the 1963 Constitution of a new article on equal protection and nondiscrimination, this section of the Declaration of Rights served as Michigan's equal protection clause. In *Gauthier v. Campbell* (1960), the Supreme Court of Michigan found that under the Constitution of 1908 this section provided equal protection guarantees similar to those in the Fourteenth Amendment to the federal Constitution.

Article 1, section 1 has occasionally surfaced to support nondelegation arguments and assure government accountability. In *Dearborn Fire Fighters Union Local No. 412, IAFF v. City of Dearborn* (1975), the Michigan Supreme Court struck down a statute providing for compulsory arbitration of labor disputes in municipal police and fire departments because the appointed chairperson of the arbitration panel was empowered to decide major political questions concerning the conditions of public employment, the levels and standards of public services, and the allocation of public resources. Since the chairperson was insulated from public accountability for his or her decisions, the statute was inconsistent with principles of representative democracy.

## SECTION 2

**Equal protection; discrimination.** No person shall be denied the equal protection of the laws; nor shall any person be denied the enjoyment of his civil or political rights or be discriminated against in the exercise thereof because of religion, race, color or national origin. The legislature shall implement this section by appropriate legislation.

This new section of the state constitution guarantees equality of treatment for the people of Michigan. The framers of the constitution were particularly concerned with the protection of the rights of African-Americans, especially in the areas of employment, education, housing, and public accommodation. The framers debated inclusion of a prohibition against gender-based discrimination, but the clause failed by a margin of 82 to 48. (One delegate noted that "women need to be discriminated against for their own benefit.") The actual language of this section was borrowed from the Hawaii Constitution.

The federal Constitutional counterpart to section 2 is the equal protection clause of the Fourteenth Amendment. However, there are certain important differences between the federal and Michigan equality guarantees. The federal clause simply guarantees equal protection; no reference is made to race or any other groups. The Michigan Constitution seems to go further and not only guarantees equality but specifically prohibits certain forms of discrimination. The Michigan Constitution also specifically protects the equal enjoyment of political and civil rights. Despite these significant linguistic differences, the Supreme Court of Michigan held in *Armco Steel Corp. v. State of Michigan* (1984) that the Michigan guarantee of equal protection is coextensive with the Fourteenth Amendment. However, a panel of the court of appeals has held that the nondiscrimination provisions of section 2 furnish greater protection of rights than the Fourteenth Amendment. In *NAACP v. City of Dearborn* (1988), the appellate court held that a finding of unconstitutional discrimination under the Michigan Constitution does not require a showing of an intention or purpose to discriminate.

The framers of the 1963 Constitution debated whether or not the constitutional prohibition against discrimination should apply to private conduct. Ultimately, it was determined that it would be up to the legislature to outlaw private discrimination and provide appropriate sanctions (Official Record, Constitutional Convention, 1961, p. 742). Section 2, therefore, provides a constitutional basis for the passage of state civil rights statutes.

The United States Supreme Court has developed an intricate "multi-tier" approach to equal protection analysis. Under the multi-tier system, legislative classifications receive different degrees of judicial deference depending on the classifications used in the legislation and the nature of the individual interest affected. The Michigan court's approach to the Michigan equal protection mirrors the federal multi-tier standard (*Manistee Bank & Trust Co. v. McGowan*, 1975; *Michigan Department of Civil Rights ex rel. Forton v. Waterford Township Department of Parks and Recreation*, 1986).

## Rational Basis Scrutiny

The lowest tier of equal protection analysis is for social or economic statutes. Laws concerning taxation or business regulation are typically placed on this tier.

Under this most deferential standard of review, the burden of proof is on the person challenging the classification to show that the classification is without some reasonable basis. In *Smith v. Employment Security Commission* (1981), the Michigan Supreme Court held that the challenger must show that the classification is arbitrary and wholly unrelated in a rational way to the objective of the statute. The usual rational basis standard embodies two tests developed in *Alexander v. City of Detroit* (1974): First, the court will ask whether the challenged enactment's classifications are based on natural distinguishing characteristics and bear a reasonable relationship to the object of legislation. Second, the court will ask whether all persons of the same class are included and affected alike, or are immunities and privileges extended to an arbitrary or unreasonable class while denying the same immunities and privileges to others of a like kind. The use of this standard was most recently affirmed in *Brittany Park Apartments v. Harrison Township* (1989).

Few statutes have been found so wanting in rationality as to fail to satisfy the essentially arbitrary test, since the court has not required statutes to be drawn with "mathematical nicety" and has allowed the legislature to make "rough accommodations" that are sometimes "illogical" or "unscientific" (*Manistee Bank & Trust Co. v. McGowan*, 1975). Yet the Michigan Supreme Court, on occasion, has struck down statutes under this most deferential standard. In *Beauty Built Construction Corp. v. City of Warren* (1965), the supreme court struck down a municipal water tax fee on the grounds the ordinance did not include and affect all persons of the same class and extended immunities and privileges to one part and denied them to others of a like kind by an unreasonable or arbitrary classification. Likewise, in *Manistee Bank & Trust Co. v. McGowan* (1975), the court invalidated Michigan's automobile guest passenger statute, and in *Longnecker v. Noordyk-Mooney, Inc.* (1975), the same fate befell the aviation guest passenger statute.

## Strict Scrutiny

The highest tier of equal protection entails "strict scrutiny" in which the court refuses to confer upon statutes the usual presumption of constitutionality. Strict scrutiny is given to statutes utilizing "suspect categories" or adversely affecting "fundamental rights." The burden of proof is on the state to show that the use of the suspect category or the effect on the fundamental right is essential to the accomplishment of a "compelling" state interest. Unlike the situation for simple rationality review, laws rarely survive strict scrutiny. The difficulty for a court is the definition of "suspect categories" and "fundamental rights."

The Michigan Supreme Court has had few opportunities to apply strict scrutiny. The court follows the United States Supreme Court in treating race, alienage, and national origin as suspect categories (*Manistee Bank & Trust*; *Michigan*

*Department of Civil Rights ex rel. Forton*), and has found that the purpose of section 2 is to duplicate the coverage of the Fourteenth Amendment (*Doe v. Michigan Department of Social Services*, 1992). Illegitimacy is also regarded as a suspect category (*Spada v. Pauley*, 1986). Like the federal courts, the Michigan courts do not treat age as a suspect category, since age cuts across racial, religious, and economic lines and bears some relation to mental and physical capacity (*Cruz v. Chevrolet Grey Iron Division of General Motors Corporation*, 1975). Wealth is also not a suspect category, and the state may constitutionally limit state funding for abortion (*Doe v. Michigan Department of Social Services*, 1992).

With respect to the fundamental rights strand of equal protection analysis, the Michigan courts agree with federal courts that the "right to travel" is correctly construed as the right to interstate migration. Thus, there is no fundamental right to choose a particular means of transportation—that is, travel by automobile (*Shavers v. Attorney General*, 1978). The right to vote is also fundamental under both federal and state equal protection standards (*Wilkins v. Ann Arbor City Clerk*, 1971).

In *Governor v. State Treasurer* (1972), a challenge to the property tax-based system of public school finance, the Michigan Supreme Court hinted that wealth might be a suspect category and education a fundamental right under state equal protection standards. Here, a plurality of the court found that Michigan's deep commitment to public education, traceable from the Northwest Ordinance to the various provisions in each state constitution, elevated education to fundamental status. The plurality also found that classification on the basis of wealth is "suspect," particularly when the classification affects a fundamental right. However, the supreme court ordered a rehearing of the case, vacated the opinions, and dismissed the complaint. Given the reversal in *Governor v. State Treasurer* and the opinion of the U.S. Supreme Court in *San Antonio Independent School District et al. v. Rodriguez et al.* (1973), a panel of the Michigan Court of Appeals has held that education is not a fundamental right and Michigan's system of school finance does not offend section 2 (*East Jackson Public Schools v. State of Michigan*, 1984).

## Heightened or Intermediate Scrutiny

Gender-based classifications reside on a unique middle tier in Michigan and federal equal protection analysis. Intermediate scrutiny requires neither the extreme deference accorded economic or social classifications nor the "inherently suspect" approach under strict scrutiny. In *Michigan Department of Civil Rights ex rel. Forton*, the Michigan court adopted the federal approach of *Craig v. Boren* (1976): Gender-based classifications must advance an "important" governmental interest and the classification must be "fairly and substantially" related to the achievement of that interest. The burden of proof is on the government to demonstrate that the use of the classification is substantially related to the important government interest.

## SECTION 3

**Assembly, consultation, instruction, petition.** The people have the right peaceably to assemble, to consult for the common good, to instruct their representatives and to petition the government for redress of grievances.

Section 3 can trace its origins to the Constitution of 1835. The major change to this section from earlier versions was the substitution of the word "government" for "legislature." The *Address to the People* indicates that the change recognizes that agencies other than the legislature are responsible for policy-making and thus should be subject to the right of petition. All 50 state constitutions have provisions similar to section 3.

There has been little litigation over this straightforward provision of the Declaration of Rights. However, in *Woodland v. Michigan Citizens Lobby* (1985), the section was construed as not guaranteeing access to private shopping malls for the purpose of gathering signatures for an initiative petition.

## SECTION 4

**Freedom of worship and religious belief; appropriations.** Every person shall be at liberty to worship God according to the dictates of his own conscience. No person shall be compelled to attend, or, against his consent, to contribute to the erection or support of any place of religious worship, or to pay tithes, taxes or other rates for the support of any minister of the gospel or teacher of religion. No money shall be appropriated or drawn from the treasury for the benefits of any religious sect or society, theological or religious seminary; nor shall property belonging to the state be appropriated for any such purpose. The civil and political rights, privileges and capacities of no person shall be diminished or enlarged on account of his religious belief.

Concern with freedom of religion and separation of church and state in Michigan dates to the Northwest Ordinance. The language of section 4 is identical to the language of its predecessor in the Constitution of 1908; and the 1908 provision is simply an improvement in the phraseology of the 1835 and 1850 Constitutions. The Michigan religion provision is much more detailed than the Establishment and Free Exercise clauses of the First Amendment to the federal Constitution and requires stricter separation between church and state. Michigan courts have read section 4 to incorporate the principle that the state shall be neutral toward religion and shall neither favor nor inhibit its pursuit (*Alexander v. Bartlett*, 1968).

Litigation involving section 4 has centered on two areas: the accommodation of religious practices in employment and religion in education. In *Michigan Department of Civil Rights ex rel. Parks v. General Motors Corporation* (1982), the state supreme court upheld a ruling of the civil rights commission requiring an employer to make "reasonable accommodations to the religious needs of employees or prospective employees where such can be done without undue hardship on the conduct of the employer's business." The burden of proof is on the employer to show that such a reasonable accommodation cannot be made. Such accommodation does not amount to an establishment of religion; rather, it is required so as not to discriminate on account of religious beliefs. A panel of the Michigan Court of Appeals found that a half-day holiday on Good Friday, negotiated through collective bargaining between a union and a county, did not violate section 4. In *Americans United for Separation of Church and State v. Kent County* (1980), the appellate court found that the holiday served the secular purpose of affording employees a longer spring vacation and did not compel anyone to attend religious services. Since the selection of Good Friday as a half day neither added to nor subtracted from the already negotiated number of holidays, the court further found that the agreement did not compel any person to pay taxes for the support of any minister, religious sect, or society.

*Alexander v. Bartlett* (1968) addressed the problem of state provision of transportation for parochial school children in light of the requirements of section 4. A panel of the court of appeals found that this state policy encourages the pursuit of education, assists parents in complying with the compulsory education law while recognizing the right of parents to send their children to accredited parochial schools, and provides a safe and efficient means of transportation to and from school. Since the primary purpose of the policy was secular and did not advance or inhibit religion, the policy was not offensive to section 4.

More recently the Michigan Supreme Court was sharply divided on the constitutionality of state certification for teachers in all schools. The court of appeals upheld the state teacher certification statute, and the supreme court affirmed the ruling by virtue of an equally divided court in *Sheridan Road Baptist Church v. Department of Education* (1986). Various justices of the supreme court suggested a number of means by which the constitutionality of state actions could be evaluated in light of section 4 and the First Amendment to the federal Constitution. Chief Justice G. Mennen Williams derived a four-part analysis: (1) plaintiff's claims must be rooted in religious belief; (2) if the regulation poses no infringement on constitutional rights, then the state action is upheld and the analysis stops; (3) any incidental burden on the free exercise of religion may be justified by a compelling state interest in the subject of the regulation; and (4) no less intrusive form of regulation may be available to the state. Justice Patricia J. Boyle suggested a balancing test with shifting burdens of persuasion. For Justice Boyle, once a plaintiff has established that a regulation burdens the exercise of religion, the state must establish that a compelling state interest is at issue and the interest cannot otherwise be served. If the plaintiff sets forth alternative means that rebut the government's assertion of necessity, then the state is required to show with greater specificity that no alternative means is available. Justice Dorothy Comstock Riley argued that the crucial question is whether the state can establish that the enforcement of its regulations is essential to the fulfillment of a compelling state interest. The state must further demonstrate how granting an exemption would unduly impair its interests and that the means selected is the least intrusive to accomplish its interests. To date then, there is no clear consensus on the correct analytical approach under section 4 or the First Amendment to state regulations affecting religion.

## SECTION 5

**Freedom of speech and of press.** Every person may freely speak, write, express and publish his views on all subjects, being responsible for the abuse of such right; and no law shall be enacted to restrain or abridge the liberty of speech or of the press.

This is Michigan's counterpart to the federal First Amendment with its protection for freedom of speech and the press. Protection for freedom of speech and press finds its origins in the Constitution of 1835. There were two major changes in the language of the 1908 Constitution. The word "express" was added to broaden the coverage of section 5 and to allow for new forms of communication beyond the traditional speaking and writing (1 *Official Record*, Committee Proposal 15, p. 466). The word "views" was substituted for the old "sentiments," because the framers believed "views" has a "sharper and more specific meaning" than the older term (*Address to the People*, p. 13).

Not all forms of expression are protected by section 5. In 1979, the Michigan Supreme Court was urged to read section 5 as protecting material that would be banned under federal constitutional standards as obscene. The supreme court agreed that in certain instances the Michigan Constitution could provide greater protection for freedom of expression than allowed under the federal standard. However, the court rejected the notion that obscenity is such an instance; instead, obscenity is an "abuse" of freedom of speech (*People v. Neumayer*). Michigan courts use the definition of obscenity set down by the United States Supreme Court in *Miller v. California*.

Prior restraints (i.e., government censorship) are regarded by Michigan and federal courts as the most serious and least tolerable infringement on freedom of speech and press (*In re Midland Publishing Co.*, 1985), but the Michigan Supreme Court has recognized that freedom of speech and press have their limitations and are not absolute rights. However, any restriction on section 5 rights must be justified by a compelling state interest in protecting or implementing the common good (*Advisory Opinion on Constitutionality of 1975 PA 227*, 1976).

## SECTION 6

**Bearing of arms.** Every person has a right to keep and bear arms for the defense of himself and the state.

This section of the Declaration of Rights remains unchanged since 1835. Judicial interpretation of section 6 is sparse; however, it is clear that this section does not create an unlimited right to possess weapons. In *People v. Smelter* (1989), a panel of the court of appeals held that the state has the right to regulate weapons and that such regulation extends not only to the establishment of conditions under which weapons may be possessed, but allows the state to prohibit weapons whose customary employment by individuals is to violate the law. The test for constitutionality of regulations is simple reasonableness. Therefore, the legislature can ban the possession of "stun guns."

## SECTION 7

**Military power subordinate to civil power.** The military shall in all cases and at all times be in strict subordination to the civil power.

Section 7 remains unchanged since the Constitution of 1835; it assures civilian control of the military. Section 7 is Michigan's response to a specific grievance against George III contained in the Declaration of Independence ("He has affected to render the military independent of, and superior to, the civil power"). There have been no judicial interpretations of section 7.

## SECTION 8

**Quartering of soldiers.** No soldier shall, in time of peace, be quartered in any house without the consent of the owner or occupant, nor in time of war, except in a manner prescribed by law.

This is Michigan's counterpart to the federal Third Amendment. The section remains basically the same from 1835. The only significant change in the wording of the section was the extension of consent to include the occupant of a house. There have been no judicial interpretations of this provision.

## SECTION 9

**Slavery and involuntary servitude.** Neither slavery, nor involuntary servitude unless for the punishment of crime, shall ever be tolerated in this state.

This section of the Declaration of Rights dates from the Constitution of 1850, predating the Thirteenth Amendment to the federal Constitution by fifteen years.

The only change in the section has been the addition of a comma after the word "slavery." The old punctuation theoretically made slavery possible for the punishment of a crime.

There have been two major references to section 9 in recent litigation. In *School District for the City of Holland v. Holland Education Association* (1968), the Michigan Supreme Court dissolved a temporary injunction against striking school teachers who had not yet signed contracts and therefore had not become public employees subject to a statute prohibiting strikes by public employees. The court reasoned that the temporary injunction as applied in such circumstances violated the state constitutional prohibition against involuntary servitude. And, in *In re Shuster* (1972), a panel of the court of appeals had little difficulty concluding that the appointment of an attorney by a circuit judge to represent an indigent defendant did not amount to involuntary servitude.

## SECTION 10

**Attainder; ex post facto laws; impairment of contracts.** No bill of attainder, ex post facto law or law impairing the obligation of contract shall be enacted.

Section 10 remains virtually unchanged since 1835. The limitations on state government contained here mirror restrictions placed on state government in Article I, section 10 of the federal Constitution. Section 10 contains three distinct limitations on the power of state government.

A bill of attainder is a legislative act that inflicts punishment without the benefit of a judicial trial. Litigation based on the prohibition against bills of attainder is rare. Michigan courts have held that reasonable restrictions or limitations on the rights of public employees—notably the right to strike—do not constitute bills of attainder (*Arnold v. Crestwood Board of Education*, 1978; *City of Detroit v. Division 26, Amalgamated Ass'n of St., Elec. Ry. & Motor Coach Emp. of America*, 1952).

The prohibition against ex post facto (literally, "after the fact") laws usually applies only to criminal laws (*People v. Chapman*, 1942). A law violates the ex post facto clause if it: (1) retroactively changes the consequences of an act after the act has occurred; (2) makes an act a more serious criminal offense; (3) increases the punishment for the offense; or (4) allows the prosecution to convict on less evidence (*People v. Moon*, 1983).

The contract clause was placed in the federal and state constitutions originally to prevent the government from passing debtor relief legislation. The existence of the contract clause does not preclude the passage of all statutes affecting the obligations of contract. Generally, the contract clause does prohibit retroactive change in the terms of a contract (*Guardian Depositors Corporation v. Brown*, 1939), and vested rights acquired under contract may not be destroyed by subsequent legislation or even by an amendment to the state constitution

(*Campbell v. Judge's Retirement Board*, 1966). But the state still retains control over remedial processes to enforce the terms of a contract (*Michigan Transportation Company v. Secretary of State*, 1971). Moreover, the state still possesses general police power to safeguard the welfare of the people, and thus reasonable legislation for the good of the people may be sustained by the courts even if the legislation has some effect on the operation of private contracts (*Michigan Transportation Company v. Secretary of State*, 1971). In *Blue Cross and Blue Shield of Michigan v. Governor* (1985), the Supreme Court of Michigan offered the following standards to determine when a state statute abridges the contract clause: (1) the state law must effect a "substantial" impairment of the contractual relationship; (2) a critical factor in determining the extent of the impairment is a history of past state regulation of the parties to the contract; (3) if the impairment is "minimal," there is no constitutional violation; and (4) if the impairment is "severe," then there must be a showing of a significant and legitimate public purpose behind the regulation, and the means adopted by the legislature to achieve the public purpose must be reasonably related to the public purpose.

## SECTION 11

**Searches and seizures.** The persons, houses, papers and possessions of every person shall be secure from unreasonable searches and seizures. No warrant to search any place or to seize any person or things shall issue without describing them, nor without probable cause, supported by oath or affirmation. The provisions of this section shall not be construed to bar from evidence in any criminal proceeding any narcotic drug, firearm, bomb, explosive or any other dangerous weapon, seized by a peace officer outside the curtilage of any dwelling house in this state.

This is Michigan's counterpart to the federal Constitution's Fourth Amendment. The Fourth Amendment and section 11 are the American response to "writs of assistance" used in colonial times. Writs of assistance were general warrants that allowed the bearer to enter any house or place and to search for undescribed contraband. These writs remained in effect for the life of the issuing sovereign and for six months thereafter. American experience holds that individual privacy is too precious to entrust to the discretion of those whose job is the detection and prevention of crime (*People v. Tyler*, 1977). The first two sentences of section 11 are handed down from Michigan's first constitution. The third sentence—the most unusual element in section 11—dates from 1936, and its placement in the state constitution was a direct result of a Michigan Supreme Court decision.

In 1919 in *People v. Marxhausen*, the Michigan Supreme Court adopted the exclusionary rule, although not required to do so by the United States Supreme Court. The exclusionary rule is a judicially created remedy that prohibits the use at trial of evidence obtained in violation of the Fourth Amendment or section 11. Fourteen years later in *People v. Stein*, the Michigan Supreme Court invoked the exclusionary rule and reversed the conviction of a defendant accused of carrying an unlicensed weapon. The legislative response was swift. A constitutional amendment (1935 Joint Resolution No.1, ratified November 3, 1936) limited the use of the exclusionary rule to bar from evidence "any firearm, rifle, pistol, revolver, automatic pistol, machine gun, bomb, bomb shell, explosive, blackjack, slingshot, billy, metallic knuckles, gas-ejecting device or other dangerous weapon or thing." A subsequent amendment (1952 Joint Resolution No. 1, ratified November 4, 1952) added "any narcotic drug or drugs" to the list.

The decision of the United States Supreme Court in *Mapp v. Ohio* in 1961 made the exclusionary rule applicable to the states as a matter of federal constitutional law. The framers of the Michigan Constitution of 1963 were aware of the federal ruling and felt that *Mapp* may have invalidated Michigan's limits on the use of the exclusionary rule (1 *Official Record*, Constitutional Convention, 1961, pp. 464–84, 488–533, 674–88). Nevertheless, the framers returned substantially to the language of the old constitution with its anti-exclusionary rule provisions. The Supreme Court of Michigan uses this constitutional history to infer a general reluctance on the part of the people to sanction broad uses of the exclusionary rule. Michigan courts recognize the supremacy of federal law; in *People v. Pennington* (1970), the Michigan Supreme Court invalidated the final sentence of Article 1, section 11 to the extent that it conflicts with federal law. However, Michigan courts will not require any greater use of the exclusionary rule than that required by federal law (*People v. Nash*, 1983; *People v. Chapman*, 1986), absent a "compelling reason" (*People v. Collins*, 1991).

Not all searches fall within the ambit of section 11 protection. Reasonable searches and seizures are permissible notwithstanding the probable cause and warrant requirements. Reasonableness is determined by examining the totality of the circumstances surrounding a search or seizure as viewed through the eyes of a reasonable and cautious police officer on the scene, guided by the officer's experience and training (*People v. Summers*, 1979).

Probable cause is determined by a magistrate or judge on the basis of a sworn affidavit setting forth all facts known through the affiant's personal observation or hearsay (*People v. Sherbine*, 1984). In Michigan, the definition of "probable cause" is guided by statute (MCL 780.653; MSA 28.1259). The magistrate must consider the reliability of the information and the credibility of the informant in determining whether or not to issue the search or arrest warrant.

The warrant requirement allows for judicial supervision of police conduct and limits the scope of the allowed search. Usually, warrants must be secured before effecting a search or seizure. There are, however, numerous exceptions recognized in Michigan to the warrant requirement. For example, consensual searches, automobile searches (*People v. Parker*, 1983), searches incident to lawful arrest (*People v. Crawl*, 1977), discovery of items in plain view (*People v. Tyler*, 1977), and exigent circumstances (*People v. Plantefaber*, 1981) all have the potential for exceptions to the warrant requirement.

## SECTION 12

**Habeas corpus.** The privilege of the writ of habeas corpus shall not be suspended unless in case of rebellion or invasion the public safety may require it.

The writ of habeas corpus is the legal method for challenging the legality of a person's confinement. The constitution does not spell out the particular types of cases in which habeas corpus is appropriate; the common law and state statutes furnish this information. Michigan's experience with the writ dates to the Northwest Ordinance of 1787 and acts passed by the territorial governments in 1820 and 1833. The Constitution of 1835 and all subsequent constitutions have protected the writ of habeas corpus. The language of the present provision is identical to the language under the Constitution of 1908. In *People v. Collins* (1971), an opinion panel of the court of appeals stated that the right to a writ of habeas corpus is absolute and that the writ cannot be denied where the preconditions spelled out in the habeas corpus act have been met. The same opinion also stated that the writ could be suspended only in the extraordinary occasions allowed by the constitution itself (i.e., in case of rebellion or invasion).

## SECTION 13

**Conduct of suits in person or by counsel.** A suitor in any court of this state has the right to prosecute or defend his suit, either in his own proper person or by an attorney.

Section 13 gives an individual the right to represent him or herself in a criminal or civil lawsuit. The origins of section 13 may be found in the Constitution of 1850. The present language of the section differs from the language of the 1908 Constitution in only one respect: the phrase "or agent of his choice" was dropped after the word "attorney." The phrase was dropped because in 1938 the Michigan Supreme Court found the word "agent" synonymous with "attorney." The 1963 Constitution dropped this excess verbiage.

The right to present a defense under this section is regarded as "fundamental" but not absolute. An accused person must comply with established rules of procedure designed to assure both fairness and reliability in the determination of guilt or innocence (*People v. Hayes*, 1984). The Michigan Supreme Court has held that the right to self-representation is not absolute and that a trial judge must use his or her discretion in allowing a person to proceed without counsel (*People v. Henley*, 1969). In criminal prosecutions—the area that has generated the most commentary on self-representation—the Michigan Supreme Court has formulated three rules to guide a trial judge in determining whether or not to allow a criminal defendant to defend him or herself. First, the defendant must make an "unequivocal" request for self-representation." This requirement is designed to prevent frivolous appeals by defendants who were represented by counsel but were convicted nonetheless. Second, the trial court must determine whether the defendant is asserting the right "knowingly, intelligently and voluntarily." The trial judge must make the defendant aware of the "dangers and disadvantages of self-representation." The trial judge may consider a defendant's mental competence in evaluating the request but should not consider technical legal skills. Third, the trial judge must determine that self-representation "will not disrupt, unduly inconvenience and burden" the court's business and the administration of justice. (*People v. Anderson*, 1976).

## SECTION 14

**Jury trials.** The right of trial by jury shall remain, but shall be waived in all civil cases unless demanded by one of the parties in the manner prescribed by law. In all civil cases tried by 12 jurors a verdict shall be received when 10 jurors agree.

Section 14 guarantees the right of trial by jury but allows for a bench trial in civil cases unless one of the parties to suit demands a jury trial. The 1963 Constitution kept the language from the 1908 Constitution but added the last sentence, allowing verdicts to be reached in civil cases when ten of the twelve jurors agree.

Since the right to a jury trial is of constitutional status, the legislature cannot make any substantial changes in its character (*People v. Bigge*, 1941). The "significant element" in the substance of a jury trial is the right to jury determination of facts (*Peasley v. Lapeer Circuit Judge*, 1964). The form in which the jury determines facts is not of vital significance, and methods, such as the special verdict, may be introduced for the ascertainment of facts (*Peasley v. Lapeer Circuit Judge*, 1964).

## SECTION 15

**Double jeopardy; bailable offenses; commencement of trial if bail denied; bail hearing; effective date.** No person shall be subject for the same offense to be twice put in jeopardy. All persons shall, before conviction, be bailable by sufficient sureties, except that bail may be denied for the following persons when the proof is evident or the presumption great:

(a) A person who, within the 15 years immediately preceding a motion for bail pending the disposition of an indictment for a violent felony or of an arraignment on a warrant charging a violent felony, has been convicted of 2 or more violent felonies under the laws of this state or under substantially similar laws of the United States or another state, or a combination thereof, only if the prior felony convictions arose out of at least 2 separate incidents, events, or transactions.

(b) A person who is indicted for, or arraigned on a warrant charging, murder or treason.

(c) A person who is indicted for, or arraigned on a warrant charging, criminal sexual conduct in the first degree, armed robbery, or kidnapping with intent to extort money or other valuable thing thereby, unless the court finds by clear and convincing evidence that the defendant is not likely to flee or present a present danger to any other person.

(d) A person who is indicted for, or arraigned on a warrant charging, a violent felony which is alleged to have been committed while the person was on bail, pending the disposition of a prior violent felony charge or while the person was on probation or parole as a result of a prior conviction for a violent felony.

If a person is denied admission to bail under this section, the trial of the person shall be commenced not more than 90 days after the date on which admission to bail is denied. If the trial is not commenced within 90 days after the date on which admission to bail is denied and the delay is not attributable to the defense, the court shall immediately schedule a bail hearing and shall set the amount of bail for the person.

As used in this section, "violent felony" means a felony, an element of which involved a violent act or threat of a violent act against any other person.

This section, as amended, shall not take effect until May 1, 1979. Amendment ratified Nov. 7, 1978.

## Double Jeopardy

Each Michigan Constitution has contained a proscription against double jeopardy. The purpose of the double jeopardy prohibition is to limit the state to having generally one chance to obtain a conviction. Without this prohibition, the state could repeatedly prosecute persons for the same crime, transforming the trial process itself into a kind of punishment (*People v. Dawson*, 1988). The Constitutions of 1850 and 1908 added language attaching protection against double jeopardy "after acquittal on the merits." Despite this limiting language, Michigan courts interpreted double jeopardy as attaching when a jury is impaneled and sworn (*People v. Tillard*, 1947; *People v. Schepps*, 1925). The framers of the 1963 Constitution recognized that Michigan court practice over the years did not square with the language of the 1850 and 1908 Constitutions (1 *Official Record*, 1961, p. 468). The framers, therefore, substituted elements of the federal Constitution's double jeopardy provisions in order to bring the Michigan Constitution into line with historical court practice. The protection against double jeopardy does not bar all retrials for the same offense. Retrial is possible when the original jury is deadlocked and cannot reach a verdict or after a mistrial prompted by "manifest necessity" (*People v. Thompson*, 1985). There is an absolute bar against retrial following an acquittal on the merits of a case, or after reversal of a trial court decision by an appellate court for reasons of insufficient evidence (*People v. Thompson*, 1985).

## Bail

The Constitution of 1835 made all persons bailable except for those accused of "capital offences" when proof was evident or the presumption great. The 1850 and 1908 Constitutions substituted "murder or treason" for "capital offences." The original version of the Constitution of 1963 maintained the murder or treason exceptions to bail. The 1978 Amendment to the bail provisions of section 15 added new exceptions to the list of bailable persons but provided for a trial within 90 days if bail was denied under this section. If a trial does not begin within 90 days after the denial of bail, and the delay was not caused by the defense, a bail hearing must be held and bail set for the accused. The supreme court has recognized that the 1978 Amendment places extensive restrictions on bail and the court appears unwilling to read these restrictions narrowly (*People v. Sligh*, 1988).

### SECTION 16

**Bail; fines; punishments; detention of witnesses.** Excessive bail shall not be required; excessive fines shall not be imposed; cruel or unusual punishment shall not be inflicted; nor shall witnesses be unreasonably detained.

This section of the constitution dates from 1835. The prohibitions against cruel or unusual punishment and excessive fines come from the Northwest Ordinance. The 1850 Constitution added language on the detention of witnesses.

There has been little interpretation of the definition of an excessive fine. In *Robison v. Miner* (1888), the Michigan Supreme Court ruled that a fine placed on a business is excessive if it seriously impairs the capacity of gaining a business livelihood.

The Michigan prohibition against cruel *or* unusual punishment differs from its Eighth Amendment counterpart, which prohibits cruel *and* unusual punishment. The wording of prohibition against cruel or unusual punishment is significant. The Michigan Supreme Court has determined that the prohibition against unusual but not necessarily cruel punishment carries with it the implication that unusually excessive punishment is covered by the clause (*People v. Sinclair*, 1971; *People v. Lorentzen*, 1971). Whether or not a particular punishment is excessive is governed by three tests. First, there is the test of proportionality: Does the punishment fit the crime? Here, the court will look to the punishments imposed in Michigan for crimes of similar seriousness. Next, the court will ask whether the punishment squares with "evolving standards of decency that mark the progress of a maturing society." The court will poll punishment patterns for the same crime in other states to see if Michigan policy is in line with the rest of the states. If Michigan policy is, then the punishment passes the evolving standards test. Finally, the court will ask whether the punishment is consistent with the goal of rehabilitation of the offender. The court works from the assumption that Michigan public policy has long recognized the goal of rehabilitation. The state constitutional provision for indeterminate sentences (Article IV, section 45) and judicial decisions on indeterminate sentences are used to underscore the importance of rehabilitation. (*People v. Lorentzen*, 1971).

There has been little reference to the detention of witnesses in Michigan law. One panel of the court of appeals has speculated that a statute providing for the detention of a material witness for the prosecution would probably run afoul of this section. The same panel also noted that the detention of witnesses is simply not feasible in this day and age due to prison overcrowding (*People v. Connor*, 1989).

### SECTION 17

**Self-incrimination; due process of law; fair treatment at investigations.** No person shall be compelled in any criminal case to be a witness against himself, nor be deprived of life, liberty or property, without due process of law. The right of all individuals, firms, corporations and voluntary associations to fair and just treatment in the course of legislative and executive investigations and hearings shall not be infringed.

The first sentence of section 17 dates from the Constitution of 1850. The second sentence was added in 1963. The *Address to the People* explains that this second sentence does not automatically import due process standards into legislative and executive investigations and hearings. Rather, it is left for the legislative and executive branches, and for the courts to develop fair rules of procedures.

## Self-Incrimination

The Michigan Constitutional law of the privilege against self-incrimination is closely tied to federal court interpretations of the Fifth Amendment to the federal Constitution and the prophylactic rules of *Miranda v. Arizona* (1966). This clause of section 17 is coextensive with the Fifth Amendment and Miranda, although in *People v. Camelio* (1984) the supreme court argued that section 17 should be "construed liberally." Michigan courts have prohibited the use of involuntary confessions at trial as an element of due process since 1929 in *People v. Cavanaugh*. By 1953 in *People v. Louzon*, the state supreme court ruled that this state constitutional privilege against self-incrimination rendered involuntary confessions inadmissible at trial. Section 17 does make confessions obtained through promises of leniency involuntary and inadmissible at trial (*People v. Camelio*, 1984). Section 17 also does not protect certain statements of codefendants at trial. Once one codefendant elects to testify against the other, the former codefendant can invoke the protection of section 17 on cross-examination (*People v. Mobley*, 1973). Like the Fifth Amendment, section 17 has been extended beyond the context of a criminal trial. The protections of section 17 protect persons in all settings in which their freedom of actions is curtailed in any significant way (*People v. Schollaert*, 1992).

The guarantee of fairness in legislative and executive investigations does not modify the scope of the privilege against self-incrimination. Therefore, officers of firms, corporations, and voluntary associations who control the documents and records of the organizations may not invoke the privilege against self-incrimination to prevent disclosure of the documents and records. The Supreme Court of Michigan believes that such an expansion of the privilege against self-incrimination would "drastically" impede the investigation of white-collar crime (*Paramount Corporation v. Miskinis*, 1984).

## Due Process

*Procedural.* Procedural due process under Article 1, section 17 is violated when there is a failure to observe that fundamental fairness essential to the very concept of justice (*People v. Thompson*, 1985; *Dodge v. Detroit Trust Company*, 1942). The kinds of procedural protections needed to satisfy the due process clause vary according to the nature of the proceeding and the nature of the interests affected by it (*Artibee v. Cheboygan Circuit Judge*, 1974): The more complex the issues addressed in a proceeding, the greater the need for procedural protections; the more substantial the interests of the affected individual, the greater the need for procedural protections.

A statute may offend the due process clause if it is too vague or overbroad. One of the core requirements of due process is adequate notice. An individual should understand what the law requires so that he or she can adjust his or her activities to conform with the law. A law enforcement officer must also understand what the law requires, such that the officer can enforce the law fairly. Vague statutes do not give an individual or a law enforcement officer adaquate notice of the requirements of the law. Michigan courts treat overbroad laws as a subset of vague laws. The "overbreadth doctrine" is seen most often in cases involving freedom of speech. Under our system of limited government under law, the government may limit individual rights and liberties only to achieve certain legitimate public goals. Important freedoms, such as freedom of speech, should be limited very carefully and as narrowly as possible. Overbroad statutes limit too much. They limit constitutionally protected words and conduct, as well as words and conduct that the government has a legitimate interest in regulating.

The theory behind the overbreadth doctrine holds that people fear prosecution and punishment and, because of this fear, they will be deterred from exercising their constitutionally protected rights and liberties. When confronted with a broad law, people will err on the side of caution. The standards for determining if a statute is "void-for-vagueness" are: (1) if the statute is overbroad, impinging on freedoms such as freedom of speech, as guaranteed by the First Amendment of the federal Constitution; (2) if the statute does not provide fair notice of the conduct proscribed; or (3) if the statute is so indefinite that it confers unstructured and unlimited discretion on the trier of fact to determine whether an offense has been committed (*People v. Hayes*, 1984; *Woll v. Attorney General*, 1980).

*Substantive.* The due process clause may also be used to effect a challenge to state regulation. In the sphere of economic regulation, Michigan courts have adopted a deferential approach to legislature. Courts recognize that the state may use its police power to enact laws promoting public health, safety, and welfare. Such laws carry a strong presumption of constitutionality, and the burden of proof to overcome this presumption rests with those challenging the law. The challengers must show that no reasonable state of facts can be ascertained that would justify the law or that the legislation bears no reasonable relationship to a legitimate government interest (*Blue Cross and Blue Shield of Michigan v. Governor*, 1985; *Romein v. General Motors*, 1990). The Michigan Supreme Court has suggested a stricter standard of review under the due process clause for regulations affecting family living arrangements. In *Charter Township of Delta v. Dinfolo* (1984), the supreme court struck down a zoning ordinance narrowly defining "family," because the ordinance lacked a fair and substantial relationship to legitimate government ends such as the preservation of family values, the maintenance of property values, and population and density control.

## Hearings and Investigations

This language was added to section 17 to assure fair treatment in legislative or executive investigations, with the recognition that such investigations have tended to assume a quasi-judicial character. The new language does not necessarily impose all the requirements of due process on such investigations. Instead, the three branches of government will develop rules of procedure appropriate to such investigations (*Paramount Pictures Corporation v. Miskinis*, 1984).

## SECTION 18

**Witnesses; competency, religious beliefs.** No person shall be rendered incompetent to be a witness on account of his opinions on matters of religious belief.

Section18 remains unchanged since the Constitution of 1850. This provision allows atheists to testify and is therefore another guarantee of religious liberty in the Michigan Constitution. Michigan courts read this section of the constitution to prohibit the questioning of witnesses in reference to a belief in a God unless it can be shown that the belief or disbelief in a God has no reference to opinions on the subject of religion. Therefore, questioning a witness about belief in God—even if done only as an oblique reminder of the fact a witness is under oath—is prohibited (*People v. Bouchee*, 1977; *People v. Hall*, 1974).

## SECTION 19

**Libels, truth as defense.** In all prosecutions for libels the truth may be given in evidence to the jury; and, if it appears to the jury that the matter charged as libelous is true and was published with good motives and for justifiable ends, the accused shall be acquitted.

The substance of section 19 dates from the Constitution of 1835. The only major change was introduced in 1850 when the 1835 language stating that a jury will determine both fact and law in a libel case was dropped. In prosecutions for libel, the defendant must first show the truth of the allegedly libelous statements before consideration is given to motive (*People v. Talbot*, 1917). Section 19 also requires that libel defendants have a reasonable opportunity to discover relevant evidence that is essential to their defense of truth (*Howe v. Detroit Free Press, Inc.*, 1992).

## SECTION 20

**Rights of accused in criminal proceedings.** In every criminal prosecution, the accused shall have the right to a speedy and public trial by an impartial jury, which may consist of less than 12 jurors in prosecutions for misdemeanors punishable by imprisonment for not more than 1 year; to be informed of the nature of the accusation; to be confronted with the witnesses against him to have compulsory process for obtaining witnesses in his favor; to have the assistance of counsel for his defense; to have an appeal as a matter of right, except as provided by law an appeal by an accused who pleads guilty or *nolo contendere* shall be by leave of the court; and, as provided by law, when the trial court so orders, to have such reasonable assistance as may be necessary to prosecute an appeal.

Amendment ratified August 8, 1972. Effective September 23, 1972. Amendment ratified November 8, 1994. Effective December 24, 1994.

Section 20 speaks to the rights of accused persons in criminal proceedings. Although the major principles of section 20 date from the Constitution of 1835, there have been some modifications. The Constitution of 1850 introduced the possibility of juries of less than twelve. The 1963 Constitution substituted the word "juror" for "men," recognizing that women can and do serve on juries. The 1963 Constitution also added the provision of appeal by right, assuring that each defendant will receive at least one appeal to a higher court. The legislature could provide for additional appeals over and above this constitutional guarantee (*People v. Pickett*, 1974).

The 1972 amendment to section 20 changed the definition of cases in which a jury of less than twelve may be used. The original wording of section 20 allowed juries of less than twelve in all courts except courts of record. Now, jury size depends on the nature of case rather than the court in which the case is tried. A jury of less than twelve may be used in prosecutions for misdemeanors punishable by prison terms of not more than one year. The 1994 amendment to section 20 limited the right to make an appeal after entering a plea of guilty or *nolo contendere*, meaning that the accused does not contest the charges lodged against him or her. Appeal after either of these pleas may be made only with the permission of the court. This amendment overturned the effect of the Michigan Supreme Court decision in *People v. Smith* (1977), which had ruled that a criminal defendant possesses the right to appeal even on convictions based upon a plea of guilty.

## Speedy Trial

Michigan courts balance four factors in determining whether or not a defendant has been denied the right to a speedy trial. These factors are: (1) the length of the delay before trial; (2) the reason for the delay; (3) the defendant's assertion of the right; and (4) the chances of prejudice to the defendant (*People v. Hill*, 1976). An unconditional guilty plea is taken as a waiver of the right to a speedy trial (*People v. Smith*, 1991). The constitutional right to a speedy trial is secured in Michigan statutory law (M.C.L.A. 768.1).

## Public Trial

The public trial clause of section 20 creates rights for both the public and the accused. There is a public interest in scrutiny of trials in order to assure that justice is administered fairly and openly. This public scrutiny also protects the accused by helping to guarantee fairness. Because there is a public interest in public trials, the accused does not have the right to waive a public trial. The public may be excluded from a criminal trial only where there is a substantial probability that prejudicial error denying the accused a right to a fair trial will result (*Detroit Free Press v. Recorder's Court Judge*, 1980). The public trial clause of section 20 is read as creating a public right of access to trials. However, the public trial clause does not encompass a right of the public or the press to attend pretrial examinations (*In re Midland Publishing Co, Inc.*, 1985).

## Impartial Jury

The right to trial by an impartial jury is regarded as "most fundamental." However, the right to trial by jury does not mean there is a corresponding, unconditional right to waiver a jury trial (*People v. Kirby*, 1992). Challenging jurors before trial and examining jurors during the course of a trial is seen as essential to securing an impartial jury. Therefore, the accused has a right to be present while the jury is impanelled or when the jury is examined. Any misconduct on the part of a jury that violates this section of the constitution is presumptively grounds for a new trial (*People v. Medcoff*, 1955).

## Nature of the Accusation

The requirement that the accused be informed of the nature of the accusations against him or her enables the accused to mount an effective defense. The Michigan Supreme Court has ruled that this constitutional right requires that the accused be given a definite statement of the time, place, and manner of committing the offense and a definite statement of the charge itself (*People v. Maki*, 1929).

## Confrontation

The confrontation clause serves as a truth finding device (*People v. Watkins*, 1991). The clause assures that: (1) witnesses will give statements under oath; (2) witnesses will be subject to cross-examination; and (3) the jury will be able to observe the witnesses as they testify, enhancing the ability of the juror to assess the witnesses' credibility (*People v. Banks*, 1991).

## Compulsory Process

The Michigan Supreme Court characterizes the compulsory process clause as the right to offer the testimony of witnesses, and to compel their attendance is, in essence, the right to present a defense (*People v. Merritt*, 1976).

## Assistance of Counsel

Following Thomas Cooley, Michigan courts have recognized that the right to counsel is perhaps the "privilege most important to the person accused of crime" (*People v. Pickens*, 1994). The right to counsel attaches after the initiation of formal adversary judicial proceedings. After the formal charge, the accused is entitled to the assistance of counsel at all "critical stages" of the prosecution. A critical stage is one where the absence of counsel might derogate from the accused's right to a fair trial. Critical stages of prosecution include the formal charge, the preliminary hearing, and the information as well as the formal trial (*People v. Bladel*, 1984).

The Michigan Constitution's guarantee of the right to counsel does not afford a greater protection than its federal constitutional counterpart when the right is invoked to make a claim of ineffective assistance of counsel. An accused person's counsel must offer something more than a "feeble and heartless defense." Under both federal and state constitutional standards, in order for a claim of ineffective assistance of counsel to succeed, a defendant must show that the counsel's performance fell below an objective standard of reasonableness and that the representation so prejudiced the defendant as to deprive him or her of a fair trial (*People v. Pickens*, 1994).

An accused person may waive the right to counsel under section 20, but Michigan courts apply strict standards to determine whether an accused person has waived the right to counsel at trial or any other critical stage of the prosecution. A waiver of the right to counsel may be proven by showing that the accused knew of the right and made an intentional and intelligent waiver of the right. The state must tell the accused person of the nature of the right to counsel and the protection that an attorney can provide. Courts will also indulge in every reasonable presumption against a waiver of the right to counsel (*People v. Leonard*, 1984).

### Right to an Appeal

The new constitutional guarantee of at least one appeal means that the state's criminal proceedings against an individual begin at the point of arraignment and continue through the right of appeal. Trial courts are under an obligation, therefore, to assign an appellate counsel for an indigent criminal defendant (*Frederick v. Presque Isle County Circuit Judge*, 1991). This right extends to convictions of city ordinance violations as well as convictions of violations of state criminal statutes (*Walber v. Wayne Circuit Judge*, 1967).

## SECTION 21

**Imprisonment for debt.** No person shall be imprisoned for debt arising out of or founded on contract, express or implied, except in cases of fraud or breach of trust.

The prohibition against imprisonment for debt was introduced in the Constitution of 1850. The framers of the 1963 Constitution modified the 1908 language and dropped exceptions concerning military fines in times of peace and the collection of money by public officers. These exceptions were considered excess verbiage since the principles contained in the exceptions were covered by other provisions of the constitution.

A decree for alimony is not considered a debt under section 21, and therefore a party in default in payment for alimony may be subject to incarceration (*Bowman v. Wayne Circuit Judge,* 1921). Taxes are not seen as contractual obligations of the taxpayer to the state (*Thompson v. Auditor General,* 1933). The government may constitutionally use the criminal sanction of imprisonment for refusal to pay taxes (*City of Detroit v. Pillon,* 1969).

## SECTION 22

**Treason; definition, evidence.** Treason against the state shall consist only of levying war against it or adhering to its enemies, giving them aid and comfort. No person shall be convicted of treason unless upon the testimony of two witnesses to the same overt act or confession in open court.

The definition of treason has remained virtually unchanged since the Constitution of 1835. There have been no interpretations of this section.

## SECTION 23

**Enumeration of rights not to deny others.** The enumeration in this constitution of certain rights shall not be construed to deny or disparage others retained by the people.

This is a new addition to the Declaration of Rights. It is identical in language and spirit to the Ninth Amendment to the federal Constitution. For both the United States and Michigan, this provision is an answer to the fear that no bill of rights could ever be a complete catalog of human freedoms under a system of limited government. Thus, the Ninth Amendment and section 23 make certain that simple omission of a right from the list in the Declaration of Rights does not mean that the right does not exist. Neither provision, though, provides an answer to the important questions of what are the sources of the unenumerated rights and who should define what the rights are and what they comprehend. Michigan courts have not used section 23 as a mechanism for the creation of new constitutional rights.

## SECTION 24

**Rights of crime victims; enforcement; assessment against convicted defendants.** (1) Crime victims, as defined by law, shall have the following rights, as provided by law:

The right to be treated with fairness and respect for their dignity and privacy throughout the criminal justice process.

The right to timely disposition of the case following the arrest of the accused.

The right to be reasonably protected from the accused throughout the criminal justice process.

The right to notification of court proceedings.

The right to attend trial and all other court proceedings the accused has the right to attend.

The right to confer with the prosecution.

The right to make a statement to the court at sentencing.

The right to restitution.

The right to information about the conviction, sentence, imprisonment, and release of the accused.

(2) The legislature may provide by law for the enforcement of this section.

(3) The legislature may provide for an assessment against convicted defendants to pay for crime victims' rights.

Amendment Ratified Nov. 8, 1988. Effective Dec. 24, 1988.

Section 24 is a bill of rights for victims of crime. The legislature has implemented section 24 in the Crime Victim's Rights Act, M.C.L.A. 780.751 et seq. Michigan courts rely on this statute rather than the provisions of section 24 in interpreting the contours of the rights of crime victims.

# Article II

## *Elections*

### SECTION 1

**Qualifications of electors; residence.** Every citizen who has attained the age of 21 years, who has resided in this state six months, and who meets the requirements of local residence provided by law, shall be an elector and qualified to vote in any election except as otherwise provided in this constitution. The legislature shall define residence for voting purposes.

All Michigan constitutions have contained language on the qualifications for voters. Article II of the Constitution of 1835 limited the right to vote to white males over the age of 21. The 1850 Constitution was amended three times, and the limitation of the franchise to white persons was omitted. The franchise was still restricted to males, but foreign-born men who had resided in the state for 25 years and indicated the intention to become citizens could vote, as could "civilized" male inhabitants of Indian descent. The Constitution of 1908 in Article III, section 1 added considerable statutory detail on voter qualifications but retained the same basic requirements. An amendment to the constitution in 1914 allowed for absentee voting, and a 1918 amendment extended the right to vote to women. The six-month durational residency requirement was a feature of all Michigan Constitutions.

Two federal constitutional developments have affected the operation of this section of the Michigan Constitution. The Twenty-Sixth Amendment to the federal Constitution, passed in 1971, lowered the voting age to eighteen. In *Dunn v. Blumstein* (1972), the United States Supreme Court invalidated one-year durational residency requirements as violative of the equal protection clause of the Fourteenth Amendment. The Supreme Court later sustained 50-day durational residency requirements (*Marston v. Lewis*, 1973; *Burns v. Forston*, 1973). The six-month requirement of section 1 is no longer considered applicable (*Attorney General Opinion No. 6081*). The current statutory requirement is 30 days.

Michigan courts consider the right to vote fundamental; any statute affecting the right to vote must be justified by a compelling state interest (*Michigan State U.A.W. Community Action Program Council v. Secretary of State*, 1972; *Wilkins v. Ann Arbor City Clerk*, 1970). Moreover, the statute must be precise in its regulation, and the state bears the burden of demonstrating that the regulation is necessary and essential and not achievable by less drastic means (*Michigan State U.A.W. Community Action Program Council*, 1972). Therefore, statutes that de-registered voters who failed to vote within the past two years (*Michigan State U.A.W. Community Action Program Council*, 1972) or that denied absentee ballots to pretrial detainees (*Arlee v. Wayne County Sheriff*, 1974) violated this section of the Michigan Constitution.

## SECTION 2

**Mental incompetence; imprisonment.** The Legislature may by law exclude persons from voting because of mental incompetence or commitment to a jail or penal institution.

This is a new section of the Michigan Constitution. Convention records indicate that the purpose of this new section is to give the legislature explicit authority to accomplish what had been long-standing Michigan practice (2 *Official Record*, p. 2214). While inmates had not been disenfranchised formally in the past, there was no statutory authorization for the provision of absentee ballots to inmates. Thus, inmates were effectively disenfranchised.

Pretrial detainees may not be excluded from voting under section 2. Since pretrial detainees are presumptively innocent and are otherwise qualified voters, a statutory scheme must allow for voting via absentee ballot (*Arlee v. Wayne County Sheriff*, 1974).

## SECTION 3

**Presidential electors; residence.** For purposes of voting in the election for president and vice president of the United States only, the legislature may by law establish lesser residence requirements for citizens who have resided in this state

> for less than six months and may waive residence requirements for former citizens of this state who have removed herefrom. The legislature shall not permit voting by any person who meets the voting residence requirements of the state to which he has removed.

This new section of the constitution acknowledges the importance of the two highest federal offices and the fact that we live in a mobile society. The state legislature is empowered to allow new residents of Michigan to vote in presidential elections only. The state may also allow former residents of Michigan to vote for president and vice-president in Michigan so long as the former residents do not meet the voting residency requirements of their new state.

There have been no judicial interpretations of this section.

## SECTION 4

> **Place and manner of elections.** The legislature shall enact laws to regulate the time, place and manner of all nominations and elections, except as otherwise provided in this constitution or in the constitution and laws of the United States. The legislature shall enact laws to preserve the purity of elections, to preserve the secrecy of the ballot, to guard against abuses of the elective franchise, and to provide for a system of voter registration and absentee voting. No law shall be enacted which permits a candidate in any partisan primary or partisan election to have a ballot designation except when required for identification of candidates for the same office who have the same or similar surnames.

Section 4 gives the state legislature general supervisory power over the electoral process. Section 4 finds its origins in Article VII, section 6 of the Constitution of 1850. The 1850 document simply allowed for the passage of laws to preserve the purity of election and to guard against abuses of the elective franchise. The 1908 Constitution preserved the 1850 language in Article III, section 8, and this section was amended in 1913 to allow for recall of elected officials. The 1963 Constitution removed the recall language and added new material on the preservation of ballot secrecy and the creation of a system of absentee voting. The final sentence of section 4 prohibits ballot designations of candidates except to avoid confusion when candidates for the same office have similar names.

The attorney general has reasoned that the purity of elections clause requires the state to institute a system of voter registration (*Attorney General Opinion No. 4644*, 1968). The clause also dictates that election procedures must try to achieve equality of treatment for all candidates (*Wells v. Kent County Board of Election Commissioners*, 1969). Thus, a state statute limiting the ballot access of minority political parties was held unconstitutional under this section (*Socialist Workers Party v. Secretary of State*, 1981). However, a statute authorizing public funding for major party candidates did not offend section 4 (*Jacobs v. Headlee*, 1984).

The Michigan Supreme Court has read section 4 to guarantee a right to a secret ballot that cannot be abrogated in the absence of a showing of fraud (*Belcher v. Mayor of Ann Arbor*, 1978). The requirement that the state should provide for a system of absentee ballots has been interpreted by one court to mean that there is a fundamental right to an absentee ballot (*Arlee v. Wayne County Sheriff*, 1974).

The prohibition against ballot designations means that nothing may appear on a ballot except: (1) party designation in partisan elections; (2) designations permitted to identify a candidate; or (3) designation of incumbency for those holding judicial office (*Wells*, 1969). The incumbency designation for judicial officers is an exception required by Article VI, section 24 of the 1963 Constitution. The purpose of the prohibition against ballot designation is to prevent "free advertising" of the qualifications of a candidate. However, to avoid confusion when candidates have similar names, the candidates' addresses, occupations, or former occupations may be included on the ballot so that voters can effectively distinguish among the candidates (*Evans v. City of Detroit Election Commission*, 1968).

## SECTION 5

**Time of elections.** Except for special elections to fill vacancies, or as otherwise provided in this constitution, all elections for national, state, county and township offices shall be held on the first Tuesday after the first Monday in November in each even-numbered year or on such other date as members of the congress of the United States are regularly elected.

Section 5 is new to the Constitution of 1963. This section abolished the spring elections that began under the Constitution of 1850, with provisions for the April election of circuit judges (Article VI, section 20) and township officers (Article XI, section 1). The Constitution of 1908 continued the tradition of spring elections for justices of the supreme court and judges of the circuit court (Article VII, sections 2 and 9), while probate judges were elected in November (Article VII, section 14). Township officers were also elected in the spring (Article VIII, section 18).

## SECTION 6

**Voters on tax limit increases or bond issues.** Whenever any question is required to be submitted by a political subdivision to the electors for the increase of the ad valorem tax rate limitation imposed by Section 6 of Article IX for a period of more than five years, or for the issue of bonds, only electors in, and who have property assessed for any ad valorem taxes in, any part of the district or territory to be affected by the result of such election or electors who are the lawful husbands or wives of such persons shall be entitled to vote thereon. All electors in the district or territory affected may vote on all other questions.

Section 6 limits voting on millage increases to property owners and their spouses. This section dates from the 1908 Constitution and in its day was quite progressive because it allowed women to vote. Today, this section is unconstitutional under federal guarantees of equal protection. In *Hill v. Stone* (1975), the U.S. Supreme Court reasoned that any law affecting the right to vote was subject to strict scrutiny (see Article I, section 2). Generally, unless an election is for narrow, special purposes, the only tolerable constitutional qualifications for voting are residence, age, and citizenship.

## SECTION 7

**Boards of canvassers.** A board of state canvassers of four members shall be established by law. No candidate for an office to be canvassed nor any inspector of elections shall be eligible to serve as a member of a board of canvassers. A majority of any board of canvassers shall not be composed of members of the same political party.

The board of state canvassers is responsible for counting votes and certifying election returns. The phrase "established by law" means that the details concerning the operation of the board will be determined by state statutes that also define the powers and duties of the board. State statutes have also established boards of canvassers at the county level.

The Constitution of 1835 had no provision for a state board of canvassers, although in elections for governor and lieutenant governor, election returns were sealed and directed to the president of the senate for public opening and publishing (Article V, section 4). Article VIII, section 4 of the 1850 Constitution introduced a board of canvassers. This board did not have its own members but was instead made up of the secretary of state, state treasurer, and commissioner of the state land office. The board determined the result of election for governor, lieutenant governor, state officers, and other officers determined by law. The Constitution of 1908 originally continued this old arrangement. A constitutional amendment adopted in 1955 created a bipartisan board of four members (Article III, section 9).

Michigan courts regard the duties of the board of canvassers as purely ministerial and clerical (*McLeod v. State Board of Canvassers*, 1942). The board is bound by election returns and cannot pass on the legality of elections (*McQuade v. Ferguson*, 1892).

## SECTION 8

**Recalls.** Laws shall be enacted to provide for the recall of all elective officers except judges of courts of record upon petition of electors equal in number to 25 percent of the number of persons voting in the last preceding election for the office of governor in the electoral district of the officer sought to be recalled. The sufficiency of any statement of reasons or grounds procedurally required shall be a political rather than a judicial question.

Recall, or the removal of an elected officer before the expiration of his or her term by a vote of the electorate, dates from a 1913 amendment to the 1908 Constitution. Michigan was among the first states to adopt recall as fundamental law; Oregon was the first in 1908. Section 8 embodies an "intensity check" to make sure that time and money are not wasted on frivolous recall petitions. In order to trigger the recall of an elected official, recall petitions must be signed by a number of voters equal to 25 percent of the number of persons voting for governor in the electoral district of the officer to be recalled. Certain offices are exempt from recall. Judges of courts of record defined in Article VI, section 19 of the 1963 Constitution may not be recalled. Details as to the exact operation of the recall are specified in state statutes.

The recall provision was originally placed in Article III, section 8 of the 1908 Constitution along with other provisions on the purity of elections. The Constitution of 1963 placed the right of recall in its own section and strengthened it by limiting the role of courts in reviewing grounds for the recall of an official. Supreme court opinions on recall under the 1908 Constitution limited recall to instances of "misfeasance, malfeasance or nonfeasance in office" (*Newberg v. Donnelly*, 1926; *People ex rel. Elliott v. O'Hara*, 1929; *Amberg v. Welsh*, 1949; *Eaton v. Baker*, 1952). In 1960 in *Wallace v. Tripp*, the Michigan Supreme Court overruled *Newberg v. Donnelly* and its progeny and determined that the sufficiency of reasons for recall is a decision for the electorate rather than the judiciary. The framers of the 1963 constitution were much aware of these decisions and feared another change of heart by the courts. The recall provision was amended to guarantee that the sufficiency of reasons for recall would remain a political rather than a judicial question (2 *Official Record*, pp. 2263–66). Michigan courts have been faithful to the intent of the framers on this point (*Mastin v. Oakland County Elections Commission*, 1983).

Courts, nevertheless, still maintain a limited role in the interpretation and supervision of the recall process. Courts will require compliance with the statutory procedures for recall and will insist that the reasons for the recall be sufficiently clear to ensure deliberate and informed action on the part of the electorate (*Noel v. Oakland County Clerk*, 1979). When the clarity of a recall petition is a close question, the issue will be resolved in favor of the proponents of the recall (*Molitor v. Miller*, 1980).

## SECTION 9

**Initiative and referendum; limitations; appropriations; petitions.** The people reserve to themselves the power to propose laws and to enact and reject laws, called the initiative, and the power to approve or reject laws enacted by the legislature, called the referendum. The power of initiative extends only to laws that the legislature may enact under this constitution. The power of referendum does not extend to acts making appropriations for state institutions or to meet deficiencies in state funds and must be invoked in the manner prescribed by law within 90 days following the final adjournment of the legislative session at which the law was enacted. To invoke the initiative or referendum, petitions signed by a number of registered electors, not less than eight percent for the initiative and five percent for the referendum of the total vote cast for all candidates for governor at the last preceding general election at which a governor was elected shall be required.

No law as to which the power of referendum properly has been invoked shall be effective thereafter unless approved by a majority of the electors voting thereon at the next general election.

Any law proposed by initiative petition shall be either enacted or rejected by the legislature without change or amendment within 40 session days from the time such petition is received by the legislature. If any law proposed by such petition shall be enacted by the legislature it shall be subject to referendum, as hereinafter provided.

If the law so proposed is not enacted by the legislature within the 40 days, the state officer authorized by law shall submit such proposed law to the people for approval or rejection at the next general election. The legislature may reject any measure so proposed by initiative petition and propose a different measure upon the same subject by a yea and nay vote upon separate roll calls, and in such event both measures shall be submitted by such state officer to the electors for approval or rejection at the next general election.

Any law submitted to the people by either initiative or referendum petition and approved by a majority of votes cast thereon at any election shall take effect 10 days after the date of the official declaration of the vote. No law initiated or adopted by the people shall be subject to the veto power of the governor, and no law adopted by the people at the polls under the initiative provisions of this section shall be amended or repealed, except by a vote of the electors unless otherwise provided in the initiative measure or by three-fourths of the members elected to and serving in each house of the legislature. Laws approved by the people under the referendum provision of this section may be amended by the legislature at any subsequent session thereof. If two or more measures approved by the electors at the same election conflict, that receiving the highest affirmative vote shall prevail.

The legislature shall implement the provisions of this section.

The initiative and referendum were added to the constitution in April 1913. The original versions of these direct democracy provisions were careful to include much statutory-type detail on procedure for initiative and referendum so that the provisions would be self-executing (i.e., not dependent on the legislature for implementation). The framers of the 1963 Constitution eliminated much of the statutory-type detail but carefully made sure that direct democracy is preserved by requiring the legislature to implement the provisions of section 9. The direct democracy provisions are still self-executing, and the legislature may not curtail or burden the rights of the people under section 9 (*Ferency v. Secretary of State*, 1980). Any statute that is unnecessary for the effective administration of these provisions is unconstitutional (*Wolverine Golf Club v. Secretary of State*, 1971).

Initiative, defined as the power to "propose legislative measures, resolutions and laws," requires a petition signed by the equivalent of at least 8 percent of the total vote cast for candidates for governor at the last preceding election at which a governor was elected. Referendum, or the power to "approve or reject any act passed by the legislature," requires a 5 percent signature threshold. The requirement of a certain percentage of voters as signatories to a petition is referred to as an "intensity check" that assures that the ballot will not be cluttered by trivial or frivolous proposals. A referendum must be invoked within 90 days after the final adjournment of the legislature at which the challenged law was enacted. If voters invoke a referendum on a law, the law cannot take effect until it is approved by a majority of voters voting on the question at the next general election.

Laws initiated by the people are sent to the legislature for consideration. The legislature has two options in considering an initiated law. The legislature may pass the law without any change within 40 days of receipt of the initiative. If the legislature passes the law, the law is subject to the referendum. Initiated laws enacted by the legislature go into effect 90 days after the end of the legislative session at which they were enacted. Article IV, section 27 applies to initiated laws enacted by the legislature. Therefore, a two-thirds vote of each house is required to give the law immediate effect (*Frey v. Director of the Department of Management and Budget*, 1987). Alternatively, the legislature may reject the law outright or propose another law on the same subject. If the legislature rejects the law, the initiated law must be sent back to the people for consideration at referendum, and, if the law is approved by the people, it goes into effect. If the legislature proposes an alternative law, the alternative must be passed with a roll call vote of each house of the legislature. Then the original initiated law and the legislative alternative are submitted to the people in a referendum at the next general election.

Once a law submitted to the people by initiative or referendum is approved, it becomes effective ten days after the election is made official. The governor cannot veto a law passed through initiative or referendum. Initiated laws can be repealed only by another initiative or by a three-fourths vote of both houses of the legislature. Laws subject to the referendum may be repealed or amended at any subsequent session of the legislature by the usual process.

The power of the initiative extends only to laws that could be enacted by the legislature under the constitution. Generally, the Michigan Supreme Court has allowed measures of questionable constitutionality to be placed before the people. The court in *Hamilton v. Secretary of State* (1920) reasoned that there was a chance that the measure would be rejected by the people anyway, and that, should the initiative succeed, there would be ample opportunity for judicial review of the initiative in actual operation. The power of referendum does not extend to acts of appropriations for state institutions or to meet deficiencies in state funds. These two exceptions have been used by the legislature, with approval from the state supreme court, to place certain taxes beyond the reach of the people by referendum. To avoid the possibility of a referendum, the legislature creates a tax, places its proceeds in a special fund, and immediately appropriates the tax to a "state institution." The state supreme court in *Detroit Automobile Club v. Secretary of State* (1925) and *Moreton v. Secretary of State* (1927) upheld this practice as beyond the power of the referendum and expanded the number of exemptions by broadly construing the term "state institutions" to include "all organized departments of the State to which the legislature has delegated or should delegate the exercise of state functions" (*County Road Association of Michigan v. Board of State Canvassers*, 1979). A deficiency in state funds refers only to an actual deficiency that exists at the time of the passage of the act. Statutes passed to cover anticipated deficiencies in state funds are subject to the referendum (*Kuhn v. Department of Treasury*, 1971).

The 40-day clock for legislative consideration of an initiative petition runs from the time the petition is received by the legislature. Simply filing the petition with the secretary of state does not start the 40-day period (*In re Proposals D & H*, 1983). The receipt of an initiative petition does not suspend the legislative process. The legislature may consider and pass measures on the same subject as an initiative petition. If a legislative action that has been submitted to the people under Article IV, section 34 and an initiative compete on the same ballot, the proposal with the highest number of votes prevails. The Supreme Court has rejected the idea that initiated laws are on a "higher plane" than legislative action (*In re Proposals D & H*, 1983).

## SECTION 10

**Limitations on terms of office of members of the United States House of Representatives and United States Senate from Michigan.** No person shall be elected to office as representative in the United States House of Representative more than three times during any twelve year period. No person shall be elected to office as senator in the United States Senate more than two times during any twenty-four year period. Any person appointed or elected to fill a vacancy in the United States House of Representatives or the United States Senate for a period of greater than one half of a term of such office, shall be considered to have been elected to serve one time in that office for the purposes of this section. This limitation on the number of times a person shall be elected to office shall apply to terms of office beginning on or after January 1, 1993.

> The people of Michigan hereby state their support for the aforementioned term limits for members of the United States House of Representatives and United States Senate and instruct their public officials to use their best efforts to attain such a limit nationwide.
>
> The people of Michigan declare that the provisions of this section shall be deemed severable from the remainder of this amendment and that their intention is that federal officials elected from Michigan will continue voluntarily to observe the wishes of the people as stated in this section, in the event any provision of this section is held invalid.
>
> This section shall be self-executing. Legislation may be enacted to facilitate operation of this section, but no law shall limit or restrict the application of this section. If any part of this section is held to be invalid or unconstitutional, the remaining parts of this section shall not be affected but will remain in full force and effect.

Section 10, along with Article IV, section 54 and Article V, section 30, were enacted during the anti-incumbent frenzy of the 1992 election. Simply stated, this section limits terms of office for members of both houses of the United States Congress. Members of the U.S. House of Representatives are limited to three terms during any twelve-year period. Members of the U.S. Senate are restricted to two terms during any 24-year period. A partial term of office counts as a term for the purposes of this section if the partial term is greater than one-half the usual term of office.

The second paragraph of this section expresses Michigan's support for national term limits. Michigan public officials are directed to work to attain nationwide term limits for members of Congress.

The third paragraph of this section is designed to preserve as much of section 10 as possible should an element of the section be struck down by a court. This paragraph declares that each element of the section exists separately and independently, such that a defect in one part need not be fatal to the entire section. This paragraph also urges Michigan's members of Congress to observe term limits voluntarily in the event an element of the section is nullified.

The final paragraph makes section 10 self-executing (i.e., it is not dependent on the legislature for implementation). In the event an element of section 10 is struck down, the remaining parts will remain in full force and effect.

Michigan's limitation on terms of office for members of Congress is unconstitutional. The Supreme Court of the United States struck down a similar amendment to the Arkansas Constitution in *U.S. Term Limits, Inc. v. Thorton* (1995). The Supreme Court offered three major reasons why term limits for members of Congress offend the federal Constitution. First, terms of office for members of Congress are fixed by Article I of the Constitution. Not even Congress itself can alter these terms, even by invoking congressional authority under Article I, section 5, clause 1 to judge the qualifications of members. Second, states cannot impose congressional term limits by invoking the powers reserved to the states under the Tenth Amendment to the federal Constitution. The Supreme Court found that the power to supplement the qualifications for members of Congress was not a power that states possessed before the adoption of the Congress. Moreover, individual state qualifications for members of Congress would undermine the vision of the framers of the Constitution of a uniform national legislature representing all the people of the United States. The court also cautioned the states that they may not accomplish term limits indirectly by disadvantaging incumbents. Finally, the Supreme Court found that term limits for members of Congress would effect such a fundamental change in the framework of American government that it must come through the vehicle of a constitutional amendment.

Despite the fact that the major elements of section 10 are unconstitutional under Article I of the federal Constitution, Michigan public officials may still follow the urging of the people and work for an amendment to the federal Constitution to secure nationwide term limits. Michigan's members of Congress may also express their sympathy with the sentiments in section 10 by voluntarily accepting term limits.

# Article III

## *General Government*

### SECTION 1

**Seat of government.** The seat of the government shall be at Lansing.

This straightforward section of the constitution establishes the state capital at Lansing. Detroit was the original capital of Michigan. An act of the state legislature in 1847 moved the capital to Lansing.

There have been no judicial interpretations of this section.

### SECTION 2

**Separation of powers of government.** The powers of government are divided into three branches; legislative, executive and judicial. No person exercising the powers of one branch shall exercise powers properly belonging to another branch except as expressly provided in this constitution.

Section 2 creates a system of separation of powers for the government of Michigan. Separation of powers is regarded as essential to the preservation of liberty. As James Madison noted in *Federalist No. 47*: "The accumulation of all powers, legislative, executive and judiciary, in the same hands, whether hereditary, self-appointed, or elective, may justly be pronounced the very definition of tyranny." The principle of separation of powers has been embodied in each of Michigan's constitutions. The 1963 Constitution uses the word "branch" rather than the old "department" of government for the sake of clarity. This substitution has been the only substantial change in the constitution.

The principle of separation of powers protects the independence of each of the three branches of government and forbids the extension of the powers of one department into another (*Civil Service Commission v. Auditor General*, 1942). For example, the judiciary must play a limited role in zoning decisions, since zoning is primarily a legislative function (*Schwartz v. City of Flint*, 1987). Likewise, the legislature and the executive branch cannot invade the powers of the judiciary by allowing the Michigan Employees Relations Commission to exercise jurisdiction over employees of the state supreme court (*In the Matter of the Petition for a Representation Election Among Supreme Court Staff Employees*, 1979). Nor can the state Open Meetings Act apply to the judicial branch (*In re 1976 PA 267*, 1977).

Most cases concerning separation of powers arise over the issue of the delegation of power by the legislature to administrative agencies. Under traditional notions of separation of powers, the legislature has sole power to make laws; administrative agencies housed in the executive branch simply implement laws. Modern legislation often seeks to solve complicated problems. Legislatures do not usually possess the expertise, foresight, and time needed to fully address all aspects of a regulatory scheme. Administrative agencies are typically given broad authorization and considerable discretion for implementing legislation and will promulgate rules and regulations that have the force of law to implement legislation. The question is at what point does this legislative delegation of power to administrative agencies amount to an unconstitutional violation of the principle of separation of powers? Michigan courts look to the "standards test" to determine whether a given delegation does violence to separations of powers. Under the standards tests, legislation must contain standards that are as reasonably precise as the subject matter requires or permits in order to govern the actions of the administrative agency (*Westervelt v. Natural Resources Commission*, 1978). Legislative standards assure that when administrative agencies promulgate rules or regulations, the agencies are merely filling in administrative details in the statutory scheme rather than making law.

## SECTION 3

**Great seal.** There shall be a great seal of the State of Michigan and its use shall be provided by law.

Michigan has always had a great seal that is used to authenticate government actions. The Constitutions of 1835, 1850, and 1908 provided that the seal would be kept by the secretary of state and used to authenticate "official acts" of the governor. The 1963 Constitution retained the great seal but allows the legislature to define the terms and conditions of its use.

## SECTION 4

**Militia.** The militia shall be organized, equipped and disciplined as provided by law.

The state militia (now the National Guard) used to rate its own article in the constitution. The Constitution of 1835 in Article IX allowed the legislature to define the organization and discipline of the militia and give the governor the power to call forth the militia. An 1870 amendment to the 1850 Constitution in Article XVII added provisions on eligibility for militia service. The 1908 Constitution retained the provisions of the militia in Article XV. The Constitution of 1963 eliminates the statutory language of earlier constitutions and entrusts the legislature to provide for the structure of the militia by state statutes.

Article V, section 2 of the Constitution of 1963 makes the governor commander-in-chief of the armed forces of the state. On occasion, there have been conflicts between statutes regulating the militia under Article III, section 4 and the governor's power as commander-in-chief. The state supreme court has ruled that in cases regarding the operation of the militia, statutes passed pursuant to Article III, section 4 prevail over the inherent powers of the governor as commander-in-chief. Thus, disciplinary action with respect to an adjutant general of the militia is handled under this specific provision of the state constitution rather than under the general provisions concerning the powers of the governor in Article V (*McDonald v. Schnipke*, 1968).

## SECTION 5

**Intergovernmental agreements; service by public officers and employees.** Subject to provisions of general law, this state or any political subdivision thereof, any governmental authority or combination thereof may enter into agreements for the performance, financing or execution of their respective functions, with any one or more of the other states, the United States, the Dominion of Canada, or any political subdivision thereof unless otherwise provided in this constitution. Any other provision of this constitution notwithstanding, an officer or employee of the state or of any such unit of government or subdivision or agency thereof may serve on or with any governmental body established for the purposes set forth in this section and shall not be required to relinquish his office or employment by reason of such service. The legislature may impose such restrictions, limitations or conditions on such service as it may deem appropriate.

Section 5 is a new section of the constitution. This section recognizes that some government functions might be most appropriately approached on a regional basis. Therefore section 5 allows for various units of state and local government to enter into agreements with each other, other states, or Canada to facilitate the performance of government functions. These agreements must be consistent with not only federal and state constitutional requirements but also with state statutes authorizing the creation of these intergovernmental agreements. Thus a Michigan county could enter into an agreement with a Wisconsin county for the joint operation of their county hospitals, but they could not form a nonprofit corporation for that purpose because the legislature had not enacted a statute authorizing that action. (*Attorney General Opinion No. 5448*, 1979)

## SECTION 6

**Internal improvements.** The state shall not be a party to, not be financially interested in, any work of internal improvement, nor engage in carrying on any such work, except for public internal improvements provided by law.

The Constitution of 1835 in Article XII, section 3 required the state government to encourage internal improvements. Extravagant use of the internal improvements clause—coupled with high state debt, oppressive taxation, and a national financial crisis—led to the constitutional convention of 1850. Article XIV, section 9 of the Constitution of 1850 specifically prohibited the state from becoming involved in internal improvements. Amendments to the 1850 constitution in 1893 and 1905 softened the absolute ban and allowed for some internal improvements for public wagon roads and the Grand River. The 1908 Constitution in Article X, section 9 continued the ban on state involvement in internal improvements, but again amendments in 1945 and 1946 allowed certain kinds of improvements such as the construction of airports, flood control and drainage projects, and reforestation programs. The framers of the Constitution of 1963 were acutely aware of the Michigan experience concerning internal improvements. Section 6 eliminates the specific constitutionally sanctioned exceptions to the general ban. Now, any public internal improvement authorized by an act of the legislature is permissible under the Michigan Constitution.

Michigan courts have been very deferential to the legislature in determining the definition of public internal improvement. The state supreme court has looked to Justice Thomas Cooley's exposition of the word "public" to outline the limits of legislative power. Necessity alone is not the test of a truly public act; the legislature may look to any activities that promote the general well-being of society and advance the happiness and prosperity of the people (*Advisory Opinion on Constitutionality of 1975 PA 301*, 1977). Michigan courts have also held that self-liquidating bonds do not fall under the general provisions of this section, since self-liquidating bonds do not obligate the general taxing power (*City of Gaylord v. Gaylord City Clerk*, 1966).

## SECTION 7

**Common law and statutes, continuance.** The common law and the statute laws now in force, not repugnant to this constitution, shall remain in force until they expire by their own limitations, or are changed, amended or repealed.

This section of the constitution finds its origins in the first section of the Schedules of the 1850 and 1908 Constitutions. The section minimized confusion and inconvenience as the state moved to a new constitutional system.

Most judicial interpretations of this section have involved changes to the common law. The common law is essentially judge-made law; it has evolved through series of judicial decisions rather than through acts of the legislature. Under section 7, both the courts and the legislature have the power to change the common law (*Placek v. City of Sterling Heights*, 1979; *Shavers v. Attorney General*, 1978). However, statutes that alter the common law must be strictly construed (*Rusinek v. Schultz, Snyder & Steel Lumber Co.*, 1981; *Morgan v. McDermott*, 1969) and will not be extended by implication (*Bandfield v. Bandfield*, 1898).

## SECTION 8

**Opinions on constitutionality by supreme court.** Either house of the legislature or the governor may request the opinion of the supreme court on important questions of law upon solemn occasions as to the constitutionality of legislation after it has been enacted into law but before its effective date.

This section is new to the constitution. Section 8 empowers the state supreme court to issue advisory opinions at the request of the governor or either house of the state legislature. There is a narrow window of opportunity during which an advisory opinion may be requested. The request must come after a piece of legislation has been enacted into law but before its effective date. Legislation that becomes effective upon the signature of the governor can never be a candidate for an advisory opinion.

The Michigan Supreme Court is usually reluctant to grant advisory opinions since this represents a departure from the traditional judicial role to decide actual controversies in which the factual record is developed by real adversary parties (*Request for Advisory Opinion on Constitutionality of 1977 PA 108, 1977*). Requests for advisory opinions must particularize any claims of unconstitutionality (*Advisory Opinion re Constitutionality 1972 PA 284*) and may not be so broad as to depend for resolution on hypothetical factual situations (*Advisory Opinion re Constitutionality of 1974 PA 272*, 1975). An advisory opinion is not binding as precedent on the court; it represents only the opinion of the signatory justices framed in a factual void (*Request for Advisory Opinion on the Constitutionality of 1979 PA 57*).

# Article IV

*Legislative Branch*

## SECTION 1

**Legislative power.** The legislative power of the State of Michigan is vested in a senate and a house of representatives.

Since Michigan's first constitution, the power to make laws has been vested in a bicameral legislature. The legislative power, simply put, is the "law-making power of a sovereign state" (*Decher v. Secretary of State,* 1920). State legislative power is plenary within the state's territorial limits, except to the extent state power has been delegated to the federal government or voluntarily restrained by the people of the state through the state constitution (*In re Brewster Street Housing Site,* 1939). Section 1 of the Constitution of 1908 was amended in 1913 to reserve to the people the powers of initiative and referendum. The Constitution of 1963 removed these provisions on direct democracy from Article 4, section 1 and placed the initiative and referendum in section 9 of Article 2.

## SECTION 2

**Senators, number, term.** The senate shall consist of 38 members to be elected from single member districts at the same election as the governor for four-year terms concurrent with the term of office of the governor.

In districting the state for the purpose of electing senators after the official publication of the total population count of each federal decennial census, each county shall be assigned apportionment factors equal to the sum of its percentage of the state's population as shown by the last regular federal decennial census computed to the nearest one-one hundredth of one percent multiplied by four and its percentage of the state's land area computed to the nearest one-one hundredth of one percent.

In arranging the state into senatorial districts, the apportionment commission shall be governed by the following rules:

(1) Counties with 13 or more apportionment factors shall be entitled as a class to senators in the proportion that the total apportionment factors of such counties bear to the total apportionment factors of the state computed to the nearest whole number. After each such county has been allocated one senator, the remaining senators to which this class of counties is entitled shall be distributed among such counties by the method of equal proportions applied to the apportionment factors.

(2) Counties having less than 13 apportionment factors shall be entitled as a class to senators in the proportion that the total apportionment factors of such counties bear to the total apportionments factors of the state computed to the nearest whole number. Such counties shall thereafter be arranged into senatorial districts that are compact, convenient, and contiguous by land, as rectangular in shape as possible, and having as nearly as possible 13 apportionment factors, but in no event less than 10 or more than 16. Insofar as possible, existing senatorial districts at the time of reapportionment shall not be altered unless there is a failure to comply with the above standards.

(3) Counties entitled to two or more senators shall be divided into single member districts. The population of such districts shall be as nearly equal as possible but shall not be less than 75 percent nor more than 125 percent of a number determined by dividing the population of the county by the number of senators to which it is entitled. Each such district shall follow incorporated city or township boundary lines to the extent possible and shall be compact, contiguous, and as nearly uniform in shape as possible.

Under the Constitution of 1835, the number of state senators was a function of the size of the state house of representatives: The membership of the senate was equal to one-third the membership of the house of representatives. This first constitutional system also provided for staggered, two-year terms of office for state senators. The Constitution of 1850 set the number of senators at 32 and retained the two-year terms of office. The Constitution of 1908 substantially maintained the 1850 scheme. Section 2 increases the number of state senators from 34 to 38 and increases the term of office to four years. State senators no longer serve staggered terms; instead, the election of state senators coincides with the election of the governor. All Michigan constitutions have required single-member senate districts and directed the preservation of county lines in the assignment of senate districts.

Section 2 also provides an elaborate formula for the apportionment of state senatorial seats. The apportionment formula for seats factors in both population and land area. For the most part, these provisions have been declared unconstitutional as a matter of federal constitutional law (see commentary at the end of section 6).

## SECTION 3

**Representatives, number, term; contiguity of districts.** The house of representatives shall consist of 110 members elected for two-year terms from single member districts apportioned on a basis of population as provided in this article. The districts shall consist of compact and convenient territory contiguous by land.

Each county which has a population of not less than seven-tenths of one percent of the population of the state shall constitute a separate representative area. Each county having less than seven-tenths of one percent of the population of the state shall be combined with another county or counties to form a representative area of not less than seven-tenths of one percent of the population of the state. Any county which is isolated under the initial allocation as provided in this section shall be joined with that contiguous representative area having the smallest percentage of the state's population. Each such representative area shall be entitled initially to one representative.

After the assignment of one representative to each of the representative areas, the remaining house seats shall be apportioned among representative areas on the basis of population by the method of equal proportions.

Any county comprising a representative area entitled to two or more representatives shall be divided into single member representative districts as follows:

(1) The population of such districts shall be as nearly equal as possible but shall not be less than 75 percent nor more than 125 percent of a number determined by dividing the population of the representative area by the number of representatives to which it is entitled.

(2) Such single member districts shall follow city and township boundaries where applicable as nearly square in shape as possible.

Any representative area consisting of more than one county, entitled to more than one representative, shall be divided into single member districts as equal as possible in population, adhering to county lines.

This section of the Constitution of 1963 sets the number of members of the state house of representatives at 110. Amendments to the 1908 Constitution had set the maximum number of senators at 110. Except for the Constitution of 1835, under which representatives served terms of a single year, terms of office have been set at two years (see commentary at the end of section 6).

## SECTION 4

**Annexation or merger with a city.** In counties having more than one representative or senatorial district, the territory in the same county annexed to or merged with a city between apportionments shall become part of a contiguous representative or senatorial district in the city with which it is combined, if provided by ordinance of the city. The district or districts with which the territory shall be combined shall be determined by such ordinance certified to the secretary of state. No such change in the boundaries of a representative or senatorial district shall have the effect of removing a legislator from office during his term.

Section 4 is new to the state constitution. This section covers the eventuality that two representative or senatorial districts may be combined between elections. In the event of an annexation or a merger in which the annexation or merger does not cross county lines, the new legislative district will be determined by city ordinance. Section 4 also guarantees that no legislator will lose his or her seat in mid-term as a result of a merger (see commentary at the end of section 6).

## SECTION 5

**Island areas, contiguity.** Island areas are considered to be contiguous by land to the county of which they are a part.

This new section of the constitution treats island areas of the state as if they were joined to the mainland county of which they are a part (see commentary at the end of section 6).

## SECTION 6

**Commission on legislative apportionment.** A commission on legislative apportionment is hereby established consisting of eight electors, four of whom shall be selected by the state organizations of each of the two political parties whose candidates for governor received the highest vote at the last general election at which a governor was elected preceding each apportionment. If a candidate for governor of a third political party has received at such election more than 25 percent of such gubernatorial vote, the commission shall consist of 12 members, four of whom shall be selected by the state organization of the third political party. One resident of each of the following four regions shall be selected by each political party organization: (1) the upper peninsula; (2) the northern part of the lower peninsula, north of a line drawn along the northern boundaries of the counties of Bay, Midland, Isabella, Mecosta, Newaygo and Oceana; (3) southwestern Michigan, those counties south of region (2) and west of a line drawn along the western boundaries of the counties of

Bay, Saginaw, Shiawassee, Ingham, Jackson and Hillsdale; (4) southeastern Michigan, the remaining counties of the state.

No officers or employes of the federal state or local governments excepting notaries public and members of the armed forces reserve, shall be eligible for membership on the commission. Members of the commission shall not be eligible for election to the legislature until two years after the apportionment in which they participated becomes effective.

The commission shall be appointed immediately after the adoption of this constitution and whenever apportionment or districting of the legislature is required by the provision of this constitution. Members of the commission shall hold office until each apportionment or districting plan becomes effective. Vacancies shall be filled in the same manner as for original appointment.

The secretary of state shall be secretary of the commission without vote, and in that capacity shall furnish, under the direction of the commission, all necessary technical services. The commission shall elect its own chairman, shall make its own rules of procedure, and shall receive compensation provided by law. The legislature shall appropriate funds to enable the commission to carry out its activities. Within 30 days after the adoption of this constitution, and after the official total population count of each federal decennial census of the state and its political subdivisions is available, the secretary of state shall issue a call convening the commission not less than 30 nor more than 45 days thereafter. The commission shall complete its work within 180 days after all necessary census information is available. The commission shall proceed to district and apportion the senate and the house of representatives according to the provisions of this constitution. All final decisions shall require the concurrence of a majority of the members of the commission. The commission shall hold public hearings as may be provided by law.

Each final apportionment and districting plan shall be published as provided by law within 30 days from the date of its adoption and shall become law 60 days after publication. The secretary of state shall keep a public record of all the proceedings of the commission and shall be responsible for the publication and distribution of each plan.

If a majority of the commission cannot agree on a plan, each member of the commission, individually or jointly with other members, may submit a proposed plan to the supreme court. The supreme court shall determine which plan complies most accurately with the constitutional requirements and shall direct that it be adopted by the commission and published as provided in this section.

Upon the application of any elector filed not later than 60 days after the final publication of the plan, the supreme court, in the exercise of original jurisdiction, shall direct the secretary of state or the commission to perform their duties, may review any final plan adopted by the commission, and shall remand such plan to the commission for further action if it fails to comply with the requirements of this constitution.

Section 6, a new addition to the constitution, sets up a commission to apportion the state legislature after the federal census.

Most of the provisions of sections 2 through 6 have been held unconstitutional by the Michigan Supreme Court in *In re Apportionment of State Legislature* (1982) as violations of the federal law of equal protection under the one-person, one vote rationale of *Reynolds v. Sims* (1964). Provisions of section 2 and section 3, which take into account land area as well as population in apportioning the legislature, violate the one-person, one-vote requirement of federal law. Since the rest of the rules in sections 2 through 6 are inextricable from the area/ population formula, they too are unconstitutional under federal law. The Michigan Supreme Court has developed principles for the apportionment of the legislature that it believes are consonant with federal requirements and the spirit of the Michigan Constitution. First, all senate and house districts must be drawn consistent with the federal principle of equality between election districts. Next, county lines should be preserved as far as possible within the federal equality principle. In counties with multiple representatives and senators, city and township lines should be preserved as far as possible. When districts must be created within a city or township, election district lines must be drawn to achieve the most compact districts possible (*In re Apportionment of State Legislature*, 1982).

## SECTION 7

**Legislators; qualifications, removal from district.** Each senator and representative must be a citizen of the United States, at least 21 years of age, and an elector of the district he represents. The removal of his domicile from the district shall be deemed a vacation of the office. No person who has been convicted of subversion or who has within the preceding 20 years been convicted of a felony involving a breach of the public trust shall be eligible for either house of the legislature.

Each Michigan Constitution has required a state legislator to be an American citizen and to reside in the district he or she represents. In 1956, the Constitution of 1908 was amended to include the additional qualification that a member of the legislature be at least 21 years of age and to exclude any person who had been convicted of subversion or a felony involving the breach of public trust from candidacy for the state legislature. Section 7 of the Constitution of 1963 substantially maintains the old language, except for removing the disqualification for subversion or felony involving a breach of public trust after 20 years.

A "qualified elector" is simply a registered voter (*Attorney General Opinion No. 6081*, 1982). Residence, for the purpose of voting and for holding seats in the state legislature, is determined by two factors: (1) the fact of physical presence and (2) the intention to remain in the district (*Attorney General Opinion No. 4931*, 1976).

## SECTION 8

**Ineligibility of government officers and employees.** No person holding any office, employment or position under the United States or this state or a political subdivision

> thereof, except notaries public and members of the armed forces reserve, may be a member of either house of the legislature.

Section 8 prevents a member of the state legislature from holding a position in the federal government, the state government or a unit of local government. However, notaries public or members of the armed forces reserve may serve in the legislature. All Michigan Constitutions contained a general prohibition on state legislators holding other simultaneous government offices, but earlier constitutions allowed different exceptions. In 1835, in Article IV, Section 8, legislators could also serve as officers of the militia, justices of the peace, associate justices of circuit, and county courts and postmasters. By 1850, in Article IV, section 6, only notaries public, officers of the militia, and township officials could also serve in the state legislature. The Constitution of 1908 maintained the same exceptions and also precluded non-excepted officers from running for the legislature. Section 8 of the 1963 Constitution now allows non-excepted officers to run for the state legislature, but successful candidates must resign their other government positions before assuming a seat in the state legislature. For example, a public school employee must resign his or her position in order to comply with this section of the constitution (*Attorney General Opinion No. 6165*, 1983).

## SECTION 9

> **Civil appointments, ineligibility of legislators.** No person elected to the legislature shall receive any civil appointment within this state from the governor, except notaries public, from the legislature, or from any other state authority, during the term for which he is elected.

Section 9 prohibits a member of the legislature from accepting any additional government appointments (with the single exception of a notary public) during his or her term of office. Prohibitions against legislators holding additional government positions have been in place since the Constitution of 1835. The Constitution of 1850, in Article IV, section 18, added three additional provisions: State legislators were prohibited from appointment to the United States Senate. All additional appointments given state legislators and all votes cast for a legislator for an additional office were declared null and void. State legislators were also prohibited from any direct or indirect interest in a state or county contract authorized during the legislator's term or for one year after. Article V, section 7 of the Constitution of 1908 mirrored the 1850 language.

The Constitution of 1963 altered elements of section 9. The 1963 section removed unnecessary language declaring additional appointments or votes for other officers null and void. The new section 9 also permits a sitting legislator to be appointed to the United States Senate. The prohibition against legislator interest in contracts was moved to a separate section of the constitution and is now a part of Article IV, section 10.

This constitutional provision serves two basic purposes: First, it prevents legislators from vote trading or logrolling in the legislature to secure a civil appointment. Second, it prevents legislators from creating new posts and running for them (*Young v. Detroit City Clerk*, 1973). Thus, the provision cannot bar a state senator from being a candidate in a mayoral primary election (*Young v. Detroit City Clerk*, 1973). Article IV, section 9 also does not bar mobility within the legislature: A sitting state representative may announce candidacy for a vacancy in the state senate (*Vaughn v. Wayne County Clerk*, 1974).

## SECTION 10

**Legislators and state officers, government contracts, conflict of interest.** No member of the legislature nor any state officer shall be interested directly or indirectly in any contract with the state or any political subdivision thereof which shall cause a substantial conflict of interest. The legislature shall further implement this section by appropriate legislation.

The constitutions of 1850 and 1908 both contained two sections prohibiting state legislators from direct or indirect interest in a contract with the state. One section generally prohibited direct or indirect interest in a contract with the state. Other sections (Article IV, section 22 of the Constitution of 1850; Article V, section 26 of the Constitution of 1908) specifically prohibited legislators from any interest in a fuel or printing contract for the state legislature. Section 10 of the Constitution of 1963 includes all state officers as well as state legislators and prohibits anyone in the service of the state from interest in any contract that causes a substantial conflict of interest. Section 10 also gives the legislature the authority to implement the section by appropriate legislation.

According to an opinion of the Attorney General, the new language of this section fundamentally alters the public policy of the state (*Attorney General Opinion No. 6468*, 1987). No longer is there a blanket prohibition against any interest in a contract with the state regardless of the extent of the interest. Now, "interest" refers to a pecuniary interest, and the personal interest must be of such substance as to induce actions on behalf of the state official in promoting his or her personal interest (*Attorney General Opinion No. 6468*). This provision helps to assure that the public will receive the best judgment of its officials untrammeled by personal interest (*Attorney General Opinion No. 6211*, 1984).

## SECTION 11

**Legislators privileged from civil arrest and civil process; limitation; questioning for speech in either house prohibited.** Except as provided by law, senators and representatives shall be privileged from civil arrest and civil process during sessions of the legislature and for five days next before the commencement and after the termination thereof. They shall not be questioned in any other place for any speech in either house. Amendment ratified Nov. 2, 1982. Effective Dec. 18, 1982.

Section 11 prevents the arrest of legislators during legislative sessions and immunizes speech made in the legislature from suit. Section 11 and its counterpart in the federal Constitution (Article I, section 6, clause 1) can trace their origins to the struggle for parliamentary supremacy in England. The immunity granted the legislators prevented the monarch from using the civil law to thwart the operation of representative government. Such a provision also protects legislators "from the trouble, worry and inconvenience of court proceedings during (legislative) session, and for a certain time before and after, so that the State could have their undivided time and attention in public affairs" (*Auditor General v. Wayne Circuit Judge, 1926*). The Constitution of 1835 privileged legislators from arrest except in cases of treason, felony, or breach of peace (Article IV, section 9) and extended the privilege for fifteen days before the start and after the end of a legislative session. The Constitution of 1850 added protection for speech made in either house of the legislature and the 1908 Constitution continued the 1850 language. The framers of the 1963 Constitution reduced the fifteen-day immunity to five days and emphasized the civil law nature of the privilege, making clear that legislators were not immune from the criminal law. The 1982 amendment added the introductory language "except as provided by law" that allows the legislature to make exceptions to the privilege from civil arrest or process.

The word "sessions" in this section encompasses more than regular sessions and special sessions when the legislature is actually sitting. Time spent on constituent contact, research, committee assignments, and other legislative business is also covered by the privilege (*Bishop v. Wayne County Circuit Judge*, 1976).

The final sentence of this section protects legislators from lawsuits based on statements made in the course of political debate in the legislature and legislative activities. A panel of the Michigan Court of Appeals has held that this immunity from suit is not so broad as to provide protection from suits for intentional torts, even if the alleged court was committed while performing legislative-related activities (*Prelesnik v. Esquina*, 1984).

## SECTION 12

**State officers compensation commission.** The state officers compensation commission is created which shall determine the salaries and expense allowances of the members of the legislature, the governor, the lieutenant governor and the justices of the supreme court. The commission shall consist of 7 members appointed by the governor. The commission shall determine the salaries and expense allowances of the members of the legislature, the governor, the lieutenant governor and the justices of the supreme court which determinations shall be the salaries and expense allowances unless the legislature by concurrent resolution adopted by 2/3 of the members elected to and serving in each house of the legislature reject them. The commission shall meet each 2 years for no more than 15 session days. The legislature shall implement this section by law. Amendment ratified Aug. 6, 1968. Effective Sept. 21, 1968.

Each Michigan Constitution has contained a section on the compensation of legislators. Article IV, section 18 of the Constitution of 1835 allowed the legislature to set legislators' salaries, provided that such compensation not exceed three dollars per day. The Constitution of 1850 maintained the three-dollar maximum but limited compensation to days of actual attendance. Legislators from the upper peninsula were allowed greater compensation for the hardship of lengthy travel. The 1850 Constitution added much statutory language on mileage and stationery allowances for members of the legislature. The Constitution of 1908 omitted the constitutional maximum on legislative salaries but also eliminated the mileage and stationery allowances. The original 1963 Constitution simply stated that the compensation and expense allowances of members of the legislature shall be determined by law.

Section 12 was amended in 1968 to create the state officers compensation commission. The commission determines salaries and expense allowance for the top officials of the three branches of state government. The decisions of the compensation commission stand unless they are rejected by concurrent resolution adopted by a two-thirds majority of both houses in the legislature.

The compensation commission may only set salaries and expense allowance; it may not determine fringe benefits. However, the commission may consider the value of fringe benefits in its determination of salary. The term "expense allowances" refers to normal reimbursable personal expenses such as food, lodging, and travel incurred on official business (*Holmes v. State Officers Compensation Commission*, 1974).

## SECTION 13

**Legislature; time of convening, sine die adjournment, measures carried over.** The legislature shall meet at the seat of government on the second Wednesday in January of each year at twelve o'clock noon. Each regular session shall adjourn without day [*sic*], on a day determined by concurrent resolution, at twelve o'clock noon. Any business, bill or joint resolution pending at the final adjournment of a regular session held in an odd numbered year shall carry over with the same status to the next regular session.

Section 13 sets the time, date, and place when the legislature convenes and the procedure by which the legislature adjourns at the end of a session. Previous

Michigan Constitutions followed the congressional model that prohibits legislative business from carrying over from one session to the next. The 1963 Constitution now allows business to be carried over to the next regular session—an innovation that the framers believed would save time and money.

The definition of "pending" business, bill, or joint resolution is contained in the Joint Rules of the Senate and the House of Representatives. "Pending" business, bill, or joint resolution is any action that has not been defeated by either house of the legislature (*Attorney General Opinion No. 6017*, 1981).

## SECTION 14

**Quorum; powers of less than quorum.** A majority of members elected to and serving in each house shall constitute a quorum to do business. A smaller number in each house may adjourn from day to day, and may compel the attendance of absent members in the manner and with penalties as each house may prescribe.

Section 14 defines a quorum and allows members in attendance to compel the appearance of absent members of legislature. There is one major difference between section 14 of the 1963 Constitution and its counterparts in earlier Michigan constitutions. The 1963 Constitution is careful to define majority in terms of members elected to and serving in each house of the legislature. This definition prevents vacant seats from being counted in computing a quorum. In 1934, six representatives and one senator were killed in the Hotel Kerns fire. The seven vacant seats had to be counted in the computation of a quorum under the 1908 Constitution (*Wilson v. Atwood*, 1935), thereby rendering it difficult to secure the required number of legislators to transact business. The new language in the 1963 Constitution allows the legislature to operate despite such a tragedy.

## SECTION 15

**Legislative council.** There shall be a bi-partisan legislative council consisting of legislators appointed in the manner prescribed by law. The legislature shall appropriate funds for the council's operations and provide for its staff which shall maintain bill drafting, research and other services for the members of the legislature. The council shall periodically examine and recommend to the legislature revision of the various laws of the state.

This is a new section of the Michigan Constitution. Section 15 establishes a legislative council that will consist of representatives of both political parties. The precise method of appointing members of the council as well as the budget and staff and staff of the council are determined by state law. The legislative council provides bill drafting and research services for both houses. Partisan or personal use of the legislative council is strictly prohibited (*Alan v. Wayne County*, 1972).

## SECTION 16

**Legislature; officers, rules of procedure, expulsion of members.** Each house, except as otherwise provided in this constitution, shall choose its own officers and determine the rules of its proceedings, but shall not adopt any rule that will prevent a majority of the members elected thereto and serving therein from discharging a committee from the further consideration of any measure. Each house shall be the sole judge of the qualifications, elections and returns of its members, and may, with the concurrence of two-thirds of all the members elected thereto and serving therein, expel a member. The reasons for such expulsion shall be entered in the journal, with the votes and names of the members voting upon the question. No member shall be expelled a second time for the same cause.

This section of the constitution allows each house of the legislature to choose its own officers and to adopt rules of procedure with one proviso: Procedural rules must not prevent a majority of members from directing a committee to terminate consideration of any measure. This proviso limits the power of legislative committees. Section 16 also makes each house the sole judge of the qualifications and election of any member and provides a mechanism whereby a member of the legislature may be expelled by his or her peers in the same house. Each Michigan Constitution has had provisions similar to those in section 16. The 1963 version defines majority in terms of members serving in the legislature and requires that the votes as well as the names of those voting on expulsion be recorded.

The power of the state legislature to make reasonable rules for its operation is regarded as an absolute power limited only by the constitution itself (*Attorney General Opinion No. 6195*, 1983). Rules of procedure adopted by the legislature and not prescribed by the constitution are not reviewable in any court (*Anderson v. Atwood*, 1935). The authority of the legislature to act as sole judge of its elections is conclusive and not subject to challenge in any court (*Attorney General ex rel. Beers v. Board of Canvassers of Seventh Senatorial District*, 1908). The power of each house to judge the qualifications of its member is continuous and runs through the entire term. This means that the legislature may at any time pass on the qualifications of its members (*McLeod v. State Board of Canvassers*, 1942). Members of the legislature have plenary power to determine when a member merits expulsion and can act to prevent a member from completing a term (*Attorney General Opinion No. 5295*, 1978).

## SECTION 17

**Committees; record of votes, public inspection, notice of hearings.** Each house of the legislature may establish the committees necessary for the efficient conduct of its business and the legislature may create joint committees. On all actions on bills and resolutions in each committee, names and votes of members shall be recorded. Such votes shall be available for public inspection. Notice of all committee hearings and a clear statement of all subjects to be considered at each hearing shall be published in the journal in advance of the hearing.

Section 17, allowing the creation of legislative committees and governing their operation, is new to the Constitution of 1963. The bulk of legislative work is performed in committee, and section 17 makes sure that members of the legislature and the public are aware of the work of committees (*Attorney General Opinion No. 5300,* 1978). Section 17 also assures that the voting records of legislative committee members shall be available for public scrutiny.

## SECTION 18

**Journal of proceedings; record of votes, dissents.** Each house shall keep a journal of its proceedings, and publish the same unless the public security otherwise requires. The record of the vote and the name of the members of either house voting on any question shall be entered in the journal at the request of one-fifth of the members present. Any member of either house may dissent from and protest any act, proceeding or resolution which he deems injurious to any person or the public, and have the reason for his dissent entered in the journal.

Each Michigan constitution has had a provision similar to Section 18. The language of this section remains unchanged from the Constitution of 1908. Roll call votes of legislators must be taken when one-fifth of the members present request such a vote. Section 18 guarantees that legislative dissenters will have the reasons for their dissent entered in the legislative journal.

The legislature has the responsibility to assure that the journal is accurate and properly kept (*McClelland v. Judge of Recorders Court of Detroit,* 1924). The journal is used by courts to make certain that the legislature follows constitutionally prescribed procedures for law making (*McClelland v. Judge of Recorder's Court of Detroit,* 1924).

## SECTION 19

**Record of votes on elections and advice and consent.** All elections in either house or in joint convention and all voted on appointments submitted to the senate for advice and consent shall be published by vote and by name in the journal.

Section 19 requires roll call votes for elections in either house and for appointments submitted to the senate for advice and consent. Earlier Michigan constitutions allowed for the same kinds of votes to be taken *viva voce* (i.e., orally). Section 19 helps constituents know how their senators and representatives vote in these two areas. There have been no interpretations of this section.

## SECTION 20

**Open meetings.** The doors of each house shall be open unless the public security otherwise requires.

Since the Constitution of 1835, Michigan has required open government. Section 20 represents a slight modification in language from its earlier counterparts. Under the Constitutions of 1835, 1850, and 1908, the doors of the legislature could be closed when "the public welfare requires secrecy." The new section 20 substitutes the more limited term "public security" to describe the situation in which access to the legislature would be limited. There have been no interpretations of this section.

## SECTION 21

**Adjournments, limitations.** Neither house shall, without the consent of the other, adjourn for more than two intervening calendar days, nor to any place other than where the legislature may then be in session.

Legislation must be approved by both houses of the legislature before presentation to the governor for signature. Section 21 keeps both houses of the legislature in session at the same time and in the same place so that neither house can thwart the legislative process by its absence. The 1963 version of this provision represents a clarification of the language in the 1908 and earlier constitutions. Earlier constitutions prohibited adjournment for more than three days, which led to disputes as to whether Sundays or holidays had to be counted (*Attorney General Opinion No. 3252* (1958).

## SECTION 22

**Bills.** All legislation shall be by bill and may originate in either house.

The federal Constitution in Article I, section 7 requires that bills for raising revenue must originate in the House of Representatives. Michigan has never had such a restriction. Since 1835, all legislation could begin in either house of the state legislature. The Constitutions of 1835 and 1850 did not limit all legislation to bills. By 1907, there was public sentiment that the legislature was undermining the legislative process through the use of joint and concurrent resolution. Thus, the Constitution of 1908 added the restriction that all legislation be by bill.

The requirement that all legislation shall be by bill means that there is one mode for the enactment of law and that mode is the procedure for the passage of law specified in the constitution (*Becker v. Detroit Savings Bank*, 1934). Therefore, legislative resolutions do not have the force of law (*Becker v. Detroit Savings Bank*, 1934).

## SECTION 23

**Style of laws.** The style of the laws shall be: The People of the State of Michigan enact.

Under Article IV, section 22 of the Constitution of 1835, Michigan laws were prefaced by "Be it enacted by the senate and house of representatives of the state of Michigan." The 1850 Constitution substituted "the People" for the houses of the legislature. Section 23 continues this tradition with a minor improvement in phraseology. This section expresses the fact that in a representative democracy the people speak through their legislature. All laws must contain this enacting clause (*People v. Dettenthaler*, 1898).

## SECTION 24

**Laws; object, title, amendments changing purpose.** No law shall embrace more than one object, which shall be expressed in its title. No bill shall be altered or amended on its passage through either house so as to change its original purpose as determined by its total content and not alone by its title.

The Constitution of 1835 did not contain a counterpart to section 24. Article IV, sections 20 and 25 of the Constitution of 1850 contained restrictions similar to those that appear in section 24, and these restrictions carried over to the Constitution of 1908.

The "object" of a law is simply its general purpose or aim (*Local No. 1644, AFSCME v. Oakwood Hospital Corp.*, 1962). The title of the law must embody three things: (1) the title must fairly indicate the purpose of the legislation; (2) the title must be a fair index of the act; and (3) the title must fairly inform the legislature and the public of the law's purpose (*Attorney General Opinion No. 6078*, 1982).

Justice Thomas Cooley in *People ex rel. Drake v. Mahaney* (1865) best explained the one object requirement of section 24:

> The history and purpose of this constitutional provision are too well understood to require any elucidation at our hands. The practice of bringing together into one bill subjects diverse in their nature, and having no necessary connection, with a view to combine in their favor the advocates of all, and thus secure the passage of several

measures, no one of which could succeed upon its own merits, was one both corruptive of the legislator and dangerous to the state.

In other words, the one object requirement prevents one extreme form of legislative logrolling. Michigan courts have held that the "one object" requirement of section 24 shall be construed reasonably and "not in so narrow or technical a manner as to frustrate legislative intent" (*City of Livonia v. Department of Social Services*, 1984; *Kuhn v. Department of Treasury*, 1971). An act may contain all matters related to its object and any provisions which "relate to, carry out and implement the principle object (*City of Livonia v. Department of Social Services*, 1984).

Section 24 also prohibits the alteration or amendment of a bill during the course of its passage so as to change its original purpose. The Constitution of 1963 added language requiring scrutiny of the content of the bill as well as its title to determine original purpose. The framers of the 1963 Constitution wanted to make sure that the public could be sure of what was before the legislature. For example, a bill that began as "housekeeping" amendments to the election law but finished as a reapportionment of the state legislature was unconstitutional under this section (*Anderson v. Oakland County Clerk*, 1984).

## SECTION 25

**Revision and amendment of laws; title references, publication of entire sections.** No law shall be revised, altered or amended by reference to its title only. The section or sections of the act altered or amended shall be reenacted and published at length.

Section 25 finds its origins in Article IV, section 25 of the Constitution of 1850. The 1908 document contained the same restrictions. The 1963 Constitu tion eliminated the wasteful requirement that the entire amended statute be reprinted. Now, only the changed parts of a statute need be printed in full.

This section gives the public and the legislature adequate notice of changes in the law (*People v. Turmon*, 1983). Justice Thomas Cooley explained the purpose of this section in *People ex rel. Drake v. Mahaney* (1865):

> The mischief remedied by [Section 25] was the enactment of amendatory statutes in terms so blind that the legislators themselves were sometimes deceived in regard to their effect, and the public, from the difficulty in making the necessary examination and comparison, failed to become apprised of changes made in the laws.

Reprinting of the entire amended section of a law also helps place the amendments in context (*Advisory Opinion on Constitutionality of 1972 PA 294*, 1973). Section 25 does not require republishing of statutes amended only by implication (*Advisory Opinion on Constitutionality of 1972 PA 294*, 1973).

## SECTION 26

**Bills; printing, possession, reading, vote on passage.** No bill shall be passed or become law at any regular session of the legislature until it has been printed or reproduced and in the possession of each house for at least five days. Every bill shall be read three times in each house before the final passage thereof. No bill shall become law without the concurrence of a majority of the members elected to and serving in each house. On the final passage of bills, the votes and names of the members voting thereon shall be entered in the journal.

Section 26 can trace its origins to Article V, section 22 of the Constitution of 1908. This section is designed to prevent hasty and careless legislative action. The five-day period gives greater publicity to legislative proceedings and allows the people time to become acquainted with proposed legislation (*Anderson v. Oakland County Clerk*, 1984).

Legislation is passed by a simple majority of the members serving in each house of the legislature. The lieutenant governor can cast a tie-breaking vote during final consideration of a bill when the senate is equally divided (*Advisory Opinion on Constitution of 1978 PA 426*, 1978).

## SECTION 27

**Laws, effective date.** No law shall take effect until the expiration of 90 days from the end of the session at which it was passed, but the legislature may give immediate effect to acts by a two-thirds vote of the members elected to and serving in each house.

Article IV, section 20 of the Constitution of 1850 was the precursor to the modern section 27. The Constitution of 1908 limited acts that could be given immediate effect to appropriations acts and acts necessary for the preservation of the public peace, health, or safety. The 90-day waiting period for an act to take effect allows for the collection of signatures for a referendum on the act of the legislature. The requirements of section 27 are clear (*Selk v. Detroit Plastics Products*, 1984): When a bill to be given immediate effect is passed by the legislature and signed by the governor, it becomes effective as law when it is filed with the secretary of state (*Attorney General Opinion No. 6201*, 1984).

## SECTION 28

**Bills, subjects at special session.** When the legislature is convened on extraordinary occasions in special session no bill shall be passed on any subjects other than those expressly stated in the governor's proclamation or submitted by special message.

Section 28 may trace its origins to the Constitution of 1908 in Article V, section 22. Only minor linguistic changes have been made. Under this section, the legislature is limited to the subjects submitted by the governor, but the governor cannot limit the legislature to the consideration of any particular bill (*Smith v. Curran*, 1934).

## SECTION 29

**Local or special acts.** The legislature shall pass no local or special act in any case where a general act can be made applicable, and whether a general act can be made applicable shall be a judicial question. No local or special act shall take effect until approved by two-thirds of the members elected to and serving in each house and by a majority of the electors voting thereon in the district affected. Any act repealing local or special acts shall require only a majority of the members elected to and serving in each house and shall not require submission to the electors of such district.

This section represents a modest revision of Article V, section 30 of the Constitution of 1908. The framers of the 1963 Constitution removed an unnecessary date and made some clarifications in language. Section 29 makes it difficult to pass local or special acts by requiring a vote by a supermajority of each house of the state legislature, plus approval by voters in the affected district before any special or local act can take effect. On the other hand, this section makes it easy to repeal a local or special act by requiring only the usual majority vote of both houses in the state legislature. These two provisions of section 29 help encourage uniformity in state legislation.

Michigan courts look to the "substance" rather than the form of an act to determine whether an act is general or special. A law may still qualify as general even if it affects only a limited class of persons or places, so long as all persons and places in similar circumstances are treated alike (*Rohan v. Detroit Racing Association*, 1946). A law that includes a classification based on county population may be sustained as a general rather than a special act when the classification applies to all counties that may reach the designated classification, and when there is a reasonable relationship between the legislative objectives and the population classification (*Avis Rent-A-Car System, Inc. v. City of Romulus*, 1977; *The Irishman's Lot, Inc. v. Secretary of State*, 1954).

## SECTION 30

**Appropriations; local or private purposes.** The assent of two-thirds of the members elected to and serving in each house of the legislature shall be required for the appropriation of public money or property for local or private purposes.

Section 30 dates from the Constitution of 1850. It is designed to prevent misuse of state power for local or private affairs but to still allow the legislature some flexibility in special circumstances. The Michigan Supreme Court has refused to construe the term "public purpose" narrowly. Generally, what constitutes a public purpose is something that has been reserved traditionally to the legislature, since the definition of a public purpose involves "considerations of economic and social philosophies and principles of political science and government" (*Gregory Marina, Inc. v. Detroit*, 1966). Thus, the realm of "private" for the purposes of this section is quite narrow. In fact, in *City of Gaylord v. Gaylord City Clerk* (1966), the state high court indicated that the fact that certain individuals benefit from an appropriation does not necessarily imply that the appropriation lacks a public purpose. This broad reading of "public purpose" was reaffirmed by the court in *Advisory Opinion on Constitutionality of 1975 PA 227* (Questions 2–10, 1976). In this decision, the court noted that only one decision under the 1963 Constitution has found an appropriation for a private purpose in violation of Article IV, section 30. In 1968 in *Advisory Opinion re Constitutionality of 1966 PA 346*, the state supreme court found a housing development fund for loans and advances to private corporations unconstitutional. Apart from this isolated decision, all other difficulties under this section date from the late nineteenth and very early twentieth centuries.

## SECTION 31

**General appropriation bills; priority, statement of estimated revenue.** The general appropriation bills for the succeeding fiscal period covering items set forth in the budget shall be passed or rejected in either house of the legislature before that house passes any appropriation bill for items not in the budget except bills supplementing appropriations for the current fiscal year's operation. Any bill requiring an appropriation to carry out its purpose shall be considered an appropriation bill. One of the general appropriation bills as passed by the legislature shall contain an itemized statement of the estimated revenue by major source in each operating fund for the ensuing fiscal period, the total of which shall not be less than the total of all appropriations made from each fund in the general appropriation bills as passed.

This section is new to the Constitution of 1963 and contains a number of provisions. First, this section defines an appropriation bill as any bill requiring the appropriation of funds to carry out the bill's purpose. Next, section 31 forces the legislature to focus on general appropriations in the budget before considering any other appropriation bill except for bills supplementing appropriations for this fiscal year's operations. Finally, the legislature must include in one of the general appropriation bills the legislature's best estimates of revenue by major source. Section 31 is designed to work with Article V, section 18, which sets forth the governor's role in the state's budget process. Among the other requirements of Article V, section 18, the governor must submit a general appropriation bill to the legislature that contains the governor's proposed expenditures. Article IV, section 31, together with Article V, section 18, allows the people to compare the legislature's and the governor's versions of state appropriations. Both these sections also operate to encourage a balanced budget by requiring the state government to match revenues and expenditures on a year-to-year basis.

Under Section 31, the legislature cannot make appropriations in advance of its ability to forecast revenues (*Board of Education of Oakland Schools v. Superintendent of Public Instruction*, 1974). The Michigan legislature does not make a fine distinction between authorization and appropriation as in the United States Congress. Under the congressional system, a budgetary authorization in a statute represents a ceiling for expenditures for a government program. Budgetary authorizations for a program may include a schedule of spending ceilings for a number of years. An appropriation is the actual amount allocated for a program in a given fiscal year. The Michigan legislature may sometimes include multi-year authorizations and appropriations in a single statute. When this happens, only the appropriation for the ensuing year is treated as a true appropriation of funds. Appropriations for subsequent years are treated as authorizations or target figures. Michigan courts believe that such a construction of Michigan spending programs is required by section 31. Any other construction would spend money in advance of the legislature's ability to forecast revenue and would violate the letter and spirit of section 31 (*Board of Education of Oakland Public Schools v. Superintendent of Public Instruction*, 1974).

## SECTION 32

**Laws imposing taxes.** Every law which imposes, continues or revives a tax shall distinctly state the tax.

Section 32 embodies the first clause of Article XIV, section 14 of the Constitution of 1850. The language of the 1850 and 1908 Constitutions is identical. The framers of the 1963 Constitution eliminated the requirement that the tax state the objects to which it is to be applied. This change recognizes that in a complicated system of general taxation, the proceeds from one general tax may be devoted to many purposes. Also eliminated was a statement that the legislature cannot fix a tax simply by reference to another law. This deletion allows the legislature to refer to income determined for federal tax purposes.

Taxes are exactions of money by government, sanctioned by law, for a public purpose (*Dukesherer Farms, Inc. v. Director of the Department of Agriculture*, 1979). Section 32 and its predecessors were designed to prevent the legislature and the people from being deceived on any measure levying a tax (*Rockwell Spring & Axle Company v. Romulus Township*, 1962).

## SECTION 33

**Bills passed; approval by governor or veto, reconsideration by legislature.** Every bill passed by the legislature shall be presented to the governor before it becomes law, and the governor shall have 14 days measured in hours and minutes from the time of presentation in which to consider it. If he approves, he shall within that time sign and file it with the secretary of state and it shall become law. If he does not approve, and the legislature has within that time finally adjourned the session at which the bill was passed, it shall not become law. If he disapproves, and the legislature continues the session at which the bill was passed, he shall return it within such 14-day period with his objections, to the house in which it originated. That house shall enter such objections in full in its journal and reconsider the bill. If two-thirds of the members elected to and serving in that house pass the bill notwithstanding the objections of the governor, it shall be sent with the objections to the other house for reconsideration. The bill shall become law if passed by two-thirds of the members elected to and serving in that house. The vote of each house shall be entered in the journal with the votes and names of the members voting thereon. If any bill is not returned by the governor within such 14-day period, the legislature continuing in session, it shall become law as if he had signed it.

Section 33 describes the operation of the veto power of the governor. The governor is given fourteen days to consider a bill. If the governor signs the bill during this period, the bill becomes law. If the governor neither signs nor returns the bill to the legislature during the fourteen-day period, the bill becomes a law without the governor's signature. If the legislature adjourns before the governor has fourteen days to consider a bill, and the governor does not sign the bill, the bill does not become law. This situation is known as the "pocket veto." If the governor refuses to sign a bill (i.e., vetoes the bill and returns it to the legislature during the fourteen-day period), the legislature has an opportunity to override the governor's veto. A two-thirds majority of each house of the legislature is required to override the governor's veto. Every Michigan constitution has permitted the governor to veto legislation. The Michigan Constitution also gives the governor the power to veto specific items in an appropriation bill. This "line item veto" is treated in Article V, section 19.

The veto power of the governor is the executive branch's participation in the lawmaking process. However, this legislative power is not "affirmative or creative, but is strictly negative and destructive," and may only be exercised within the letter of the constitutional grant of authority (*Wood v. State Administrative Board*, 1931).

The governor has a full fourteen-day period to consider a bill. If a governor's term expires before the end of the fourteen-day period, his or her successor will have the remainder of the fourteen days to consider the bill and exercise the veto (*Attorney General Opinion No. 6114*, 1982).

The requirement of a two-thirds majority to override a veto applies to initiated laws as well as laws instigated by the legislature. Requiring a three-fourths majority of the legislature to override a veto of an initiated law would violate the letter of section 33 and unconstitutionally enlarge the role of the governor in the lawmaking process (*Attorney General Opinion No. 6102*, 1982).

The legislature must override a governor's veto during the same session at which a bill is passed. If the legislature has adjourned sine die, and the governor has used the veto or the pocket veto, the legislature cannot attempt to override the veto at the next session. Instead, the legislature must start the process of legislating all over again and reintroduce the bill at the next session (*Attorney General Opinion No. 6629*, 1990). Legislative sessions are defined in Article IV, section 13.

Under section 33, a bill becomes effective as law when it is filed with the secretary of state. Under this reading of section 33, the governor may exercise the line-item veto even after a bill is signed, so long as the line-item veto occurs prior to the bill's filing with the secretary of state (*Attorney General Opinion No. 6707*, 1991).

The procedures for overriding a governor's veto also apply to the line-item veto. If the governor vetoes a particular appropriation, the override is the only way for the legislature to restore funds to the program

## SECTION 34

**Bills, referendum.** Any bill passed by the legislature and approved by the governor, except a bill appropriating money, may provide that it will not become law unless approved by a majority of the electors voting thereon.

This section permits the legislature to allow the people to have the final word on whether or not a bill becomes a law. A bill passed by the legislature and signed by the governor may contain a provision that prohibits the bill from becoming law unless the bill is approved in a referendum by a majority of voters voting on the question. Only appropriation bills are excepted. This section was introduced in the Constitution of 1908.

The legislature may enact a law pursuant to section 34 even after initiative petitions have been filed. The provisions on the initiative in Article II, section 9 do not prevent the legislature from considering measures on the same subject as an initiative petition. If an initiated law and a legislative action on the same subject compete on a ballot, the proposal with the highest number of votes prevails (*In re Proposals D & H*, 1983).

## SECTION 35

**Publication and distribution of laws and judicial decisions.** All laws enacted at any session of the legislature shall be published in book form within 60 days after the final adjournment of the session, and shall be distributed in the manner provided by law. The prompt publication of judicial decisions shall be provided by law. All laws and judicial decisions shall be free for publication by any person.

The Constitution of 1850 required the speedy publication of all statutes of a public nature and such statutes deemed expedient by the legislature. The 1908 Constitution introduced the 60-day deadline. The present section 35 represents simply an improvement of language over the 1908 document.

Judicial decisions of Michigan courts are regarded as public property. Therefore, they are not protected by copyright (*Attorney General Opinion No. 1976*, 1955).

## SECTION 36

**General revision of laws; compilation of laws.** No general revision of the laws shall be made. The legislature may provide for a compilation of the laws in force, arranged without alteration, under appropriate heads and titles.

Michigan constitutions have prohibited a general revision of the laws since 1850. At the same time, the compilation of laws in force under appropriate titles and headings has been permitted. The 1963 Constitution placed the issue of the compilation of the laws completely in the hands of the legislature. The codification of Michigan laws under appropriate titles is not regarded as a general revision of law and is constitutionally permissible under this section (*Attorney General Opinion No. 2330*, 1955).

## SECTION 37

**Administrative rules, suspension by legislative committee.** The legislature may by concurrent resolution empower a joint committee of the legislature, acting between sessions, to suspend any rule or regulation promulgated by an administrative agency subsequent to the adjournment of the last preceding regular legislative session. Such suspension shall continue no longer than the end of the next regular legislative session.

This section is new to the Constitution of 1963. Section 37 provides for a legislative check on the operation of administrative agencies. Both houses of the legislature may agree to empower a joint committee to suspend any rule or regulation of an administrative agency. The joint committee functions between legislative sessions.

Michigan courts do not perceive section 37 as a general authorization for a legislative veto (*Request for Advisory Opinion on Constitutionality of 1977 PA 108*, 1977). Instead, this power is strictly limited to the oversight of administrative rules or regulations promulgated after adjournment. The usual vehicle for suspending, revoking, or amending an administrative rule is by a bill enacted in conformity with the constitution (*Request for Advisory Opinion on Constitutionality of 1977 PA 108*, 1977).

## SECTION 38

**Vacancies in office.** The legislature may provide by law the cases in which any office shall be vacant and the manner of filling vacancies where no provision is made in this constitution.

Since 1850, the legislature has been allowed to determine when an office is vacant and prescribe the way in which that vacancy will be filled when the constitution does not provide a method for filling the vacancy. Section 38 is simply an improvement in language from earlier constitutions. There have been no interpretations of this section.

## SECTION 39

**Continuity of government in emergencies.** In order to insure the continuity of state and local governmental operations in periods of emergency only, resulting from disasters occurring in this state caused by enemy attack on the United States, the legislature may provide by law for prompt and temporary succession to the powers and duties of public offices, of whatever nature and whether filled by election or appointment, the incumbents of which may become unavailable for carrying out the powers and duties of such offices; and enact other laws necessary and proper for insuring the continuity of governmental operations. Notwithstanding the power conferred by this section, elections shall always be called as soon as possible to fill any vacancies in elective office temporarily occupied by operation of any legislation enacted pursuant to the provisions of this section.

Section 39 allows the legislature to provide a way for vacancies in public office to be filled in the event the persons elected or appointed to public office cannot fulfill the duties of office due to an emergency caused by an enemy attack on the United States. However, the legislature must call an election as soon as possible to fill any vacancies in elected offices. The legislature is also given power under this section to enact other laws necessary and proper to ensure the continuing operation of state and local government during time of emergency.

Michigan first addressed the issue of the continuity of government in case of emergency in a 1959 amendment to the 1908 Constitution. Section 39 is an improvement in language from the 1959 amendment. There have been no interpretations of this section.

## SECTION 40

**Alcoholic beverages; age requirement; liquor control commission; excise tax; local option.** A person shall not sell or give any alcoholic beverage to any person who has not reached the age of 21 years. A person who has not reached the age of 21 years shall not possess any alcoholic beverages for the purpose of personal consumption. An alcoholic beverage is any beverage containing one-half of one percent or more alcohol by volume.

Except as prohibited by this section, (t)he legislature may by law establish a liquor control commission which, subject to statutory limitations, shall exercise complete control of the alcoholic beverage traffic within this state, including the retail sales thereof. The legislature may provide for an excise tax on such sales. Neither the legislature nor the commission may authorize the manufacture or sale of alcoholic beverages in any county in which a majority of electors voting thereon shall prohibit the same. Amendment ratified Nov. 7, 1978. Effective Dec. 23, 1978.

The Michigan Constitutions of 1835, 1850, and 1908 were silent on state regulation of the production, sale, and consumption of alcoholic beverages. By the late nineteenth century, the Temperance Movement swept the United States, and Michigan was no exception. In 1916, a constitutional amendment was proposed via initiative to prohibit the nonmedicinal manufacture, sale, or use of alcoholic beverages. Nationwide prohibition became a reality in 1919 as a result of the Eighteenth Amendment to the federal Constitution. The 1908 Constitution was amended again via the initiative in 1932 to permit the sale of alcoholic beverages subject to state regulation through a liquor control commission. The framers of the 1963 Constitution adopted the principles of the 1932 amendment except for some improvements in language. The constitution was amended again in 1978—once more via the initiative—to establish 21 as the legal drinking age. The 1978 amendment also defined an alcoholic beverage as a beverage containing 0.005 percent or more alcohol by volume.

The Michigan Supreme Court sees the 1978 amendment as embodying three principles: (1) state public policy prohibits persons under the age of 21 from possessing alcohol for the purpose of personal consumption; (2) other persons are prohibited from selling or giving away alcohol to persons under 21; and (3) the liquor control commission exercises complete control over the state's alcoholic beverage traffic (*Longstreth v. Gensel*, 1985). Section 40 does not mean that state government preempts all local control over the regulation of the liquor business (*Stafford's Restaurant, Inc. v. City of Oak Park*, 1983). Therefore, for example, cities can adopt policies of approving fewer liquor licenses than the maximum number permitted by statute.

## SECTION 41

**Lotteries.** The legislature may authorize lotteries and permit the sale of lottery tickets in the manner provided by law. Amendment ratified May 16, 1972. Effective July 1, 1972.

Each Michigan constitution—including the original version of the 1963 Constitution—prohibited the legislature from authorizing any lottery or permitting the sale of lottery tickets. The constitution was amended at a special election in May 1972 to allow for the state lottery. There have been no interpretations of the amended version of Section 41.

## SECTION 42

**Ports and port districts; incorporation, internal.** The legislature may provide for the incorporation of ports and port districts, and confer power and authority upon them to engage in work of internal improvements in connection therewith.

Section 42 remains unchanged from Article VIII, section 30 of the Constitution of 1908. There have been no interpretations of this section.

## SECTION 43

**Bank and trust company laws.** No general law providing for the incorporation of trust companies or corporations for banking purposes, or regulating the business thereof, shall be enacted, amended or repealed except by a vote of two-thirds of the members elected to and serving in each house.

Although the Constitution of 1835 allowed the legislature to pass acts of incorporation, banking was first addressed in 1850. This section represents a modification of Article XII, section 9 of the Constitution of 1908. The 1963 document eliminated as unnecessary a final sentence prohibiting the legislature from authorizing the issuance of bank notes or paper credit to serve as money.

The requirement of an extraordinary majority of the legislature for the regulation of banking is a product of historic distrust of banks. Unlike today's banks, the banks of 1850 did not provide security or interest to depositors, and state bank notes that circulated as money were only as sound as the bank's ability to pay (*Attorney General Opinion No. 6115*, 1983). Since savings and loan associations are not banks, regulation of savings and loan associations does not require the two-thirds majority of section 43 (*Attorney General Opinion No. 6115*).

## SECTION 44

**Trial by jury in civil cases.** The legislature may authorize a trial by a jury of less than 12 jurors in civil cases.

Michigan constitutions have allowed juries of less than twelve persons since 1850. The Constitution of 1963 limited the use of juries of less than twelve persons to civil cases. The word "juror" replaced the word "men" in 1963 to reflect the fact that women can and do serve on juries.

The "clear and unambiguous language" of section 44 does not designate a number of jurors nor the number required to reach a verdict. Therefore, a state statute authorizing juries of six, with the agreement of five jurors necessary to reach a verdict, is constitutional (*Fisher v. Hatcher*, 1973).

## SECTION 45

**Indeterminate sentences.** The legislature may provide for indeterminate sentences as punishment for crime and for the detention and release of persons imprisoned or detained under such sentences.

Michigan introduced indeterminate sentences through a 1902 amendment to the 1850 Constitution. Michigan had attempted to create a system of indeterminate sentences by statute in 1861. The state supreme court struck down the law in 1892 in *People v. Cummings* on the grounds that the state offended the principle of separation of powers. The court reasoned that the decision of the parole board to release a prisoner compromised the power of the governor to grant pardons. The decision in *Cummings* led to the constitutional amendment. The language in section 45 is simply an improvement of the language of Article V, section 28 of the Constitution of 1908.

An indeterminate sentence is a sentence of a range of time (e.g., ten to twenty years). The sentence may be terminated at any time after the minimum amount of time is served. The purpose of an indeterminate sentence "is to reform criminals and to convert bad citizens into good citizens, and thus protect society" (*Oakland County Prosecuting Attorney v. Department of Corrections*, 1981). When a prisoner has demonstrated by his or her behavior that he or she is ready to return to society, then the prisoner is released on parole but remains under the supervision of the state.

The Michigan Supreme Court has held that the power granted to the legislature under section 45 is sufficient to sustain a law creating an early release program to alleviate prison overcrowding (*Oakland County Prosecuting Attorney v. Department of Corrections*).

## SECTION 46

**Death penalty.** No law shall be enacted providing for the penalty of death.

The Michigan legislature banned the death penalty by statute in 1846. Section 46 elevates the ban to constitutional status. There have been no judicial interpretations of this section.

## SECTION 47

**Chaplains in state institutions.** The legislature may authorize the employment of chaplains in state institutions of detention or confinement.

Michigan constitutions have authorized the employment of chaplains for those confined in state institutions since 1850.

Section 47 creates an exemption to the general rule that the state may not inquire of an applicant for state employment or a candidate for promotion in a state agency his or her religious beliefs or nonbeliefs (*Attorney General Opinion No. 5856*, 1981). Obviously, it is appropriate to ask prison chaplains about their religious affiliations.

## SECTION 48

**Disputes concerning public employees.** The legislature may enact laws providing for the resolution of disputes concerning public employees, except those in the state classified civil service.

The Constitutions of 1850 and 1908 allowed the legislature to establish "courts of conciliation." Section 48 allows for the legislature to establish via statute a mechanism for the resolution of disputes concerning public employees. Civil service employees are covered by their own system in Article XI.

Michigan's Public Employment Relations Act (M.C.L. 423.200; M.S.A. 17.455) was enacted in 1965 to resolve disputes among public employees as allowed under this section. Disputes involving public employees are typically resolved under the terms of the Public Employment Relations Act (PERA), rather than the constitutional grant of authority to the legislature in section 48. However, because section 48 specifically grants power to the state legislature in this area, the Michigan Supreme Court has consistently held that PERA prevails over conflicting legislation, charters, and ordinances in the face of contentions by cities, counties, public universities, and school districts that other law—or provisions of the state constitution itself—carve out exceptions to PERA (*Local 1383 of the International Association of Fire Fighters v. City of Warren and Police and Civil Service Commission for the City of Warren*, 1981).

The power of the legislature under section 48 is limited by general concerns for separation of powers. Therefore, statutes passed pursuant to section 48 may not reach certain employees of the judiciary (*In the Matter of the Petition for a Representation Election Among Supreme Court Staff Employees*, 1979).

## SECTION 49

**Hours and conditions of employment.** The legislature may enact laws relative to the hours and conditions of employment.

The Constitution of 1908 permitted the legislature to regulate hours and conditions of employment for women and children. The 1908 Constitution was amended in 1920 to allow the legislature to pass similar laws for men. There have been no interpretations of this section.

## SECTION 50

**Atomic and new forms of energy.** The legislature may provide safety measures and regulate the use of atomic energy and forms of energy developed in the future, having in view the general welfare of the people of this state.

This section is new to the Constitution of 1963. This section does not add anything to the traditional police powers of the state. Section 50 recognizes the development of new energy forms and alerts the legislature to the possible need for regulation in this area. The federal government has provided for the comprehensive regulation of nuclear power, and some federal laws may preempt some Michigan laws on the subject of nuclear power (*Marshall v. Consumers Power Company*, 1975).

## SECTION 51

**Public health and general welfare.** The public health and general welfare of the people of the state are hereby declared to be matters of primary public concern. The legislature shall pass suitable laws for the protection and promotion of the public health.

This section is new to the Constitution of 1963. Section 51 does not add anything to the traditional police powers of the state—it simply highlights the importance of public health and welfare.

Section 51, coupled with the traditional public policy of Michigan, does, however, limit the legislature to such acts as exhibit a public purpose (*W.A. Foote Memorial Hospital, Inc. v. City of Jackson Hospital Authority*, 1973).

## SECTION 52

**Natural resources; conservation, pollution, impairment, destruction.** The conservation and development of the natural resources of the state are hereby declared to be of paramount public concern in the interest of the health, safety and general welfare of the people. The legislature shall provide for the protection of the air, water and other natural resources of the state from pollution, impairment and destruction.

This section is new to the Constitution of 1963 and remarkably foresighted. In a controversial decision, a majority of the Michigan Supreme Court held that section 52 creates a mandatory legislative duty to act to protect the state's natural resources (*State Highway Commission v. Vanderkloot*, 1973). However, this mandatory duty does not entail writing specific environmental protection provisions into every piece of legislation; a general act on environmental protection satisfies the command of section 52 (*State Highway Commission v. Vanderkloot*).

While Section 52 "clearly and unambiguously" vests in the state legislature the authority to preserve and protect Michigan's natural resources, it does not mandate any particular organizational or administrative structure for the accomplishment of that task. Section 52 also does not mean that the issue of environmental protection should be dominated by one branch of government rather than another (*House Speaker v. Governor*, 1993).

## SECTION 53

**Auditor general; appointment, qualifications, term, removal, post audits.** The legislature by a majority vote of the members elected to and serving in each house, shall appoint an auditor general, who shall be a certified public accountant licensed to practice in this state, to serve for a term of eight years. He shall be ineligible for appointment or election to any other public office in this state from which compensation is derived while serving as auditor general and for two years following the termination of his service. He may be removed for cause at any time by a two-thirds vote of the members elected to and serving in each house. The auditor general shall conduct post audits of financial transactions and accounts of the state and all branches, departments, offices, boards, commissions, agencies, authorities and institutions of the state established by this constitution or by law, and performance post audits thereof.

Each Michigan constitution has provided for an auditor general. Until 1963, the auditor general was elected at a statewide election. Section 53 adds new language on the selection of the auditor general and the responsibilities of the office.

Section 53 now provides that the auditor general is appointed by a majority vote of both houses of the legislature for an eight-year term. The legislature may also remove the auditor general for cause at any time. These provisions of section 53 place the auditor general in the legislative branch of government. To prevent any conflicts of interest, the auditor general cannot hold any state or local office during his or her term of office and for two years after that. The auditor general must be a licensed certified public accountant. He or she is charged with auditing the financial transactions of state government. The auditor general is a constitutional officer, and restrictions on the authority of the auditor general may only be imposed by the state constitution itself or statute enacted pursuant to the constitution (*Attorney General Opinion No. 6613*, 1990).

The auditor general upon direction by the legislature may employ independent accounting firms or legal counsel and may make investigations pertinent to the conduct of audits. He shall report annually to the legislature and to the governor and at such other times as he deems necessary or as required by the legislature. He shall be assigned no duties other than those specified in this section.

This paragraph allows the legislature to authorize the auditor general to employ independent accounting firms and lawyers to help in the work of the office. However, the legislature lacks the power to direct the auditor general to hire any particular accounting firm or legal counsel (*Attorney General Opinion No. 6613*, 1990). The auditor general makes annual reports to the legislature and the governor. The legislature may require other reports but is prohibited from assigning any other duties to the auditor general except those contained in section 53. The frequency with which the auditor general audits state agencies is up to the discretion of the auditor general unless required to perform certain audits by the legislature (*Attorney General Opinion No. 4637*, 1968).

> Nothing in this section shall be construed in any way to infringe the responsibility and constitutional authority of the governing boards of the institutions of higher education to be solely responsible for the control and direction of all expenditures from the institutions' funds.

This fourth paragraph of Section 53 emphasizes the constitutional independence of the governing boards of Michigan's institutions of higher education. The authority of the governing boards of universities and colleges is set forth in Article VIII, sections 5 and 6.

> The auditor general, his deputy and one other member of his staff shall be exempt from classified civil service. All other members of his staff shall have classified civil service status.

This paragraph simply exempts the auditor general, deputy, and one other staff member from Michigan's classified civil service.

## SECTION 54

**Limitations on terms of office of state legislators.** No person shall be elected to the office of state representative more than three times. No person shall be elected to the office of state senate more than two times. Any person appointed or elected to fill a vacancy in the State House of Representatives or the State Senate for a period greater than one half of a term of such office, shall be considered to have been elected to serve one time in that offce for the purpose of this section. This limitation on the number of times a person shall be elected to office shall apply to terms of office beginning on or after January 1, 1993.

This section shall be self-executing. Legislation may be enacted to facilitate the operation of this section, but no law shall limit or restrict the application of this section. If any part of this section is held to be invalid or unconstitutional, the remaining parts of this section shall not be affected but will remain in full force and effect. Amendment approved November 3, 1992. Amendment Effective December 19, 1992.

Section 54 places limits on the number of terms a state representative or a state senator may hold. A state representative may serve only three terms of office. A state senator may serve only two terms of office. Partial terms count for the purposes of this section if more than one-half of the term of the office is served. Section 54 is self-executing (i.e., it is not dependent on the legislature for implementation).

While term limits for members of Congress have been struck down as offensive to the federal Constitution (*U.S. Term Limits, Inc. v. Thorton*, 1995), term limits for state representatives enacted by the states have no similar federal constitutional defect.[1]

[1] See the commentary for Article II, section 10.

# Article V

*Executive Branch*

## SECTION 1

**Executive power.** The executive power is vested in the governor.

Michigan has always placed the executive power of the state in the office of the governor. The executive power may be described as the power to carry out legislative policies enacted into law (*Wyandotte Savings Bank v. Eveland,* 1956). The current version of section 1 represents a slight change in wording over the Constitution of 1908. The 1963 Constitution eliminated the modifier "chief" from "executive power."

## SECTION 2

**Principal departments.** All executive and administrative offices, agencies and instrumentalities of the executive branch of state government and their respective functions, powers and duties, except for the office of governor and lieutenant governor and the governing bodies of institutions of higher education provided for in this constitution, shall be allocated by law among and within not more than 20 principle departments. They shall be grouped as far as practicable according to major purposes.

Subsequent to the initial allocation, the governor may make changes in the organization of the executive branch or in the assignment of functions among its units which he considers necessary for efficient administration. Where these changes require the force of law, they shall be set forth in executive orders and submitted to the legislature. Thereafter the legislature shall have 60 calendar days of a regular session, or a full regular session if of shorter duration, to disapprove each executive order. Unless disapproved by a majority of members elected to and serving in each house, each order shall become effective at a date thereafter to be designated by the governor.

This section is new to the Constitution of 1963. The framers of the constitution believed that a thorough restructuring of the executive branch was needed to make it more accountable and efficient. As one convention delegate put it, "the structure of the executive branch is incredibly and unnecessarily complex and, in terms of direct authority and control, the governor is chief executive in name only" (2 *Official Record*, 1961, p. 1837). Section 2 requires that the 126 various state administrative agencies, boards, commissions, and departments be grouped into no more than twenty principle departments. The agencies are to be grouped together according to their major purposes. The office of governor and lieutenant governor and the governing bodies of state colleges and universities are not grouped into any of the twenty departments.

Section 2 also spells out how the agencies are to be grouped together. The legislature makes the initial allocation of agencies among the twenty principal departments. Thereafter, the governor may make changes in the organization of the executive branch in the interest of efficient administration. When the proposed changes require the force of law, the governor must set forth the changes in an executive order and submit the executive order to the legislature. The legislature must have 60 days to consider the changes contained in the executive order. The executive order becomes effective unless it is vetoed by both houses of the legislature.

Section 12 of Schedule and Temporary Provisions gave the legislature two years after the effective date of the new constitution to make the initial allocation of agencies. If the legislature failed in its task, the governor was empowered to make the allocation through executive order. The legislature reorganized state administrative agencies into nineteen principal departments in the Executive Organization Act of 1965 (M.C.L.A. section 16.101 et seq.).

Section 2 is regarded as vesting broad legislative power in the governor to effectuate executive reorganization in the interest of efficiency. The framers of the 1963 Constitution believed that the legislature had failed in the past to accomplish executive reorganization and that the governor was in the best position to reorganize the executive branch given his or her "intimate knowledge of the problems." There are three important limitations on the power of the governor in this area: First, the exercise of legislative power by the governor is clearly limited in section 2. Second, the legislature possesses concurrent power to transfer functions and powers of executive agencies. And third, the governor's ability to reorganize the executive branch is subject to legislative veto (*Soap and Detergent Association v. Natural Resources Commission*, 1982).

Despite these limitations, the governor does have the power to decide that changes are needed in the structure of the executive branch and to carry out those changes through an executive order. The governor's power to reorganize the executive branch is coequal to that of the legislature. The only way the legislature may undo the governor's reorganization is through a properly supported legislative veto (*House Speaker v. Governor*, 1993).

## SECTION 3

**Single heads of departments; appointment, term.** The head of each principal department shall be a single executive unless otherwise provided in this constitution or by law. The single executives heading principal departments shall include a secretary of state, a state treasurer and an attorney general. When a single executive is head of a principal department, unless elected or appointed as otherwise provided in this constitution, he shall be appointed by the governor by and with the advice and consent of the senate and he shall serve at the pleasure of the governor.

When a board or commission is at the head of a principal department, unless elected or appointed as otherwise provided in this constitution, the members thereof shall be appointed by the governor by and with the advice and consent of the senate. The term of office and procedure for the removal of such members shall be as prescribed in this constitution or by law.

Terms of office of any board or commission created or enlarged after the effective date of this constitution shall not exceed four years except as otherwise authorized in this constitution. The terms of office of existing boards and commissions which are longer than four years shall not be further extended except as provided in this constitution.

This section is new to the Constitution of 1963, and it describes the appointment and terms of office for the leadership of principal departments. A single individual is in charge of each principal department unless the constitution or state law provides otherwise. With the exception of the secretary of state, state treasurer, and attorney general, the governor, with advice and consent of the senate, is given the power to appoint heads of principal departments. The head of a principal department who has been appointed by the governor serves at the pleasure of the governor and may be removed from office by the governor at any time.

A board or commission may also head a principal department. Here, too, the governor appoints members of the board or commission unless the constitution calls for another mechanism. The constitution or state law provides the terms of office and the procedures for removal from office for members of boards or commissions. Generally, the term of office for any board or commission created or enlarged after the effective date of the constitution is four years.

Like section 2, this section of the constitution is not self-executing. The Executive Organization Act implemented the constitutional requirements of this section (*McDonald v. Schnipke*, 1968).

## SECTION 4

**Commissions or agencies for less than two years.** Temporary commissions or agencies for special purposes with a life of no more than two years may be established by law and need not be allocated within a principal department.

This new section of the constitution allows for the creation of temporary agencies and commissions for special purposes. These temporary agencies or commissions cannot last more than two years, and they need not be placed within one of the twenty principal departments organized under section 2. There have been no interpretations of this section.

## SECTION 5

**Examining or licensing board members, qualifications.** A majority of the members of an appointed examining or licensing board of a profession shall be members of that profession.

Section 5 is new to the 1963 Constitution. It guarantees that the boards providing licenses or examinations of professionals shall be members of the same profession. This section expresses the belief that members of the same profession are best equipped to judge and regulate their own profession (*Nemer v. Michigan State Board of Registration for Architects, Professional Engineers and Land Surveyors*, 1969).

## SECTION 6

**Advice and consent to appointments.** Appointment by and with the advice and consent of the senate when used in this constitution or laws in effect or hereafter enacted means appointment subject to disapproval by a majority vote of the members elected to and serving in the senate if such action is taken within 60 session days after the date of such appointment. Any appointment not disapproved within such period shall stand confirmed.

This new section defines the meaning of "appointment by and with the advice and consent of the senate" when used either in the constitution or statutes enacted by the legislature. The senate is given 60 days to consider an appointment. The senate may confirm the appointment by a simple majority vote. If the senate has not disapproved the appointment within the allowed 60 days, the appointment is considered confirmed despite the senate's silence.

The governor may make appointments even when there are less than 60 days left in the legislature's session. Although under Article IV, section 13, *legislative* business does not carry over to the next legislature, the Michigan Supreme Court has held that when the senate gives its advice and consent, it is performing an *executive* function (*Attorney General ex rel. Dust v. Oakman,* 1901). Therefore, a 60-day period in which the senate can exercise its advice and consent carries over both to the next session of the legislature and the ensuing legislature (*Attorney General Opinion No. 6120,* 1983). A governor-elect, however, may upon taking office withdraw a nomination made by the predecessor governor if the nomination has not yet been confirmed by the senate (*Attorney General Opinion No. 6120,* 1983).

The governor has sole prerogative to select individuals for appointment. The governor's choice is limited only by specific legal qualifications for the office (*People ex rel. Attorney General v. Galbraith,* 1910). Section 6 does not contain standards for the senate to follow in granting its advice and consent. The senate has absolute authority to reject a nomination for any reason whatsoever (*Attorney General Opinion No. 5994,* 1981). In performing its advice and consent function, the senate may seek all available information relevant to the ability and likelihood of an appointee to administer effectively an office in the public interest (*Attorney General Opinion No. 5994,* 1981).

## SECTION 7

**Vacancies in office; filling, senatorial disapproval of appointees.** Vacancies in any office, appointment to which requires advice and consent of the senate, shall be filled by the governor by and with the advice and consent of the senate. A person whose appointment has been disapproved by the senate shall not be eligible for an interim appointment to the same office.

Section 7 finds its origins in the provisions of the 1835 (Article V, section 12), 1850 (Article VIII, section 3), and 1908 (Article VI, section 10) constitutions that allowed the governor to fill vacancies in office when the senate was not in session. Section 7 emphasizes the role of senate and its advice and consent function in the appointment process. The last sentence of section 7 is new: It prevents a senate-rejected nominee from serving as an interim appointee for the same office. A gubernatorial appointment may assume office after taking the oath of office for the position. The appointee will continue to hold the office unless the appointee is rejected by the senate (*Attorney General Opinion No. 4531,* 1966).

## SECTION 8

**Principal departments, supervision of governor; information from state officers.** Each principal department shall be under the supervision of the governor unless otherwise provided by this constitution. The governor shall take care that the laws be faithfully executed. He shall transact all necessary business with the officers of

> government and may require information in writing from all executive and administrative state officers, elective and appointive, upon any subject relating to the duties of their respective offices.

Since 1835, the governor has been charged with the responsibility of taking care that the laws are faithfully executed. Each Michigan constitution has allowed the governor to request information in writing from state officers in the executive branch. The 1963 Constitution added the first sentence of section 8 that places each principal department under the supervision of the governor.

Because the governor can require information in writing from executive-branch state officers and can get legal advice from the attorney general, the Michigan Supreme Court has ruled that the governor may not employ outside counsel at the expense of the state to advise him on drafting proposed legislation (*Cahill v. Board of State Auditors*, 1901).

> The governor may initiate court proceedings in the name of the state to enforce compliance with any constitutional or legislative mandate, or to restrain violations of any constitutional or legislative power, duty or right by any officer, department or agency of the state or any of its political subdivisions. This authority shall not be construed to authorize court proceedings against the legislature.

This second paragraph of section 8 is new to the Constitution of 1963. This section allows the governor to resort to the courts to compel compliance with constitutional and statutory command. The governor cannot use this power to initiate court proceedings against the legislature.

## SECTION 9

> **Principal departments, location.** Single executives heading principal departments and the chief executive officers of principal departments headed by boards or commissions shall keep their offices at the seat of government except as otherwise provided by law, superintend them in person and perform duties as prescribed by law.

Article VII, section 8 of the Constitution of 1835 required the governor, secretary of state, treasurer, and auditor general to keep their offices at the seat of government. The 1850 Constitution added the offices of superintendent of public instruction, attorney general, and commissioner of the land office to the list. By 1908, the lieutenant governor, too, was required to keep his or her office at the state capital. The 1908 Constitution also added the requirement that each of these officials personally superintend his or her office, and carry out such duties as required by law. Section 9 of the Constitution of 1963 now requires the heads of principal departments and the chief executive officer of a principal department headed by a board or commission to keep their offices at the seat of government. However, the legislature may authorize an exception to this requirement. These state officers are require to superintend their offices in person. There have been no interpretations of this section.

## SECTION 10

**Removal or suspension of officers; grounds, report.** The governor shall have power and it shall be his duty to inquire into the condition and administration of any public office and the acts of any public officer, elective or appointive. He may remove or suspend from office for gross neglect of duty or for corrupt conduct in office, or for any other misfeasance or malfeasance therein, any elective or appointive state officer, except legislative or judicial, and shall report the reasons for such removal or suspension to the legislature.

The Constitution of 1835 made no provision for gubernatorial removal of state officials. Both the Constitutions of 1850 and 1908 allowed the governor to remove state officials but only when the legislature was not in session. Section 10 increases the power of the governor by eliminating the limitation of the removal power to times when the legislature is not in session. The removal power does not extend to legislative or judicial officers.

The governor may only remove officials for the causes specified in the constitution (*People ex rel. Johnson v. Coffey*, 1927). In other contexts, Michigan courts have argued that where removal is for "official misconduct," "misfeasance," or "mal-administration," the misconduct must be such that it affects the administration of the office and is directly related to the rights and interests of the public (*Krajewski v. City of Royal Oak*, 1983). The removal power of the governor is linked to the governor's duty to inquire into the actions of public officials. The governor must provide the official a "reasonable opportunity" to make a defense (*People ex rel. Clardy v. Balch*, 1934). If the governor acts within the law, the decision of the governor is final. However, if the governor acts "arbitrarily or capriciously," the "faithful" officer is entitled to judicial review and redress (*People ex rel. Johnson v. Coffey*, 1927).

The removal power of the governor does not extend to removal of the adjutant general of the Michigan National Guard. Removal of officers of the National Guard is covered under statutes passed pursuant to Article III, section 4, which empowers the legislature to provide for the discipline of the militia (*McDonald v. Schnipke*, 1968). Removal of members of local boards of education is governed by Article VII, section 33, not Article V, section 10 (*Attorney General Opinion No. 5395*, 1978).

## SECTION 11

**Provisional appointments to fill vacancies due to suspension.** The governor may make a provisional appointment to fill a vacancy occasioned by the suspension of an appointed or elected officer, other than a legislative or judicial officer, until he is reinstated or until the vacancy in filled in the manner prescribed by law or this constitution.

Section 11 allows the governor to make a temporary appointment to fill a vacancy created by the suspension of a state officer. The temporary appointment lasts until the suspended officer is reinstated or until the vacancy is filled as prescribed by statute or the constitution. The power to make temporary appointments does not extend to legislative or judicial officers. The Constitution of 1850 introduced the provisional appointment power of the governor, and the 1908 document continued the 1850 language. Section 11 is simply a revision of language. There have been no interpretations of this section.

## SECTION 12

**Military powers.** The governor shall be commander-in-chief of the armed forces and may call them out to execute the laws, suppress insurrection and repel invasion.

Since Michigan's first constitution, the governor has been commander-in-chief of the armed forces of the state. The current section 12 is simply an improvement in language. Section 12 does not empower the governor to remove or otherwise discipline officers of the militia. Removal and discipline of officers of the militia is covered by Article III, section 4 of this constitution (*McDonald v. Schnipke*, 1968).

## SECTION 13

**Elections to fill vacancies in legislature.** The governor shall issue writs of election to fill vacancies in the senate or house of representatives. Any such election shall be held in a manner prescribed by law.

Michigan's governor has always been permitted to issue writs of election to fill vacancies in the state senate or house of representatives. The second sentence of section 13 is new and recognizes that the legislature has the power to prescribe the way in which the election will be held. The governor has discretion to determine whether a special election will be held or to allow the vacancy to be filled at the next general election. There have been no interpretations of this section.

## SECTION 14

**Reprieves, commutations and pardons.** The governor shall have power to grant reprieves, commutations and pardons after convictions for all offenses, except cases of impeachment, upon such conditions and limitations as he may direct, subject to procedures and regulations prescribed by law. He shall inform the legislature annually of each reprieve, commutation and pardon granted, stating reasons therefor.

The Constitution of 1835 allowed the governor to grant reprieves and pardons except in cases of impeachment. Both the 1850 and 1908 Constitutions also excluded treason from pardonable offenses and allowed the governor to place conditions and limitations on a reprieve, commutation, or pardon subject to procedures and limitations required by law. These constitutions also required the governor to inform the legislature of any actions taken in the area. The Constitution of 1963 made only one substantive change in the pardon power of the governor: Treason is no longer excluded and is treated as any other crime.

Michigan courts have "jealously guarded the governor's prerogative" contained in section 14 (*People v. Whalen*, 1981). Any law that infringes on the governor's power to pardon, grant reprieves, or commute sentences would be declared unconstitutional and void (*People v. Freleigh*, 1952; *Rich v. Chamberlain*, 1895). For example, judges cannot reduce valid sentences without infringing on the governor's power (*People v. Whalen*, 1981; *People v. Fox*, 1945). However, a statute releasing certain prisoners due to jail overcrowding does not infringe on the governor's power, because sentence reductions due to jail overcrowding are a response to general conditions rather than the unique characteristics of the affected prisoner, as in the case of a pardon, reprieve or commutation (*Kent County Prosecutor v. Kent County Sheriff*, 1987).

A governor may place conditions on the commutation of a sentence, and a prisoner accepting the benefit of a commutation must accept the conditions (*Meyers v. Jackson*, 1929). Valid conditions that may be placed on a commutation include: reimbursement (*People v. Marsh*, 1900) or leaving the state or the United States never to return (*In re Cammarata*, 1955).

## SECTION 15

**Extra sessions of legislature.** The governor may convene the legislature on extraordinary occasions.

Section 15 remains unchanged from the Constitution of 1908. In calling a special session of the legislature, the governor outlines the purposes for the session, and these purposes limit the legislative agenda. However, once called into special session, the governor cannot limit the legislature to consideration of any particular bill. The legislature has broad freedom of action within the purposes stated by the governor (*Smith v. Curran*, 1934).

## SECTION 16

**Legislature other than at seat of government.** The governor may convene the legislature at some other place when the seat of government becomes dangerous from any cause.

This section allows the governor to convene the legislature outside the state capital when the capital becomes dangerous from any cause. The 1908 Constitution had limited this power to times when the capital became dangerous from "disease or a common enemy." There have been no interpretations of this section.

## SECTION 17

**Messages and recommendations to legislature.** The governor shall communicate by message to the legislature at the beginning of each session and may at other times present to the legislature information as to the affairs of the state and recommend measures he considers necessary or desirable.

Each Michigan constitution has required the governor to communicate with the legislature and to make recommendations for action by the legislature. Section 17 is a revision of the language of the Constitution of 1908, which required an outgoing governor to address the incoming legislature. This requirement was eliminated as a source of potential embarrassment to the new governor. There have been no interpretations of this section.

## SECTION 18

**Budget; general and deficiency appropriation bills.** The governor shall submit to the legislature at a time fixed by law, a budget for the ensuing fiscal period setting forth in detail, for all operating funds, the proposed expenditures and estimated revenue of the state. Proposed expenditures from any fund shall not exceed the estimated revenue thereof. On the same date, the governor shall submit to the legislature general appropriation bills to embody the proposed expenditures and any necessary bill or bills to provide new or additional revenues to meet proposed expenditures. The amount of any surplus created or deficit incurred in any fund during the last preceding fiscal period shall be entered as an item in the budget and in one of the appropriation bills. The governor may submit amendments to appropriation bills to be offered in either house during consideration of the bill by that house, and shall submit bills to meet deficiencies in current appropriations.

This new section of the constitution provides for a balanced budget and an orderly budget process. The legislature sets a date by which the governor must submit a budget. The budget covers the next fiscal year and must set forth in detail all proposed expenditures and estimated revenue for the upcoming year. Proposed expenditures must not surpass estimated revenue. In other words, the governor must submit a balanced budget to the legislature. The same day the governor submits the budget, the governor must also submit to the legislature two kinds of proposed legislation. First, the governor must submit a general appropriation bill that includes all proposed expenditures. An appropriation is money set aside by formal action for specific use. Appropriations must be done on a year-by-year basis since the dynamics of the budget, fiscal policy, and spending goals and priorities change each year (*Board of Education of Oakland Schools v. Superintendent of Public Instruction*, 1974). Second, the governor also submits any new and necessary revenue-raising bills needed to meet the proposed expenditures.

Section 18 also spells out the way in which any surplus or deficit from the preceding fiscal year must be handled. Any surplus or deficit from the past year must appear as an item in the next budget and in one of the appropriation bills: Any surplus is credited to estimated revenues; any deficit is an initial charge against expenditures. Thus, the legislature cannot create an economic stabilization fund that is funded by automatically depositing a year-end surplus into the fund. Any transfer of money to a special fund must be by an appropriation item without reference to any surplus (*Attorney General Opinion No. 5204*, 1977).

Section 18 allows the governor to submit amendments to appropriation bills as the bills are considered by each house of the legislature. The governor must also submit additional bills to the legislature to cover any deficiencies in current appropriations.

## SECTION 19

**Disapproval of items in appropriation bills.** The governor may disapprove any distinct item or items appropriating moneys in any appropriation bill. The part or parts approved shall become law, and the item or items disapproved shall be void unless re-passed according to the method prescribed for the passage of other bills over the executive veto.

Section 19 gives the governor a "line-item veto" for appropriations. The line-item veto is a state innovation: The President of the United States possesses no similar power. The governor may veto any particular item appropriating money in any appropriation bill. An "item" in an appropriation bill contains the subject and amount of an appropriation. The item may be a single line or a numbered paragraph in an appropriation bill (*Attorney General Opinion No. 6684*, 1991). The decision of the governor stands unless the line-item veto is overridden by a two-thirds vote of each house of the legislature. The line-item veto was introduced in the 1908 Constitution. By the time of the 1908 Constitution, thirty other states had adopted line-item vetoes, and Michigan followed their example.

The veto power of the governor is a legislative power and must be narrowly construed to avoid doing violence to the concept of separation of powers. Thus, the governor can merely approve or disapprove an appropriation item, he or she cannot reduce the amount of the appropriation (*Wood v. State Administrative Board*, 1931). The governor cannot approve part of an item of appropriation while disapproving another part of the same item. For example, the governor cannot veto a source of funding for an item without simultaneously vetoing the expenditure derived from that source (*Attorney General Opinion No. 5852*, 1981). The veto power also does not extend to disapproving provisions that place conditions or restrictions upon items of appropriations (*Attorney General Opinion No. 6684*, 1991). In other words, the line-item veto must be exercised in a "take-it-or-leave-it" fashion with respect to a particular item.

## SECTION 20

**Reductions in expenditures.** No appropriation shall be a mandate to spend. The governor, with the approval of the appropriating committees of the house and senate, shall reduce expenditures authorized by appropriations whenever it appears that actual revenues for a fiscal period will fall below the revenue estimates on which appropriations for that period were based. Reductions in expenditures shall be made in accordance with procedures prescribed by law. The governor may not reduce expenditures of the legislative and judicial branches or from funds constitutionally dedicated for specific purposes.

Section 20 is new to the Constitution of 1963, and it helps government maintain control over state expenditures in the interests of a balanced budget. The governor, with the approval of the appropriations committees of each house of the legislature, must cut expenditures when it appears that actual revenues will fall short of the estimated revenues. The legislature retains authority to dictate the procedures used to make reductions in expenditures. Section 20 is careful to preserve separation of powers. The governor cannot reduce expenditures of the legislature or the judiciary. The governor also cannot touch expenditures from funds created by the constitution and dedicated for specific purposes.

The first sentence of section 20 is designed to allow departments to reduce expenditures in the interests of efficiencies and economies. If money can be saved in the implementation of a program through efficient administration, then it should be saved (*Attorney General Opinion No. 6607*, 1989). However, this provision does not allow departments to reduce or eliminate services or programs mandated by the legislature (*Attorney General Opinion No. 6607*, 1989).

Section 20 is read as giving the governor the discretion to reduce the expenditure of all bodies receiving appropriations, except those exempted by the constitution. Revenue-sharing payments are considered expenditures and may be reduced. The governor may reduce the expenditures of some agencies to a greater extent than others subject, of course, to approval by the legislature's appropriating committees (*Michigan Association of Counties v. Department of Management and Budget*, 1984).

## SECTION 21

**State elective executive officers; term, election.** The governor, lieutenant governor, secretary of state and attorney general shall be elected for four-year terms at the general election in each alternate even-numbered year.

The lieutenant governor, secretary of state and attorney general shall be nominated by party conventions in a manner prescribed by law. In the general election one vote shall be cast jointly for the governor and lieutenant governor nominated by the same party.

Vacancies in the office of the secretary of state and attorney general shall be filled by appointment by the governor.

Section 21 provides for the election and terms of office for four major state officers. The 1963 Constitution reduced the number of state officers elected at statewide elections and increased the term of office for the remaining officers from two to four years. The governor, lieutenant governor, secretary of state, and attorney general are elected in each alternating even-numbered year. The election of these four statewide officers never conflicts with the election of President of the United States. The four major state officers are nominated by the political parties, and the candidates for governor and lieutenant governor run as a team and are elected as a team. The governor is given the power to appoint a secretary of state or attorney general in the event of a vacancy in office. The legislature may not, consistent with this section, pass a law allowing the governor to fill a vacancy in the office of lieutenant governor by appointment with advice and consent of the senate (*Attorney General Opinion No. 4625*, 1968).

## SECTION 22

**Governor and lieutenant governor, qualifications.** To be eligible for the office of governor or lieutenant governor a person must have attained the age of 30 years, and have been a registered elector in this state for four years next preceding his election.

Section 22 simply sets the legal eligibility requirements for governor and lieutenant governor. Since 1850, candidates for these offices must be at least 30 years old. The present language on "registered elector" takes the place of requirements for United States citizenship and state residency. Obviously, to be a registered Michigan voter, one must be an American citizen and a resident of the state of Michigan. There have been no interpretations of this section.

## SECTION 23

**State elective executive officers, compensation.** The governor, lieutenant governor, secretary of state and attorney general shall each receive compensation provided by law in full payment for all services performed and expenses incurred during his term of office. Such compensation shall not be changed during the term of office except as otherwise provided in this constitution.

From 1850 to 1948, the salaries for major state officers were written into the constitution. The 1908 Constitution was amended in 1948 to allow the legislature to set the salary for major state officers. The 1963 Constitution follows the 1948 practice. Each Michigan constitution has prohibited changes in salaries during the term of office. There have been no interpretations of this section.

## SECTION 24

**Executive residence.** An executive residence suitably furnished shall be provided at the seat of government for the use of the governor. He shall receive an allowance for its maintenance as provided by law.

This new section of the constitution provides for a place of residence at the state capital for the governor. All details concerning the residence, including an allowance for its maintenance, are left to the legislature. There have been no interpretations of this section.

## SECTION 25

**Lieutenant governor; president of the senate, tie vote, duties.** The lieutenant governor shall be president of the senate, but shall have no vote, unless they be equally divided. He may perform duties requested of him by the governor, but no power vested in the governor shall be delegated.

The lieutenant governor has always been the presiding officer of the senate. There has been much debate on the role of the lieutenant governor in case of a tie vote in the senate. The 1908 Constitution specifically prohibited the lieutenant governor from voting in the senate. The 1963 Constitution allows the lieutenant governor a vote in case of a tie. Section 25 of Article V appears to conflict with Article IV, section 26, which requires that bills be passed by a majority of members elected to and serving in each house of the legislature. The Michigan Supreme Court has held that the specific provisions of the power of the lieutenant governor of section 25 prevail over the general provisions of Article IV, section 26. Therefore, the lieutenant governor may cast a tie-breaking vote whenever the senate is deadlocked (*Advisory Opinion on Constitutionality of 1978 PA 426*, 1978).

## SECTION 26

**Succession to governorship.** In case of the conviction of the governor on impeachment, his removal from office, his resignation or his death, the lieutenant governor, the elected secretary of state, the elected attorney general and such other persons designated by law shall in that order be governor for the remainder of the governor's term.

In case of the death of the governor-elect, the lieutenant governor-elect, the secretary of state-elect, the attorney general-elect and such other persons designated by law shall become governor in that order at the commencement of the governor-elect's term.

If the governor or the person in line of succession to serve as governor is absent from the state, or suffering under an inability, the powers and duties of the office of the governor shall devolve in order of precedence until the absence or inability giving rise to the devolution of powers ceases.

The ability of the governor or person acting as governor shall be determined by a majority of the supreme court on joint request of the president pro tempore of the senate and the speaker of the house of representatives. Such a determination shall be final and conclusive. The supreme court shall upon its own initiative determine if and when the inability ceases.

Every Michigan constitution has provided for the lieutenant governor to succeed the governor in case of death, resignation, or impeachment. The 1963 Constitution lengthens the line of succession after the lieutenant governor. Section 26 adds new paragraphs covering the eventuality of gubernatorial disability. There have been no interpretations of this section.

## SECTION 27

**Salary of successor.** The legislature shall provide that the salary of any state officer while acting as governor shall be equal to that of the governor.

Section 27 simply revises the language of the 1908 Constitution. Section 27 precludes the State Officers Compensation Commission from fixing the salary of any officer while that officer is acting as governor (*Attorney General Opinion No. 5195*, 1977).

## SECTION 28

**State transportation commission; establishment; purpose; appointment, qualifications, and terms of members; director of state transportation department.** There is hereby established a state transportation commission, which shall establish policy for the state transportation department transportation programs and facilities, and such other public works of the state, as provided by law.

The state transportation commission shall consist of six members, not more than three of whom shall be members of the same political party. They shall be appointed by the governor by and with the advice and consent of the senate for three-year terms, no three of which shall expire in the same year, as provided by law.

The director of the state transportation department shall be appointed as provided by law and shall be the principal executive officer of the state transportation department and shall be responsible for executing the policy of the state transportation commission. Amendment ratified Nov. 7, 1978. Effective Dec. 23, 1978.

The 1963 Constitution originally established a bipartisan state highway commission of four members that was charged with administration of the state highway department and control over state highways and highway facilities. The 1978 amendment created the office of director of the state transportation department. The director is appointed by the governor and is charged with executing the policy of the transportation commission. The state transportation commission is composed of six members appointed by the governor with advice and consent of the senate. The commission is bipartisan. Commissioners serve three-year, staggered terms so that not more than three commissioners may be replaced in any year. The state transportation commission's responsibility is limited to the setting of policy. A policy decision is a decision of a general nature, it is not a command to take specific action. The legislature cannot grant nonpolicy making powers to the state transportation commission without infringing on the constitutional role of the director of the state transportation department (*Attorney General Opinion No. 5547*, 1979).

## SECTION 29

**Civil rights commission; members, term, duties, appropriation.** There is hereby established a civil rights commission which shall consist of eight persons, not more than four of whom shall be members of the same political party, who shall be appointed by the governor, by and with the advice and consent of the senate, for four-year terms not more than two of which shall expire in the same year. It shall be the duty of the commission in a manner which may be prescribed by law to investigate alleged discrimination against any person because of religion, race, color or national origin in the enjoyment of the civil rights guaranteed by law and by this constitution, and to secure the equal protection of such civil rights without such discrimination. The legislature shall provide an annual appropriation for the effective operation of the commission.

The commission shall have power, in accordance with the provisions of this constitution and of general laws governing administrative agencies, to promulgate rules and regulations for its own procedures, to hold hearings, administer oaths, through court authorization to require the attendance of witnesses and the submission of records, to take testimony, and to issue appropriate orders. The commission shall have other powers provided by law to carry out its purposes. Nothing contained in this section shall be construed to diminish the right of any party to direct and immediate legal or equitable remedies in the courts of this state.

Appeals from final orders of the commission, including cease and desist orders and refusals to issue complaints, shall be tried de novo before the circuit court having jurisdiction provided by law.

Section 29 is new to the Constitution of 1963. It establishes an eight-member bipartisan commission to investigate charges of discrimination and to secure the equal protection of civil rights. Section 29 does not define civil rights; civil rights are derived from the federal Constitution and statutes, the Michigan Constitution and state statutes, and the common law (*Beech Grove Investment Company v. Civil Rights Commission*, 1968). Commissioners are appointed by the governor with the advice and consent of the senate. They serve four-year, staggered terms such that only two terms shall expire in a single year. The legislature is required to provide an annual appropriation sufficient for the effective operation of the commission.

The civil rights commission was included in the constitution because of a perception that the legislature was unwilling to create such a commission by statute. The framers sought to create a commission with enough power to survive legislative attempts to eviscerate it but with enough limits on its power so that it could not become an arbitrary, unchecked fourth branch of government (*Walker v. Wolverine Fabricating and Manufacturing Company*, 1985). The civil rights commission's duty to investigate claims of discrimination comes from the constitution itself and requires no enabling legislation. In fact, in its sphere of authority, the civil rights commission is supreme in the exercise of the powers conferred by the constitution (*Attorney General Opinion No. 5353*, 1978). The legislature, though, retains the power to prescribe the manner in which the commission will operate (*Beech Grove Investment Company v. Civil Rights Commission*, 1968).

The commission is empowered to make rules and regulations for its procedures subject to the requirements of the constitution and laws governing the operation of administrative agencies. The commission can hold hearings, administer oaths, take testimony, and issue appropriate orders. The commission may also go to court to get subpoenas to compel the attendance of witnesses at hearings and the submission of records. The legislature may give the commission additional powers to help carry out its purposes. Despite the existence of the civil rights commission, any party may go directly to court for a legal or equitable remedy.

Section 29 provides for appeals from the civil rights commission. Appeals go from the commission to the circuit court having jurisdiction. The case before the circuit court is tried "de novo." There has been much debate over the meaning of trial de novo. Some framers of the constitution believed that de novo review required a completely new hearing with new evidence in the circuit court. Others seemed to think that de novo review meant a trial in the circuit court based on the record established in the hearing before the civil rights commission. The Michigan Supreme Court has held that de novo review means that the circuit courts take a fresh look at the evidence and testimony in the record before the commission and determine whether the commission's findings of fact and conclusions of law are supported by competent material and substantial evidence (*Walker v. Wolverine Fabricating and Manufacturing Company*, 1985).

## SECTION 30

**Limitations on terms of executive officers.** No person shall be elected more than two times to each office of the executive branch of government: governor, lieutenant governor, secretary of state or attorney general. Any person appointed to or elected to fill a vacancy in the office of governor, lieutenant governor, secretary of state or attorney general for a period of greater than one half of a term of such office, shall be considered to have been elected to serve one time in that office for the purposes of this section. This limitation on the number of times a person shall be elected to office shall apply to terms of office beginning on or after January 1, 1993.

This section shall be self-executing. Legislation may be enacted to facilitate the operation of this section, but no law shall limit or restrict the application of this section. If any part of this section is held to be invalid or unconstitutional, the remaining parts of this section shall not be effected but will remain in full force and effect. Amendment approved November 3, 1993. Amendment effective December 19, 1992.

Section 30 places a two-term limit on the number of terms the governor, lieutenant governor, secretary of state, and attorney general may serve. Partial terms count for the purposes of this section if more than half of the term of office was served. The United States Supreme Court has struck down term limits for members of Congress (*U.S. Term Limits, Inc. v. Thorton*, 1995) but section 30 should present no federal Constitution difficulties.[2]

[2] See the commentary for Article II, section 10.

# Article VI

## *Judicial Branch*

### SECTION 1

**Judicial power in court of justice; divisions.** The judicial power of the state is vested exclusively in one court of justice which shall be divided into one supreme court, one court of appeals, one trial court of general jurisdiction known as the circuit court, one probate court, and courts of limited jurisdiction that the legislature may establish by a two-thirds vote of the members elected to and serving in each house.

The judicial power is the inherent authority of courts to decide cases between contending parties, to make binding orders or judgments (*Underwood v. Mc-Duffee*, 1867), and to enforce final judgments by appropriate processes (*Anway v. Grand Rapids Railroad Company*, 1920). Courts also possess nonadjudicatory, administrative powers to accomplish "housekeeping" chores necessary for the administration of justice. For example, the Michigan Supreme Court assigns judges, advances judicial education, maintains judicial statistics, and supervises the practice of law within the state. The supreme court also prepares and submits a judicial budget and urges its adoption by the legislative and executive branches (*Wayne Circuit Judges v. Wayne County*, 1969). These additional, nonadjudicatory powers are regarded as inherent powers necessary to maintain the system of separation of powers required by the constitution.

The structure of the judicial branch of Michigan's government has varied considerably since 1835. Michigan's first constitution followed the federal model and vested the judicial power in one supreme court and in such other courts that may be created by the legislature. The Constitution of 1850 retained the language on one supreme court but added new constitutionally created judicial entities: circuit courts, probate courts, and justices of the peace. The legislature was empowered to create civil and criminal municipal courts in cities. The 1908 Constitution again placed the judicial power in the supreme court, circuit courts, probate courts, and justices of the peace. The legislature could create additional courts inferior to the supreme court by a two-thirds vote.

The language of the 1963 Constitution emphasizes the unitary nature of the state court system; that is, there is but one court of justice—the judicial branch of the state government—and that court consists of a number of divisions (*Buback v. Governor*, 1968). For example, the legislature created a court of limited jurisdiction called the district court. Consistent with the requirement of the unity of court there is only one district court. The individual district courts that appear in Michigan communities are merely administrative units of the unitary district court (*Judges of the 74th Judicial District v. Bay County*, 1971). Section 1 also creates an intermediate court of appeals, placed between the trial courts and the supreme court, to hear appeals. Justices of the peace are eliminated from the new constitution, but the legislature still retains the power to create by super majority vote courts of limited jurisdiction.

## SECTION 2

**Justices of the supreme court; number, term, nomination, election.** The supreme court shall consist of seven justices elected at non-partisan elections as provided by law. The term of office shall be eight years and not more than two terms of office shall expire at the same time. Nominations for justices of the supreme court shall be in the manner prescribed by law. Any incumbent justice whose term is to expire may become a candidate for re-election by filing an affidavit of candidacy, in the form and manner prescribed by law, not less than 180 days prior to the expiration of his term.

Section 2 describes the state supreme court. The supreme court consists of seven justices chosen at nonpartisan elections. The nomination process for candidates for the supreme court is governed by state statute, which allows for candidates for justice to be nominated at the conventions of the political parties. *Committee for Constitutional Reform v. Secretary of State* (1986) contested the openly partisan process of nomination for supreme court justices on the grounds that it undermines the constitutional requirement of a nonpartisan judiciary. However, the Michigan Supreme Court ruled that the plain language of section 2, along with evidence from the debates at the 1962 Constitutional Convention, gives the legislature the discretion to provide for the nomination of candidates for justice at political party conventions. An incumbent justice can become a candidate for reelection by filing an affidavit of candidacy not less than 180 days before the expiration of his or her term. This self-nomination provision helps to remove sitting justices from external political considerations.

A supreme court justice serves a term of precisely eight years, no less, no more (*Kelley v. Riley*, 1983). The terms of the justices are staggered, such that only two justices are selected every two years. Staggered terms help provide continuity on the court and offer some insulation from majoritarian pressures.

The Michigan Supreme Court has undergone great evolution since 1835. The original supreme court was appointed by the governor with the advice and consent of the state senate. The number of justices on the supreme court was up to the legislature, and judges held their offices for seven years. The 1850 Constitution represented an important transition in the history of the supreme court. For six years after 1850, the supreme court ceased to exist as an independent court. Justices of the circuit courts sat together and formed an *ad hoc* supreme court. After the passage of six years, the legislature could organize a new supreme court consisting of one chief justice and three associate justices. The new supreme court was to be chosen by popular election. These new justices of the supreme court would serve eight-year, staggered terms. The 1908 Constitution required a chief justice but left the number of associate justices up to the legislature. The constitution required staggered terms of office but left it to the legislature to prescribe the length of the term.

## SECTION 3

**Chief justice; court administrator; other assistants.** One justice of the supreme court shall be selected by the court as its chief justice as provided by rules of the court. He shall perform duties required by the court. The supreme court shall appoint an administrator of the courts and other assistants of the supreme court as may be necessary to aid in the administration of the courts of this state. The administrator shall perform duties assigned by the court.

This section is new to the state constitution. The justices of the supreme court are allowed to select, under court-created rules, their own chief justice. The supreme court is empowered to appoint an administrator for the state court system and other assistants for the purpose of court administration. There have been no interpretations of this section.

## SECTION 4

**General superintending control over courts; writs; appellate jurisdiction.** The supreme court shall have general superintending control over all courts; power to issue, hear and determine prerogative and remedial writs; and appellate jurisdiction as provided by the rules of the supreme court. The supreme court shall not have the power to remove a judge.

Section 4 describes the powers of the supreme court. The supreme court is given supervisory control over all Michigan courts. Examples of the supervisory functions of the state supreme court include: the assignment of judges, the advancement of judicial education, the maintenance of judicial statistics, the division of judicial business, and the governance of the practice of law within Michigan (*Wayne Circuit Judges v. Wayne County*, 1969). Section 4, in conjunction with section 30 of this Article, gives the supreme court the authority to discipline members of the state judiciary. The supreme court has read section 4 as bestowing a more general grant of supervisory authority than section 30 (*In the Matter of Probert*, 1981). As the court reasoned in *In re Huff* (1958), the power of superintending control is hampered by no specific rules or means for its exercise. Section 4 does prohibit the supreme court from removing a judge, but this prohibition does not preclude the supreme court's imposition of a conditional suspension of a judge or an indefinite injunction against a judge's exercise of the powers and duties of office (*In the Matter of Probert*, 1981).

The court can hear and issue prerogative and remedial writs. Writs are the written documents through which the court issues its commands. The supreme court's power to issue writs is given by the constitution and cannot be limited by statute (*Milliard ex rel. Reuter v. City of Bay City*, 1952). The appellate jurisdiction is the ability of the supreme court to review the actions of inferior courts (*In re Certified Question from the United States Court of Appeals for the Sixth Circuit*, 1989). The supreme court may hear cases on appeal under rules the court establishes for itself.

The 1835 Constitution was silent as to the supreme court's jurisdiction. The 1850 and 1908 Constitutions gave the supreme court superintending control over Michigan courts. These constitutions also listed out the kinds of writs the supreme court could issue. Section 4 of this constitution represents a modification of the 1908 language.

## SECTION 5

**Court rules; distinctions between law and equity; master in chancery.** The supreme court shall by general rules establish, modify, amend and simplify the practice and procedure in all courts of this state. The distinction between law and equity proceedings shall, as far as practicable, be abolished. The office of master in chancery is prohibited.

Beginning in 1850, the Michigan Supreme Court has had the constitutional authority to make, amend, and simplify general rules of practice in the state courts.

The 1850 and 1908 Constitutions gave the legislature the authority to abolish the distinction between law and equity. The legislature, in the Judicature Act of 1915, empowered the supreme court to abolish the law-equity distinction between law and equity procedures but prohibited the joining of legal and equitable causes of action. The 1963 Constitution gives the supreme court the power to achieve complete abolition of the distinction between law and equity.

The Michigan Supreme Court has held that section 5 must be construed liberally to aid in the efficient administration of the judicial system. The legislature may not interfere with judicially created rules of practice and procedure; the supreme court may, however, choose to acquiesce to or adopt legislatively generated rules (*Buscaino v. Rhodes*, 1971).

Courts of equity traditionally had jurisdiction over cases in which the courts of law could not afford an adequate remedy. Courts of equity—driven by considerations of justice and fairness—heard cases involving the specific performance of contracts, the reformation of written instruments, and the setting aside of deeds (*Bridge Street & Allendale Gravel-Road, Co. v. Hogadone*, 1908). Abolishing the distinction between legal and equitable actions streamlines the judicial system and prevents waste and duplication. The office of master in chancery has been prohibited since 1850.

A master in chancery was an assistant to a chancellor or a judge deciding a case in equity. A master in chancery could hear testimonies, compute damages, and make reports to the judge or chancellor (*Frank v. Schultz*, 1940; *Maas Brothers, Inc. v. Weitzman*, 1939). The prohibition on the office of master in chancery guarantees that litigants will receive the benefit of having their case heard before the judge who will render the ultimate decision.

## SECTION 6

**Decisions and dissents; writing, contents.** Decisions of the supreme court, including all decisions on prerogative writs, shall be in writing and shall contain a concise statement of the facts and reasons for each decision and reasons for each denial of leave to appeal. When a judge dissents in whole or in part he shall give in writing the reasons for his dissent.

The Constitutions of 1850 and 1908 required written decisions from the supreme court. These constitutions also required written decisions from dissenting justices. Section 6 is a revision of the language of the earlier constitutions.

A dissenting opinion in *American Independent Party v. Secretary of State* (1976) explained the functions of written opinions, which articulate the law as it applies in a case. Written opinions help assure thoughtful review of the facts and law in a case. The checking of holdings in similar cases, the setting down of reasons for the decision, and the evaluation of competing arguments may not ensure a good decision but certainly increase the probability of one.

## SECTION 7

**Staff; budget; salaries of justices; fees.** The supreme court may appoint, may remove, and shall have general supervision of its staff. It shall have control of the preparation of its budget recommendations and the expenditure of moneys appropriated for any purpose pertaining to the operation of the court or the performance of activities of its staff except that the salaries of the justices shall be established by law. All fees and perquisites collected by the court staff shall be turned over to the state treasury and credited to the general fund.

Since 1835, the Michigan Supreme Court has had the power to appoint clerks to help in the work of the court. The 1908 Constitution allowed the supreme court to appoint a clerk, a reporter of decisions, and a court crier but added a provision prohibiting the court from appointing any other public official. The 1908 Constitution also introduced the language requiring all fees and perquisites collected by the court to be turned over to the state treasury and credited to the general fund. The 1963 Constitution strengthens the control of the supreme court over all of its employees. The court now appoints and supervises its entire staff. A new provision allows the court to prepare its own budget recommendations and control the expenditure of funds appropriated for court activities except for the salaries of the justices. Generally, the revisions of 1963 enhance the independence of the supreme court.

In a concurring opinion in *Matter of Petition for a Representation Election of Supreme Court Employees* (1979), Chief Justice Coleman argued that the specific provisions of section 7 stand as an exception to the power of the legislature in Article 4, section 48 to regulate public employment outside the civil service. Therefore the supreme court has complete control over its entire staff.

## SECTION 8

**Court of appeals; election of judges, divisions.** The court of appeals shall consist initially of nine judges who shall be nominated and elected at nonpartisan election from districts drawn on county lines and as nearly as possible of equal population, as provided by law. The supreme court may prescribe by rule that the court of appeals sit in divisions and for terms of court and the times and places thereof. Each such division shall consist of not fewer than three judges. The number of judges comprising the court of appeals may be increased, and the districts from which they are elected may be changed by law.

Section 8, new to the constitution, describes the composition of Michigan's intermediate appellate court—the court of appeals. Section 8 gives the supreme court the power to allow the court of appeals to sit in panels (divisions) of no less than three judges. The legislature may increase the number of judges on the court of appeals and change the districts from which they are elected by statute.

Election districts for the court of appeals must respect county borders (i.e., an election district must consist of either a county or a group of counties). These county-based election districts must be as nearly as possible of equal population (*In re Districting for Court of Appeals*, 1964). The legislature is required to redraw election district lines when it becomes "obvious" (from federal census figures, for example) that the election districts are no longer of approximately equal population (*Attorney General Opinion No. 6153*, 1983).

## SECTION 9

**Judges of court of appeals, terms.** Judges of the court of appeals shall hold office for a term of six years and until their successors are elected and qualified. The terms of office for the judges in each district shall be arranged by law to provide that not all terms will expire at the same time.

Section 9 is new to the Constitution of 1963. It sets the term of office for judges of the court of appeals and requires that the terms of office for the judges by staggered, such that only a fraction of the judges may be replaced in any given election. There have been no interpretations of this section.

## SECTION 10

**Jurisdiction, practice and procedure of court of appeals.** The jurisdiction of the court of appeals shall be provided by law and the practice and procedure therein shall be prescribed by rules of the supreme court.

This new section continues the description of the operation of Michigan's intermediate appellate court. The legislature defines the jurisdiction of the court of appeals by statute; that is, the legislature has the authority to prescribe in what cases and under what circumstances appeals may be taken (*In re Butterfield Estate*, 1980). The supreme court prescribes the rules for practice and procedure in the court of appeals, as permitted by this section and section 4 of this Article (*People v. Blachura*, 1973).

## SECTION 11

**Circuit courts; judicial circuits, sessions, number of judges.** The state shall be divided into judicial circuits along county lines in each of which there shall be elected one or more circuit judges as provided by law. Sessions of the circuit court shall be held at least four times in each year in every county organized for judicial purposes. Each circuit judge shall hold court in the county or counties within the circuit in which he is elected, and in other circuits as may be provided by rules of the supreme court.

The number of judges may be changed and circuits may be created, altered and discontinued on recommendation of the supreme court to reflect changes in judicial activity. No change in the number of judges or alteration or discontinuance of a circuit shall have the effect of removing a judge from office during his term.

Section 11 describes the circuit courts—Michigan's trial courts of general jurisdiction. The legislature divides the state into judicial circuits along county lines. At least one circuit judge is elected for each circuit. A circuit judge holds court within the circuit to which he or she was elected, but the circuit judge may hold court in other circuits as provided by supreme court rules. The number of judicial circuits may be changed at the recommendation of the supreme court, depending on the amount of judicial activity. The creation of new circuits and judgeships allows the courts to keep abreast of changing population and economic conditions in order to serve all sections of the state efficiently (*Eason v. Secretary of State*, 1979). In creating new circuits, the legislature must respect county lines. The legislature may not divide a circuit made up of two or more counties into election districts with each district electing a circuit judge (*Attorney General Opinion No. 6592*, 1988).

The present system of circuit courts descends from the system that began in 1850 and continued in 1908. The Constitution of 1963 represents a revision of Article 7, section 8 of the 1908 constitution that eliminates unnecessary language.

## SECTION 12

**Circuit judges; nomination, election, term.** Circuit judges shall be nominated and elected at non-partisan elections in the circuit in which they reside, and shall hold office for a term of six years until their successors are elected and qualified. In circuits having more than one circuit judge their terms of office shall be arranged by law to provide that not all terms will expire at the same time.

This section describes the nomination, election, and term of office for circuit judges. The legislature is required to create a system of staggered terms for circuits with more than one judge, such that all terms cannot expire in the same election year. Staggered terms were introduced to avoid lengthy and confusing ballots and to prevent a large turnover in judges, a circumstance that may have detrimental effects on the administration of justice. In creating new judgeships, the legislature may vary the length of a new judge's term in order to maintain the required system of staggered terms (*Eason v. Secretary of State*, 1979).

Michigan has elected its circuit judges since 1835 when circuit judges were chosen at partisan elections for four-year terms. The 1850 Constitution increased the term of office to six years and added a provision prohibiting circuit judges from being elected to a nonjudicial office during the judge's term and for one year after the expiration of the term. The Constitution of 1908 continued the 1850 structure.

## SECTION 13

**Circuit courts; jurisdiction, writs, supervisory control over inferior courts.** The circuit court shall have original jurisdiction in all matters not prohibited by law; appellate jurisdiction from all inferior courts and tribunals except as otherwise provided by law; power to issue, hear and determine prerogative and remedial writs; supervisory and general control over inferior courts and tribunals within their respective jurisdictions in accordance with rules of the supreme court; and jurisdiction of other cases and matters as provided by rules of the supreme court.

Section 13 describes the jurisdiction of the circuit courts. Circuit courts are primarily trial courts, but they can hear appeals from inferior courts and tribunals (i.e., from Michigan's courts of limited jurisdiction). The circuit courts also supervise the inferior courts within their jurisdiction according to the rules prescribed by the state supreme court. The legislature may regulate the original and appellate jurisdiction of the circuit courts. Section 13 finds its origins in the Constitution of 1850 in Article VI, section 8. A constitutional amendment in 1893 allowed the supreme court to assign by rule other "cases and matters" to circuit courts. The Constitution of 1908 adopted the 1850 language as amended.

The constitutional grant of original subject matter jurisdiction to the circuit courts is broad. Circuit courts possess original jurisdiction over all matters so long as jurisdiction is not expressly prohibited by constitution or statute. Courts read statutes restricting the jurisdiction of the circuit courts carefully and with the presumption that jurisdiction is retained and that any intent to divest the court of jurisdiction must be clearly and unambiguously stated (*Campbell v. St. John Hospital*, 1990; *Solomon v. Lewis*, 1990).

The constitution clearly authorizes legislative curtailment of the appellate authority of the circuit courts. The extent of the appellate jurisdiction of the circuit courts over inferior tribunals (such as the small claims division of the district court) is the exclusive province of the legislature (*Marshall v. Pech*, 1980). Circuit courts can review probate court orders on the civil commitment of mental patients and may compel a hospital administrator by a writ of mandamus to hold an evidentiary hearing for the release of a patient (*Teasel v. Department of Mental Health*, 1984).

In order to supervise inferior tribunals, circuit courts may enter orders of superintending control. Petitioning the circuit court for an order of superintending control is the vehicle by which litigants may challenge the generalized practice of an inferior court (*Cahill v. 15th District Judge*, 1974; *City of Detroit v. Recorder's Court Judge*, 1981). The supreme court has codified the way in which circuit courts control inferior tribunals in court rules. Inferior court judges are bound to obey an order of superintending control with proper jurisdiction, even if it is clearly incorrect (*In re Hague*, 1982).

## SECTION 14

**County clerks; duties, vacancies; prosecuting attorneys, vacancies.** The clerk of each county organized for judicial purposes or other officer performing the duties of such office as provided in a county charter shall be clerk of the circuit court for such county. The judges of the circuit court may fill a vacancy in an elective office of county clerk or prosecuting attorney within their respective jurisdictions.

Since 1835, the county clerk has served as the clerk of the circuit courts. The 1963 Constitution rewrote Article VII, section 13 of the 1908 Constitution to recognize the possibility that under some county charters, some officer other than the county clerk may be empowered to be clerk of the circuit court. Since 1850, circuit court judges could fill vacancies in the offices of clerk or prosecuting attorney within their jurisdiction. The circuit judges possess the sole authority to fill vacancies in the offices of clerk or prosecuting attorney. The court's appointee will hold office for the unexpired portion of the term of office (*Attorney General Opinion No. 47*, 1935).

## SECTION 15

**Probate courts; districts, jurisdiction.** In each county organized for judicial purposes there shall be a probate court. The legislature may create or alter probate court districts of more than one county if approved in each affected county by a majority of electors voting on the question. The legislature may provide for the combination of the office of probate judge with any judicial office of limited jurisdiction within a county with supplemental salary as provided by law. The jurisdiction, powers and duties of the probate court and of the judges thereof shall be provided by law. They shall have original jurisdiction in all cases of juvenile delinquents and dependents, except as otherwise provided by law.

Probate courts are courts of limited jurisdiction (*In re Macomber*, 1990) that traditionally handle matters concerning wills and estates. The Constitution of 1835 required the establishment of probate courts in each organized county. The 1850 Constitution added provisions requiring the election of probate judges for four-year terms and allowing the legislature to prescribe the powers, duties, and jurisdiction of the probate courts. The 1908 Constitution added cases concerning juvenile delinquents and dependents to the jurisdiction of the probate courts.

The 1963 Constitution revises earlier language on probate courts in the interest of flexibility. The legislature may now combine counties into probate districts if approved by a majority of voters in each affected county. The legislature may also combine the duties of probate judge with the duties of any judge of a court of limited jurisdiction within a county. A judge performing the extra duties will receive additional salary. These provisions were designed to aid judicial administration in smaller counties.

The probate court has no inherent powers. The phrase "provided by law" in this section means that the legislature must do the entire job of implementing the provisions of this section (*Buback v. Governor,* 1968). The constitution and statutes give the probate court jurisdiction over children (*Hendrickson v. Moghissi,* 1987; *Fritts v. Krugh,* 1958).

## SECTION 16

**Probate judges; nomination, election, terms.** One or more judges of probate as provided by law shall be nominated and elected at non-partisan elections in the counties or the probate districts in which they reside and shall hold office for terms of six years and until their successors are elected and qualified. In counties or districts with more than one judge the terms of office shall be arranged by law to provide that not all terms will expire at the same time.

This section describes the nomination, election, and term of office of probate judges. Although probate judges hold court in probate districts or counties, probate judges are state officers (*People ex rel. Douvielle v. Board of Supervisors of Manistee County,* 1879). In areas with multiple district judges, a system with staggered terms of office is created. The constitution has required the election of probate judges since 1850. The 1963 Constitution, a revision of the 1908 language, increases the term of office from four to six years.

## SECTION 17

**Judicial salaries and fees.** No judge or justice of any court of this state shall be paid from the fees of his office nor shall the amount of his salary be measured by fees, other moneys received or the amount of judicial activity of his office.

This section is new to the constitution. Section 17 prohibits the use of fees to pay judges' salaries and requires that a judge's salary cannot be dependent on the amount of litigation handled in the judge's court. This provision is designed to increase the fairness or the perception of fairness of the judicial process. There have been no interpretations of this section.

## SECTION 18

**Salaries; uniformity, changes during term.** Salaries of justices of the supreme court, of the judges of the court of appeals, of the circuit judges within a circuit, and of the probate judges within a county or district, shall be uniform, and may be increased but shall not be decreased during a term of office except and only to the extent of a general salary reduction in all other branches of government.

> Each of the judges of the circuit court shall receive an annual salary as provided by law. In addition to the salary received from the state, each circuit judge may receive from any county in which he regularly holds court an additional salary as determined from time to time by the board of supervisors of the county. In any county where additional salary is granted, it shall be paid at the same rate to all circuit judges regularly holding court therein.

The first paragraph of Section 18 is new. It requires uniform salaries for all judges within a district. Salaries are defined as a fixed annual or periodic payment depending upon the time and not upon the amount of services rendered (*Beach v. Kent*, 1905). This new paragraph was added to eliminate salary disparities caused by staggered terms and to prevent disparate treatment by counties of judges within a circuit (*Kohn v. Wayne County*, 1975). This paragraph also removes a restriction from Article XVI, section 3 of the 1908 Constitution that prohibited an increase in salaries of public officers (except circuit judges) during their terms of office. Section 18 also prohibits the reduction of the salary of judges except as part of a general salary reduction in all other branches of government.

The second paragraph of this section is a revision of Article VII, section 12 of the Constitution of 1908. This second paragraph allows counties to supplement the salaries of their circuit judges with the proviso that the supplements be uniform among the circuit's judges. This paragraph was designed to prevent the legislature from prohibiting contributions to salaries from the counties within a circuit (*Deneweth v. State Treasurer*, 1971). However, this paragraph only applies to judges regularly holding court in a circuit; it does not apply to judges temporarily assigned to a circuit (*Kohn v. Wayne County*, 1975; *Lamb v. Board of Auditors of Wayne County*, 1926). Longevity pay to judges by counties is not considered salary but a kind of fringe benefit and therefore does not offend section 18 (*Elliott v. Genesee County*, 1988).

## SECTION 19

> **Courts of record; seal, qualifications of judges.** The supreme court, the court of appeals, the circuit court, the probate court and other courts designated as such by the legislature shall be courts of record and each shall have a common seal. Justices and judges of courts of record must be persons who are licensed to practice law in this state. No person shall be elected or appointed to a judicial office after reaching the age of 70 years.

Section 19 defines Michigan's courts of record, adding the new court of appeals to the roster, and gives the qualification for office for these courts. A court of record is a court whose proceedings are recorded for perpetual memory. Courts of record have the power to punish, through fines or imprisonment, contempt of court. The Supreme Court, circuit courts, and probate courts have been courts of record since 1850. A 1955 amendment to the 1908 Constitution required justices of the supreme court and judges of the circuit courts to be licensed to practice law in Michigan and under the age of 70 at election or appointment.

Justices and judges must be licensed to practice law. However, loss or suspension of the license of a sitting judge does not automatically warrant discipline against the judge (*In re Kapcia*, 1978).

The age qualification for judges and justices applies to all courts in Michigan, including courts not of record (*Hackett v. Kress*, 1965). A city clerk may refuse to accept nominating petitions for a candidate for judicial office if that candidate does not meet the age qualification (*Ball v. Thomas*, 1965).

## SECTION 20

**Removal of domicile of judge.** Whenever a justice or judge removes his domicile beyond the limits of the territory from which he was elected or appointed, he shall have vacated his office. Amendment ratified Aug. 6, 1968. Effective Sept. 21, 1968.

Section 20 requires justices and judges to live in the area from which they were elected. If a judge moves outside this area, he or she is considered as having vacated the office. Michigan has had this kind of residency requirement since 1850. Section 20 was amended in 1968 to add the words "or appointed" to take into account the possibility of interim appointments to office. There have been no interpretations of this section.

## SECTION 21

**Ineligibility for other office.** Any justice or judge of a court of record shall be ineligible to be nominated for or elected to an elective office other than a judicial office during the period of his service and for one year thereafter.

Section 21 is designed to help divorce judges from the political arena. No justice or judge of a court of record can run for a nonjudicial office during his or her term of office and for one year after the expiration of that term. The Constitutions of 1850 and 1908 introduced a similar provision for circuit court judges only. There have been no interpretations of this section.

## SECTION 22

**Incumbent judges, affidavit of candidacy.** Any judge of the court of appeals, circuit court or probate court may become a candidate in the primary election for the office of which he is the incumbent by filing an affidavit of candidacy in the form and manner prescribed by law. Amendment ratified Aug. 1968. Effective Sept. 21, 1968.

Section 22 is new to the constitution. Incumbent judges of the court of appeals, circuit courts, and probate courts may become candidates for reelection in a primary by filing an affidavit of candidacy. The form and manner in which the affidavit is filed is up to the legislature. This provision eliminates the need for incumbent judges to file nominating petitions and helps to remove judges from the political process (*Committee for Constitution Reform v. Secretary of State*, 1986). The 1968 amendment to section 22 deleted the word "elected" that had preceded "judge of." This change overturns the effect of the supreme court decision in *Burdick v. Secretary of State* (1964), which held that only judges who had secured their offices through election were entitled to the benefits of incumbency. This amendment gives appointed judges the same benefit as their elected colleagues.

## SECTION 23

**Judicial vacancies, filling; appointee, term; successor; new offices.** A vacancy shall occur in the office of judge of any court of record or in the district court by death, removal, resignation or vacating the office, and such vacancy shall be filled by appointment by the governor. The person appointed by the governor shall hold office until 12 noon of the first day of January next succeeding the first general election after the vacancy occurs, at which election a successor shall be elected for the remainder of the unexpired term. Whenever a new office of judge in a court of record, or in the district court, is created by law, it shall be filled by election as provided by law. The supreme court may authorize persons who have been elected and served as judges to perform judicial duties for limited periods or specific assignments. Amendment ratified Aug. 6, 1968. Effective Sept. 21, 1968.

This section governs how unexpected vacancies are filled. The Constitution of 1835 contained no provision for filling vacancies in judicial office. The Constitutions of 1850 and 1908 both permitted the governor to fill vacancies through appointment. The gubernatorial appointee would hold office until a successor could be elected and qualified for office. The 1963 Constitution initially introduced a new method of filling vacancies. Judicial vacancies would be filled at either the general election or a special election, as determined by the state legislature. The supreme court of the state could appoint retired judges or others who have served as judges to fill vacancies until a successor was elected. These temporary appointees were ineligible for election to fill the vacancy. This change reflected the people's strong preference for an elected judiciary. The 1968 amendment was a product of the fact that the original system embarrassed the operation of government by leaving important judicial offices without their own regular incumbent for long periods of time (*Schwartz v. Secretary of State*, 1974). While the governor's traditional power to fill vacancies was restored, the 1968 amendment was careful to provide that new judicial offices are to be filled by election to prevent collusion between the legislature and the governor to create a new judgeship for a favored appointee (*Schwartz v. Secretary of State*, 1974).

The scope of the governor's appointment power was considered in the bizarre case of *Kelley v. Riley* (1983). Justice Blair Moody won reelection to the supreme court but died soon after the election. The lame-duck governor appointed Dorothy Comstock Riley to fill Blair Moody's seat until the next November election. The incoming governor contended that his predecessor's power to fill vacancies only extended until the end of Justice Moody's old term and not into the first year of his new term. The supreme court agreed. The appointment power of the governor under section 23 operates only within the term in which the vacancy arose. The supreme court felt this limited view of the appointment power was dictated by the injustice that could arise from extended appointed terms and Michigan's historical preference for an elected judiciary.

## SECTION 24

**Incumbent judges, ballot designation.** There shall be printed upon the ballot under the name of each incumbent justice or judge who is a candidate for nomination or election to the same office the designation of that office. Amendment ratified Aug. 6, 1968. Effective Sept. 21, 1968.

Section 24 descends from a 1939 amendment to section 23 of Article VII of the 1908 Constitution. This section allows incumbent justices and judges to be designated as such when they run for reelection. Section 24 was amended in 1968 to delete the word "elected" that had preceded the phrase "incumbent justice or judge." This change overturns the effect of the supreme court decision in *Burdick v. Secretary of State* (1964), which held that only judges who had secured their offices through election were entitled to the benefits of incumbency. This amendment gives appointed judges the same benefit of a ballot designation as their elected colleagues.

## SECTION 25

**Removal of judges from office.** For reasonable cause, which is not sufficient ground for impeachment, the governor shall remove any judge on a concurrent resolution of two-thirds of the members elected to and serving in each house of the legislature. The cause for removal shall be stated at length in the resolution.

Section 25 describes a way to remove a judge from office for grounds that would be insufficient for impeachment. The state supreme court may still discipline a judge for misconduct in office even if the legislature fails to pass the concurrent resolution (*Ransford v. Graham*, 1964). Michigan has permitted removal of judges by way of joint resolution since 1835.

## SECTION 26

**Circuit court commissioners and justices of the peace, abolition; courts of limited jurisdiction.** The offices of circuit court commission and justice of the peace are abolished at the expiration of five years from the date this constitution becomes effective or may within this period be abolished by law. Their jurisdiction, compensation and powers within this period shall be as provided by law. Within this five-year period, the legislature shall establish a court or courts of limited jurisdiction with powers and jurisdiction defined by law. The location of such court or courts, and the qualifications, tenure, method of election and salary of the judges of such court or courts, and by what governmental units the judges shall be paid, shall be provided by law, subject to the limitations contained in this article.

Statutory courts in existence at the time this constitution becomes effective shall retain their powers and jurisdiction, except as provided by law, until they are abolished by law.

Section 26, which is new to the constitution, revises Michigan's system of courts of limited jurisdiction. This section abolishes the offices of circuit court commissioner and justice of the peace five years after the effective date of the constitution or sooner if the legislature so chooses. New courts of limited jurisdiction will then be created by the legislature. The legislature will also define the powers, jurisdiction, and location of these courts as well as the qualifications, term of office, method of election, and salary for the judges of these courts. The second paragraph of this section maintains other courts created by the legislature until the legislature abolishes these courts or transfers their duties to another court. The legislature implemented the requirements of section 26 in M.C.L.A. 600.8101.

The phrase "method of election" in this section must be read in conjunction with other sections of this constitution governing elections. Article II governs elections in general, and Article VI, section 24 addresses the issue of ballot designations for incumbent justices or judges. For the purposes of section 26, "method of election" means the power of the legislature to provide for the details of election within the framework of the requirements of the entire judicial article (*Wells v. Kent County Board of Election Commissioners*, 1969).

## SECTION 27

**Power of appointment to public office.** The supreme court, the court of appeals, the circuit court, or any justices or judges thereof, shall not exercise any power of appointment to public office except as provided in this constitution.

Since 1850 and through 1908, circuit court judges were prohibited from making any appointments to public office except for filling vacancies in the office of county clerk or prosecuting attorney. Section 27 is a revision of this prohibition with an extension of its application to the supreme court and the court of appeals, unless the constitution elsewhere allows courts to make appointments. The constitution does give the courts certain powers of appointment. Section 3 of this article allows the supreme court to appoint an administrator of the courts and other assistants. Section 7 gives the supreme court the power to appoint its staff, and under section 14, circuit judges may fill vacancies in the offices of county clerk and prosecuting attorney. Section 23 of this article also empowers the supreme court to authorize persons who have been elected and served as judges to perform judicial duties for limited periods of time.

The prohibition in section 27, along with the supreme court's powers under section 23, makes it unconstitutional for a circuit judge to appoint a retired judge to hear a case, even if both parties to the litigation agree to the appointment (*Brockman v. Brockman*, 1982).

## SECTION 28

**Administrative action, review.** All final decisions, finding, rulings and orders of any administrative officer or agency existing under the constitution or by law, which are judicial or quasi-judicial and affect private rights or licenses, shall be subject to direct review by the courts as provided by law. This review shall include, as a minimum, the determination of whether such final decisions, findings, rulings and orders are authorized by law; and, in cases in which a hearing is required, whether the same are supported by competent, material and substantial evidence on the whole record. Findings of fact in workmen's compensation proceedings shall be conclusive in the absence of fraud unless otherwise provided by law.

In the absence of fraud, error of law or the adoption of wrong principles, no appeal may be taken to any court from any final agency provided for the administration of property tax laws from any decision relating to valuation or allocation.

Section 28 is new to the constitution and, as the Address to the People describes it, recognizes the "increased significance assumed by administrative law in the legal system of the state in recent years." This section provides for direct judicial review of final decisions made by administrative agencies when these decisions affect private rights or licenses. Courts may review administrative findings of fact and conclusions of law except in workmen's compensation claims when findings of fact are considered conclusive in the absence of fraud (unless legislation provides otherwise). The second paragraph of section 28 limits judicial review of property tax valuation or allocation. Only in cases of fraud or the adoption of wrong principles can an appeal be taken from an agency administering the property tax to a court. Section 28 is supplemented by Michigan's Administrative Procedures Act.

Section 28 speaks to "final" decisions of administrative agencies. The definition of "final" for the purposes of section 28 is a complicated matter. The supreme court recognizes that "final" is an "abstruse and infinitely uncertain term" and that its meaning cannot be ascertained by resort to simple dictionary definitions. The definition of "final" takes its meaning from the context in which it is employed. Given these considerations, an order for partial and immediate utility rate relief is not a "final" decision for the purposes of section 28 (*Great Lakes Steel Division of National Steel Corporation v. Michigan Public Service Commission*, 1982).

In *Michigan Employment Relations Commission v. Detroit Symphony Orchestra* (1974), the Michigan Supreme Court summarized how courts look at administrative decisions under section 28. Section 28 requires a thorough judicial review of an administrative decision that entails the qualitative and quantitative evaluation of the evidence considered by the agency. This review must include an examination of the whole record of the decision-making process—not just those portions of the record that support the administrative agency. The supreme court also admonished courts reviewing agency decisions to be careful to accord due deference to administrative expertise and not displace an agency's choice between two reasonably differing views.

Michigan courts read the phrase "as provided by law" in section 28 to mean that the legislature has substantial control over the mechanics of how administrative decisions are to be appealed (*McAvoy v. H. B. Sherman Company*, 1977; *Viculin v. Department of Civil Service*, 1971).

## SECTION 29

**Conservators of the peace.** Justices of the supreme court, judges of the court of appeals, circuit judges and other judges as provided by law shall be conservators of the peace within their respective jurisdictions.

Michigan judges have served as conservators of the peace since 1850. Section 29 is simply a revision of the language of Article VII, section 18 of the 1908 Constitution. As conservators of the peace, justices and judges are charged with maintaining public order. They may effect legal arrests (*City of Lincoln Park v. Sigler*, 1970) and carry concealed weapons (*Attorney General Opinion No. 537*, 1947).

## SECTION 30

**Judicial tenure commission; selection; terms; duties; power of supreme court.** (1) A judicial tenure commission is established of nine persons selected for three-year terms as follows: Four members shall be judges elected by the judges of the courts in which they serve; one shall be a court of appeals judge, one a circuit judge, one a probate judge and one a judge of a court of limited jurisdiction. Three shall be members of the state bar who shall be elected by the members of the state bar of whom one shall be a judge and two shall not be judges. Two shall be appointed by the governor; the members appointed by the governor shall not be judges, retired judges or members of the state bar. Terms shall be staggered as provided by rule of the supreme court. Vacancies shall be filled by the appointing power.

(2) On recommendation of the judicial tenure commission, the supreme court may censure, suspend with or without salary, retire or remove a judge for conviction of a felony, physical or mental disability which prevents the performance of judicial duties, misconduct in office, persistent failure to perform his duties, habitual intemperance or conduct that is clearly prejudicial to the administration of justice. The supreme court shall make rules implementing this section and providing for confidentiality and privilege of proceedings. Enactment ratified Aug. 6, 1968. Effective Sept. 21, 1968.

Section 30 was added to the constitution in 1968 after ratification at a special election. This section creates a nine-member judicial tenure commission made up of four judges, three lawyers, and two lay persons. Michigan judges elect the judicial members, members of the state bar elect the representatives of the legal profession, and the governor appoints the representatives of the citizenry. The members serve three-year, staggered terms. Vacancies on the commission are filled through the appointment power of the governor. The judicial tenure commission makes recommendations to the supreme court on the discipline of judges. The supreme court is given the power to provide for the staggering of the terms of the members of the commission, to make rules for implementing this section, and to provide for the confidentiality and privileged nature of the proceedings. The supreme court has implemented section 30 through court rules.

The judicial tenure commission conducts investigations and holds hearings on matters of alleged judicial misconduct. The combination of investigatory and disciplinary functions in the commission does not necessarily offend due process of law (*In the Matter of Mikesell*, 1976). The hearings conducted by the commission are governed by constitutional standards on due process appropriate to an administrative setting (*In the Matter of Del Rio*, 1977). The Michigan Constitution in Article I, section 17 provides the state guarantee of due process of law. The standard of proof used in judicial tenure cases is the preponderance of evidence standard, the same standard of proof used in criminal trials (*In re Loyd*, 1985). The disciplinary process of section 30 may begin after a conviction of a crime. The process need not wait until all appeals of that conviction are exhausted (*In the Matter of Callahan*, 1984).

Although the judicial disciplinary proceedings of section 30, and the court rules used to implement them, resemble civil proceedings, they are seen as fundamentally different from all other legal proceedings. The proceedings do not impose a criminal penalty or exact damages (*In re Jenkins*, 1991). The purpose of the proceedings is to maintain high standards of judicial fitness and competency and keep public confidence in the judiciary (*In re Loyd*, 1986). Because of this interest in the preservation of the integrity of the judiciary, the judicial tenure commission may not terminate proceedings against a judge simply because the judge has voluntarily left office (*In the Matter of Probert*, 1981).

The judicial tenure commission must make individual findings in individual cases. No conduct, however serious, warrants automatic removal from office. Section 30 gives the commission the choice whether and to what extent to recommend discipline against an offending judge (*In re Kapcia*, 1978).

The judicial tenure commission ultimately makes only recommendations to the state supreme court. The supreme court alone under section 30 possesses the power to decide what, if any, disciplinary action may be taken against a judge (*In the Matter of Del Rio*, 1977). The supreme court exercises *de novo* review over findings and conclusions of the commission (*In re Somers*, 1971). The four kinds of discipline the supreme court can impose—censure, suspension, removal, or retirement—do not empower the court to issue a permanent injunction against an individual holding judicial office (*In the Matter of Callahan*, 1984; *In the Matter of Probert*, 1981).

# Article VII

## *Local Government*

### SECTION 1

**Counties; corporate character, powers and immunities.** Each organized county shall be a body corporate with powers and immunities provided by law.

Mention of counties first appeared in the Constitution of 1850. Section 1 is simply a revision of the language of Article VIII, section 1 of the 1908 Constitution. Counties, along with cities, townships, and villages, are geographic areas organized as subunits of the state government. They facilitate local government.

Counties in Michigan can only exercise the powers granted to them under the state constitution or by state statute (*Alan v. Wayne County,* 1972; *Mosier v. Wayne County Board of Auditors,* 1940). Sections 1, 2, 7, and 8 of Article VII are not self-executing but require legislative action for them to take effect (*County Commissioners of Oakland County v. Oakland County Executive,* 1980).

### SECTION 2

**County charters.** Any county may frame, adopt, amend or repeal a county charter in a manner and with powers and limitations to be provided by general law, which shall among other things provide for the election of a charter commission. The law may permit the organization of county government in form different from that set forth in this constitution and shall limit the rate of ad valorem property taxation for county purposes, and restrict the powers of charter counties to borrow money and contract debts.Each charter county is hereby granted power to levy other taxes for county purposes subject to limitations and prohibitions set forth in this constitution or law. Subject to law, a county charter may authorize through its regularly constituted authority to adopt resolutions and ordinances relating to its concerns.

### *Election of Charter Commissions*

The board of supervisors by a majority vote of its members may, and upon petition of five percent of the electors shall, place upon the ballot the question of electing a commission to frame a charter.

### *Approval of Electors*

No county charter shall be adopted, amended or repealed until approved by a majority of electors voting on the question.

Section 2 is new to the constitution, and it provides for home rule for Michigan's counties. This addition to the constitution is designed to allow the counties to adjust their governmental structures to address specific problems (*Address to the People*).

The first paragraph of section 2 allows a county to write, amend, and repeal a county charter. The legislature sets forth in a statute the way in which a county goes about writing, amending, and repealing a charter and governs the content of the county charter. This statute must provide for the election of a county charter commission. The statute may allow county governments to differ in form from that described in the constitution. Before adoption of the 1963 Constitution, county governments existed only in a strict commission form (i.e., a board of commissions was the sole governing body of the county). Section 2 makes it clear that the legislature may provide for other forms of county governance (*Lucas v. Wayne County Election Commission,* 1985). The legislature must set a limit on the property tax rate for county purposes and must restrict the power of the charter county to borrow money and contract debts. In light of this constitutional requirement, the legislature cannot pass any statute that provides for the unlimited ability to contract debt (*Alan v. Wayne County,* 1972). Charter counties may levy other kinds of taxes subject to restrictions set forth in the constitution or state law. A county charter, subject to state law, may authorize the county government to adopt resolutions and ordinances relating to the concerns of the county. This provision means that the county government does not have to wait for specific permission from the state legislature to act on matters of concern to the county.

The second paragraph of section 2 describes how a county goes about electing a commission to write a county charter. The county board of supervisors may, by majority vote, place a question on the ballot on the election of a charter commission. Such a question must be placed on the ballot if 5 percent of the county's registered voters so petition.

The third paragraph of section 2 requires a majority vote of registered oters in order to adopt, amend, or repeal a charter. The majority is calculated on the basis of the number of voters voting on the question of the county charter.

Section 2 is not self-executing; it therefore requires implementation by state statute. The Michigan legislation complied with the provisions of section 2 by passing the Charter Counties Act (M.C.L.A. 45.501 et seq.). Section 2 must be read in harmony with other sections of Article VII that relate to county governance (*Lucas v. Wayne County Election Commission*, 1985).

## SECTION 3

**Reduction of size of county.** No organized county shall be reduced by the organization of new counties to less than 16 townships as surveyed by the United States, unless approved in the manner prescribed by law by a majority of electors voting thereon in each county to be affected.

This section prohibits the reduction in the size of a county in order to create new counties unless the majority of voters in each affected county approves the reduction. Limitations such as this have appeared in Michigan Constitutions since 1835.

Michigan courts have encountered the organization of new counties only under the Constitution of 1850. In *Board of Supervisors of Bay County v. Edmunds* (1905), the Michigan Supreme Court held that taking territory from one county and adding it to another came under the purview of this section.

## SECTION 4

**County officers; terms, combination.** There shall be elected for four-year terms in each organized county a sheriff, a county clerk, a county treasurer, a register of deeds and a prosecuting attorney, whose duties and powers shall be provided by law. The board of supervisors in any county may combine the offices of county clerk and register of deeds in one office or separate them at pleasure.

Section 4 provides for the election of certain county officers. Under the Constitution of 1835, the governor appointed a prosecuting attorney for each county. Voters chose the county sheriff, treasurer, coroner, register of deeds, and surveyor. All county officials held office for two-year terms. By 1850, the prosecutor and the county clerk had become elected officials. The 1908 Constitution continued the 1850 system but allowed the county board of supervisors to unite the offices of clerk and register of deeds. The 1963 Constitution revises the Constitution of 1908 by increasing the term of office for these county officials from two to four years.

Section 4 must be read in harmony with section 2 of this article. Although under Section 2 state law may permit a county to frame a county government different from that specified in the constitution, a county government must include the named section 4 elected officials (*Lucas v. Wayne County Election Commission,* 1985).

The prosecutor is the chief law enforcement officer of the county. While the office of prosecuting attorney is created by Article VII, the duties and powers of the office are established by statute. Since the prosecutor is chief law enforcement officer, Michigan courts allow the prosecutor broad discretion in the choice of statutes under which to bring a prosecution (*People v. Ford,* 1982).

The sheriff is a peace officer charged with enforcing the laws enacted by the legislature under the police power (*Fraternal Order of Police, Ionia County Lodge No. 157 v. Bensiger,* 1983). By providing for the office of sheriff, the state has constitutionally delegated the duty of law enforcement to the county (*Brownstown Township v. Wayne County,* 1976). Section 4 gives the office of sheriff constitutional status. The state legislature has defined the powers of the sheriff in state statutes (M.C.L.A. 51.70 et seq.).

The board of supervisors is entitled under this section to combine the offices of county clerk and register of deeds in a single office. This permission to unite the offices does not mean that the board of supervisors is empowered to eliminate either office (*Attorney General Opinion No. 6726,* 1992). A county cannot combine the two offices until after the expiration of the terms of office for both offices (*Attorney General Opinion No. 6688,* 1991).

## SECTION 5

**Offices at county seat.** The sheriff, county clerk, county treasurer and register of deeds shall hold their principal offices at the county seat.

Since 1850, Michigan has required county officials to maintain their offices at the county seat. The 1963 Constitution added the modifier "principal" to office to allow county officials to establish additional offices in other parts of the county. The 1963 Constitution also dropped "judge of probate" from the list of county officials. Probate judges are properly regarded as judicial, not county, officials.

Under section 5, only the buildings that house the offices of sheriff, county clerk, county treasurer, and register of deeds must be located at the county seat. Buildings that contain other county government offices, such as the department of social services, may be located outside the county seat (*Kyes v. Allegan County Board of Commissioners,* 1974).

## SECTION 6

**Sheriffs; security, responsibility for acts, ineligibility for other office.** The sheriff may be required by law to renew his security periodically and in default of giving such security, his office shall be vacant. The county shall never be responsible for his acts, except that the board of supervisors may protect him against claims by prisoners for unintentional injuries received while in his custody. He shall not hold any other office except in civil defense.

Section 6 governs the county sheriff. The Constitution of 1835 provided for a county sheriff who would hold no other office. This constitution also allowed the legislature to require the sheriff to renew his security and freed the county from responsibility for the actions of the sheriff. The 1850 and 1908 Constitutions retained this basic framework. The 1963 Constitution deletes the prohibition against the sheriff holding other offices to allow the sheriff to hold a civil defense position. The constitution also allows the county board of supervisors to protect the sheriff from lawsuits by prisoners who were unintentionally injured while in the sheriff's custody.

While section 6 specifically exempts the county from liability for the actions of the sheriff, the county may be responsible for the actions of other county employees who work in conjunction with the sheriff (*Lockaby v. Wayne County,* 1979).

The prohibition against the sheriff holding another office only applies to a government office. A sheriff may simultaneously hold a political office, such as executive committee treasurer of a county political party (*Attorney General Opinion No. 4969,* 1976).

## SECTION 7

**Boards of supervisors; members.** A board of supervisors shall be established in each organized county consisting of one member from each organized township and such representation from cities as provided by law.

Section 7 describes the membership of the county board of supervisors. The constitution has required representation for cities on the board of supervisors since 1850. The 1963 Constitution simply revises the 1908 language.

Section 7 has been the source of much constitutional debate in Michigan. As written, this section is designed to create a system of representation by townships and cities on county boards of supervisors. The constitutional problem with section 7 is that its system of representation makes no reference to population. When this section was placed in the constitution, the United States Supreme Court had only begun to wrestle with the problem of malapportionment. While the one-person, one-vote standard was applicable to state legislative districts (*Reynolds v. Sims,* 1964), there was some doubt as to whether this standard would be applicable to subunits of the state government. In 1968 in *Avery v.*

*Midland County*, the United States Supreme Court settled the issue by holding that the equal protection clause of the Fourteenth Amendment requires that political units with general governmental powers over an entire geographic area prohibits apportionment among single-member districts of substantially unequal population. For a while, the Michigan Supreme Court seemed to believe that *Avery* rendered all of section 7 unconstitutional (*In re Advisory Opinion re Constitutionality of 1966 P.A. 346*, 1968). However in 1982, the supreme court reconsidered its opinion in *Apportionment of Wayne County, County Board of Commissioners*. The supreme court disregarded its statements in the advisory opinion because advisory opinions do not carry precedential value (see Article III, section 8). In *Apportionment of Wayne County*, the supreme court preserved elements of section 7. The supreme court recognized that the Michigan Constitution has historically limited the power of state legislature to shape county boards of commissioners by requiring representation by cities and townships. Therefore, the supreme court held that the state legislature cannot provide for representation on county boards other than from townships and cities, except to the extent required by the one-person, one-vote principle of the Fourteenth Amendment's equal protection clause.

## SECTION 8

**Legislative, administrative, and other powers and duties of boards.** Boards of supervisors shall have legislative, administrative and such other powers and duties as provided by law.

Since 1850, the state legislature has been allowed to delegate power to the board of supervisors of a county. The 1963 Constitution simply revises the phraseology of the 1908 document.

Section 8 allows the legislature to delegate powers to county boards of supervisors. Under section 8, a county may only possess such powers given to it under the Michigan Constitution or by state statute (*Alan v. Wayne County*, 1972). County boards of supervisors, like legislatures, can raise money and distribute funds among various departments. Courts will not usually interfere with the discretionary actions of a county, as judicial intervention in legislative affairs offends principles of separation of powers (*Lucas v. Wayne County Board of Commissioners*, 1983).

## SECTION 9

**Compensation of county officers.** Boards of supervisors shall have exclusive power to fix the compensation of county officers not otherwise provided by law.

Beginning in 1850, the constitution has given the county board of supervisors the sole power to set the compensation for county officers, unless state law provides otherwise. The 1963 Constitution continues this tradition. The 1963 Constitution eliminated a sentence governing the responsibility for adjusting claims against the county. Such claims are now addressed by state statute.

Despite the power granted counties in section 9, the Michigan Supreme Court has ruled that counties must bear the costs for compensating private attorneys assigned to represent indigent defendants in appealing their convictions (*Frederick v. Presque Isle County Circuit Judge,* 1991). The supreme court has believed that the county must assume these costs because the county traditionally has been the primary unit in Michigan's criminal justice system. Also, under Article I, section 20 of the Constitution of 1963, criminal defendants are given a right to an appeal and reasonable assistance of counsel necessary to perfect that appeal.

The final phrase in section 9, "not otherwise provided by law," is clearly designed to place a limit on the power granted to the board of supervisors (*Vetter v. Fowler,* 1911).

## SECTION 10

**Removal of county seat.** A county seat once established shall not be removed until the place to which it is proposed to be moved shall be designated by two-thirds of the members of the board of supervisors and a majority of electors voting thereon shall have approved the proposed location in the manner prescribed by law.

Section 10 prohibits moving the county seat unless the new site is approved by a two-thirds majority of the board of supervisors and a majority of voters voting on the question. This prohibition first appeared in the Constitution in 1850.

The only interpretation of section 10 dates from the nineteenth century. Since counties are permitted to move the county seat by following the prescribed procedure, a county need not wait for the legislature to authorize the county to begin the process to move the county seat. A county is entitled to move the county seat even if the state legislature originally fixed the county seat at the time the county was organized (*Bagot v. Supervisors of Antrim,* 1880).

## SECTION 11

**Indebtedness, limitation.** No county shall incur any indebtedness which shall increase its total debt beyond 10 percent of its assessed valuation.

Michigan has limited the indebtedness of counties since 1850. The 1850 and 1908 Constitutions limited the indebtedness of counties to three percent. The 1908 Constitution allowed counties with an assessed valuation of $5,000,000 to incur an indebtedness of 5 percent. The 1963 Constitution increases the limit for all counties to 10 percent to give the counties greater power to meet modern problems. The *Address to the People* explained:

> Counties are now extending their credit for both primary and secondary purposes. Secondary obligations are incurred by placing the full faith and credit of the county behind bonds of cities and townships to enable them to borrow at the lowest possible interest rate for the construction of water and sewer systems and other public works.

The framers believed that this secondary debt could easily exceed the old three percent limitation.

The Michigan Supreme Court reads section 11 in harmony with section 34 of this article, which requires liberal construction of the constitution and laws affecting local government. At the same time, however, courts are mindful that limitations on government must be construed to protect the life, liberty, and property of the citizen (*Alan v. Wayne County*, 1972). The words "any indebtedness" in this section includes obligations of every character whereby the county agrees, or is bound, to pay a sum of money to another (*Young v. Ann Arbor*, 1934). In light of the intention of the framers of this section, any indebtedness clearly includes the secondary obligations of the county when it backs up the bonds of other units of government with a pledge of full faith and credit (*Alan v. Wayne County*, 1972). Since the limitation on indebtedness is a constitutional limitation, the legislature cannot change the definition of indebtedness by mere statute (*Alan v. Wayne County*, 1972).

## SECTION 12

> **Navigable streams, permission to bridge or dam.** A navigable stream shall not be bridged or dammed without permission granted by the board of supervisors of the county as provided by law, which permission shall be subject to such reasonable compensation and other conditions as may seem best suited to safeguard the rights and interests of the county and political subdivisions therein.

Section 12 traces its origins to sentiments in the Northwest Ordinance and the Constitutions of 1850 and 1908. The section was originally designed to further the policy of the Northwest Ordinance, which proclaimed that "the navigable waters leading into the Mississippi and the St. Lawrence, and the carrying places between the same, shall be common highways and forever free" (*In re Martiny Lakes Project*, 1968; *Shepard v. Gates*, 1883). The 1963 version is basically a revision of the 1850 language. The only major substantive change is the deletion of a provision that emphasized that this section could not be used to preclude the legislature from improving the navigation of any stream or prejudice the rights of individuals to free navigation. The framers of the 1963 Constitution saw this provision as adding nothing to the power of the legislature. More importantly, the traditional emphasis on navigation was seen as limiting.

Deletion of the mention of navigation allows consideration of other public uses of waterways, such as recreation or the preservation of natural habitats.

## SECTION 13

**Consolidation of counties, approval by electors.** Two or more contiguous counties may combine into a single county if approved in each affected county by a majority of the electors voting on the question.

Section 13 is new to the state constitution. It allows two or more adjoining counties to combine into a single county if the majority of voters in each affected county, voting on the issue of combination, approve. There have been no interpretations of this section.

## SECTION 14

**Organization and consolidation of townships.** The board of supervisors of each organized county may organize and consolidate townships under restrictions and limitations provided by law.

Under Article X, section 11 of the Constitution of 1850, the county board of supervisors was permitted to lay out highways, construct bridges, and organize townships under limitations and restrictions furnished by the state legislature. The 1908 counterpart to section 14 governed only the organization and consolidation of townships. Provision for highway and bridge construction was moved to a separate section and made a concern of the state legislature. The 1963 Constitution revises the 1908 language.

Decisions of a board of supervisors to reorganize a township are regarded as political and final so long as the board of supervisors complies with all statutory requirements (*Attorney General v. Page*, 1878).

## SECTION 15

**County intervention in public utility service and rate proceedings.** Any county, when authorized by its board of supervisors shall have the authority to enter or to intervene in any action or certificate proceeding involving the services, charges or rates of any privately owned public utility furnishing services or commodities to rate payers within the county.

Section 15 is new to the Constitution of 1963. It allows a county, when authorized by its board of supervisors, to participate in any action regarding services, rates, and charges of public utility companies that serve the people of the county. Under the Constitution of 1908, public utilities and public utility franchises were the special concern of cities, villages, and townships. In 1955 in *Wayne County v. Michigan Public Service Commission,* the supreme court refused to allow a county to represent county gas users before the public service commission. Section 15 negates this decision.

## SECTION 16

**Highways, bridges, culverts, airports; road tax limitation.** The legislature may provide for the laying out, construction, improvement and maintenance of highways, bridges, culverts and airports by the state and by the counties and townships thereof; and may authorize counties to take charge and control of any highway within their limits for such purposes. The legislature may provide the powers and duties of counties in relation to highways, bridges, culverts and airports; may provide for county road commissions to be appointed or elected, with powers and duties provided by law. The ad valorem property tax imposed for road purposes by any county shall not exceed in any year one-half of one percent of the assessed valuation for the preceding year.

Under Article IV, section 49 of the Constitution of 1850, the legislature was allowed to provide for the construction, improvement, and maintenance of highways, bridges, and culverts by counties and townships. The legislature could also provide a board of supervisors and county road commissions for these purposes. Counties were limited to a tax of two dollars for every thousand dollars' valuation for highways, bridges, and culverts. The 1908 Constitution maintained this basic structure but increased the tax limit to five dollars per one thousand dollars' valuation. The 1963 Constitution revises the 1908 language to conform to the present county highway system and to recognize county responsibility for airports. The same tax limit is maintained but expressed in the contemporary language of percents.

Section 16 recognizes that with the advent of the automobile, the building and maintenance of roads is no longer solely and exclusively a matter of local concern. Instead, good roads are a matter of general public interest and statewide importance (*City of Dearborn v. Michigan Turnpike Authority,* 1955).

However, section 16 must be read in harmony with Article 7, section 29. While the legislature and counties have responsibility for county roads under section 16, section 29 reserves regulatory powers to the townships and requires township consent when a public utility seeks to use roads within a township (*Union Township v. City of Mount Pleasant,* 1968; *Attorney General Opinion No. 5953,* 1981).

## SECTION 17

**Townships; corporate character, powers and immunities.** Each organized township shall be a body corporate with powers and immunities provided by law.

Both the 1850 and 1908 Constitutions spoke to the legal status of townships. A township is a municipal corporation and, as such, is an instrumentality of the state for the purposes of local government (*Hanslovsky v. Township of Leland*, 1937). The qualifications for township status and the steps for organizing a locality as a township are set forth in Michigan statutes, notably the Charter Township Act (M.C.L.A. sections 42.1 et seq.).

Townships have no police power of their own; they may exercise only such powers as given to them by the state (*Brandon Township v. North-Oakland Residential Service, Inc.*, 1981; *Lake Township v. Sytsma*, 1970) through the state constitution or state statute (*Hanselman v. Killeen*, 1984).

## SECTION 18

**Township officers; term, powers and duties.** In each organized township there shall be elected for terms of not less than two not more than four years as prescribed by law a supervisor, a clerk, a treasurer, and not to exceed four trustees, whose legislative and administrative powers and duties shall be prescribed by law.

The Constitution of 1850 was the first constitution to address the governance of townships. Article XI, section 1 of the 1850 Constitution provided for the annual election of a township supervisor, clerk, school inspector, commissioner of highways, overseer of highways, and up to four constables. This constitution in Article IV, section 38 also permitted the state legislature to delegate appropriate administrative and legislative powers to townships. The Constitution of 1908 lengthened the term of office of township officials to two years and provided for the office of justice of the peace. The 1963 Constitution revises the 1908 system. The legislature may now extend the term of office for township officials to four years. The new constitution also recognizes the new office of township trustee. The highway commissioner is now a constitutional officer, therefore reference to that post is deleted from section 18. The 1963 Constitution also abolished the office of justice of the peace in Article VI, section 26. This office, too, is deleted from section 18.

Township boards are government bodies of limited and special jurisdiction (*Hanslovsky v. Township of Leland*, 1937).

## SECTION 19

**Township public utility franchises.** No organized township shall grant any public utility franchise which is not subject to revocation at the will of the township, unless the proposition shall first have been approved by a majority of the electors of such township voting thereon at a regular or special election.

The Constitution of 1908 was the first constitution to treat the issue of townships and public utility franchises. Section 19 simply revises the language of Article VIII, section 19 of the 1908 Constitution.

Under the Constitution of 1908, public utilities included only those utilities for supplying water, light, heat, power, and transportation. Other public works, such as the operation of a sewer system, were not considered public utilities but rather government projects for the public health and safety. As such, these public works were not governed by the limitations in the 1908 counterpart to section 19 (*Holland v. Clerk of Garden City*, 1941). Similarly today, drain districts do not need to be granted a franchise under Section 19 when they undertake to construct a sewer system in the interest of public health (*Butcher v. Grosse Ile Township*, 1970).

## SECTION 20

**Townships, dissolution; villages as cities.** The legislature shall provide by law for the dissolution of township government whenever all the territory of an organized township is included within the boundaries of a village or villages notwithstanding that a village may include territory within another organized township and provide by law for the classification of such village or villages as cities.

Section 20 is new to the Constitution of 1963. It is designed to prevent two local governments from governing the same area. The legislature may dissolve a township government whenever all the land area of an organized township is included within the boundaries of a village or villages. The legislature may then reclassify the village or villages as cities. This mechanism retains for the people of the affected villages representation on the county board of supervisors. There have been no interpretation of this section.

## SECTION 21

**Cities and villages; incorporation, taxes, indebtedness.** The legislature shall provide by general laws for the incorporation of cities and villages. Such laws shall limit their rate of ad valorem property taxation for municipal purposes, and restrict the powers of cities and villages to borrow money and contract debts. Each city and village is granted power to levy other taxes for public purposes, subject to limitations and prohibitions provided by this constitution or by law.

Section 21 empowers the legislature to pass laws for the incorporation of cities and villages. These laws must limit the rate of property taxes for local purposes and set limits on the ability of cities and villages to borrow money and contract debt. Cities or villages can levy other taxes as well as the property tax, but these taxes may be subject to limitation by this constitution or a state statute. Section 21 is a revision of Article VIII, section 20 of the Constitution of 1908.

Section 21 clearly sets aside the incorporation of cities and villages for the state legislature (*Midland Township v. State Boundary Commission*, 1975). The Home Rule Cities Act (M.C.L.A. 117.1 et seq.) is the general law governing the incorporation of cities and villages. Under section 21, the only process for creating a new, hitherto nonexistent city is the process of incorporation (*Township of Farmington v. State Boundary Commission*, 1971).

The state legislature and section 21 grant cities the power to tax. Therefore, municipal officials can seek revenue from whatever taxes the city can devise, subject only to the state legislature's constitutionally ordained limitation on the rate of taxes for municipal purposes (*Dooley v. City of Detroit*, 1963).

Section 21 limits the power to tax to public purposes. Public funds cannot be used to advance a private enterprise (*McManus v. Petoskey*, 1911). What constitutes a public purpose is a difficult question that Michigan courts answer on the basis of the facts of an individual case (*Gregory Marina, Inc. v. Detroit*, 1966). Generally, courts defer to the political branches' definition of a public purpose, and even acts of municipal governments are accorded a presumption of validity. A public purpose can be any action of organized government that makes government subserve the general well-being of society and advance the present and prospective happiness and prosperity of the people (*Horton v. City of Kalamazoo*, 1977).

## SECTION 22

**Charters, resolutions, ordinances; enumeration of powers.** Under general laws the electors of each city and village shall have the power and authority to frame, adopt and amend its charter, and to amend an existing charter of the city or village heretofore granted or enacted by the legislature for the government of the city or village. Each such city and village shall have power to adopt resolutions and ordinances relating to municipal concerns, property and government, subject to the constitution and law. No enumeration of powers granted to cities and villages in this constitution shall limit or restrict the general grant of authority conferred by this section.

Section 22 establishes home rule for Michigan cities and villages. Cities and villages are given the power to pass ordinances relating to municipal concerns, property, and government, limited only by the constitution and state law. The Constitution of 1850 in Article IV, section 38 allowed the legislature to delegate to organized townships and incorporated villages and cities legislative and administrative power appropriate to municipal concerns. Michigan established a general system of home rule in the Constitution of 1908. Section 22 is a revision of Article VII, section 21 of the Constitution of 1908. This new language is designed to be a more positive statement of municipal powers in light of Michigan's successful experience with home rule (*Address to the People*).

Municipal corporations have no inherent power; they are created by the state and derive their authority from the state. An ordinance enacted by the governing body of a home rule city is valid only if it is consistent with the powers conferred by the state in the constitution and statutes and if it falls within the scope of authority delegated by the electorate in the city's charter (*Bivens v. City of Grand Rapids*, 1993). A city charter is like a city constitution, and the city cannot validly enact an ordinance that contradicts the limitations expressed in the city's charter (*Jackson Common Council v. Harrington*, 1910). But so long as local municipalities do not circumvent the constitution, a state statute, or their charters, courts cannot hinder the cities' exercise of police power (*People v. Krezen*, 1986).

## SECTION 23

**Parks, boulevards, cemeteries, hospitals.** Any city or village may acquire, own, establish and maintain, within or without its corporate limits, parks, boulevards, cemeteries, hospitals and all works which involve the public health and safety.

Section 23 empowers municipalities to acquire, own, and maintain certain kinds of property that involve public health or safety. Section 23 is a revision of Article VIII, section 22 of the Constitution of 1908. The 1963 Constitution deleted the obsolete word "almshouses" from the list of municipal properties and works.

Section 23 is not self-executing; that is, implementation of the powers granted to cities requires enabling legislation from the state (*Saubaugh v. City of Dearborn*, 1969; *Parr v. Ladd*, 1949). The state legislature has addressed section 23 powers in a series of statutes.[3] The acquisition of property by municipalities is governed by the eminent domain provision of Article X, section 2 of this constitution.

Section 23 should be read in harmony with section 22 of this article. When these two sections of the constitution are read together, Michigan courts hold that the list of itemized powers contained in section 23 is not exclusive (*Saubaugh v. City of Dearborn*, 1969). The meaning of "public health or safety" has been broadened to include public health and necessity (*In re Petition of City of Detroit for Condemnation of Lands for Airport*, 1944).

---

[3] For buildings, grounds, and parks, see M.C.L.A. section 100.1 et seq. (fourth class cities) and section M.C.L.A. 67.4 et seq. (villages). For cemeteries, see M.C.L.A. section 95.1 et seq. (cities); section 117.4 et seq. (home rule cities); 67.55 et seq. (villages). For hospitals, see M.C.L.A. section 100.2 et seq. (fourth class cities); section 331.1 et seq. (community hospitals); section 117.4 et seq. (home rule cities); section 67.5 (villages).

The phrase "within or without its corporate limits" means that a city or village may acquire, own, establish, or maintain public works outside municipal geographic boundaries, including territory within the borders of another municipality (*Toebe v. City of Munising*, 1937). This phrase covers even the acquisition and operation of public works in another state (*Saubaugh v. City of Dearborn*, 1969).

## SECTION 24

**Public service facilities.** Subject to this constitution, any city or village may acquire, own or operate, within or without its corporate limits, public service facilities for supplying water, light, heat, power, sewage disposal and transportation to the municipality and the inhabitants thereof.

Any city or village may sell and deliver heat, power or light without its corporate limits in amounts not exceeding 25 percent of that furnished by it within the corporate limits, except as greater amounts may be permitted by law; may sell and deliver water and provide sewage disposal services outside of its corporate limits in such amount as may be determined by the legislative body of the city or village; and may operate transportation lines outside the municipality within such limits as may be prescribed by law.

Article VIII, section 23 of the Constitution of 1908 allowed Michigan municipalities to own and operate public utilities and set the 25 percent sale limit on the water, heat, light, power, or transportation services created by the public utilities. A 1944 amendment to the 1908 Constitution permitted municipalities to sell and deliver water outside the municipalities in an amount set by the governing body of the city or village. Section 24 of the Constitution of 1963 revises the 1908 language in two major ways. In the first paragraph, sewage disposal is added to the list of municipal services. This addition was a response to the decision of the Michigan Supreme Court in *Holland v. Clerk of Garden City* (1941), which held that a sewage treatment system was not a public utility for the purposes of the 1908 Constitution. In the second paragraph, the state legislature is given the power to increase the limitation on the sale of heat, light, or power service. This addition is designed to help prevent the duplication of power plants in neighboring areas (*Address to the People*). The 1963 version of this section also deleted a provision preventing cities and villages of under 25,000 inhabitants from owning and operating transportation facilities. The framers of the new section 24 thought that this prohibition was unnecessary and worked to prevent small municipalities from entering into joint transit projects with private companies or neighboring cities or villages (*Address to the People*).

The first paragraph of section 24 gives municipalities the power to operate public utilities subject to the limitations in the state constitution. The second paragraph allows municipalities to sell to outside parties up to 25 percent of the heat, power, or light generated by municipal public utilities. The state legislature, however, may increase this limit. A municipality has more discretion on the operation of water and sewer facilities. Municipalities may sell or deliver water and sewer services in whatever amounts the governing body of the municipality sees fit. Finally, the second paragraph allows a municipality to operate transportation lines outside the municipality, subject to limits set by the state legislature in statutes.

Like other sections of Article VII concerning local government, section 24 is not self-executing (*Thompson v. City of Dearborn*, 1957). The state legislature has implemented the powers in section 24 in a series of statutes.[4] Moreover, even though the first words of section 24 refer simply to constitutional limits, operation of a public utility by a municipality is not exempt from state statutory *law* (*Northville Coach Line, Inc. v. City of Detroit*, 1966).

Michigan courts have given municipalities considerable latitude in structuring the rates and operations of their public utilities. As the Michigan Supreme Court stated in 1918, this constitutional prerogative of municipalities is granted in general terms, and it would be unwise and practically impossible for courts to interfere in the business judgments involved in the operation of public utilities (*Andrews v. City of South Haven*, 1915). Municipalities have the power to fix just and equitable rates for the supply of a service such as electricity (*Wolgamood v. Village of Constantine*, 1942). These rates are presumed to be reasonable in the absence of a showing that they are arbitrary, capricious, or unreasonable (*Oakland County v. City of Detroit*, 1978). Municipalities may make distinctions between residents and nonresidents in providing public utility services (*Oakland County v. City of Detroit*, 1978). Courts will uphold these distinctions even in light of equal protection challenges, since these classifications are judged under the lenient rational basis standard of review (see Article I, section 2).

## SECTION 25

**Public utilities; acquisition, franchises, sale.** No city or village shall acquire any public utility furnishing light, heat or power, or grant any public utility franchise which is not subject to revocation at the will of the city or village, unless the proposition shall first have been approved by three-fifths of the electors voting thereon. No city or village may sell any public utility unless the propositions shall have first been approved by a majority of the electors voting thereon, or a greater number if the charter shall so provide.

---

[4] For public utilities in home rule cities, see M.C.L.A. section 117.4c. For the powers of fourth class cities, see M.C.L.A. section 91.1 et seq. For sewers, drains, and water-courses, see M.C.L.A. section 101.1 et seq. (fourth class cities); section 124.251 (municipal water supply and sewerage disposal systems); section 67.12 (villages). For village heat, light, water, and power, see M.C.L.A. section 78.24.

Section 25 governs the acquisition and sale of public utilities providing light, heat, or power. Conditions are placed on the acquisition or franchise of such public utilities. A city or village cannot acquire or franchise a public utility that cannot be revoked at the discretion of the city or village, unless the decision to acquire or franchise has been approved by a three-fifths majority of voters voting on the question. Cities or villages cannot sell any public utility without approval by a majority of voters voting on the question. A city or village charter may require more than a majority vote in order to approve sale.

Section 25 is a revision of Article VIII, section 25 of the Constitution of 1908. The framers of the 1963 Constitution retained the supermajority vote to acquire or franchise a public utility because of the tremendous commitment of public funds to such projects. The framers also added new language requiring voter approval of the sale of public utilities. Here, only a majority of voters need approve the sale of a municipally owned utility. The reason for the simple majority vote was the belief that the considerations for the sale of a utility differ from the considerations for acquisition. When a utility is sold, the framers reasoned, the major considerations are largely restricted to a judgment on whether the sale is desirable and whether the sales price is satisfactory (*Address to the People*).

According to the Michigan Supreme Court, a public franchise is a special privilege of a public nature conferred by governmental authority upon individuals as such or artificial personalities called corporations (*Lansing Township v. City of Lansing*, 1959). A franchise is also a contract (*City of Niles v. Michigan Gas and Electric Co.*, 1935).

Only public utilities providing light, heat, or power, as specified in the first sentence, are governed by the provisions of section 25. Cable television, therefore, is not considered a public utility (*Continental Cablevision of Michigan, Inc. v. City of Roseville*, 1988; *White v. City of Ann Arbor*, 1979). The courts have been unwilling to expand the list of public utilities governed by section 25 because of the requirement that all public utility franchises be revocable at the will of the municipality. The courts believe that this requirement would substantially increase the risks for private entrepreneurs making large investments in projects such as cable television. The risks may become so great as to deter or effectually prohibit private companies from making these investments (*White v. City of Ann Arbor*, 1979).

Extensions of a public utility, such as the purchasing of an additional power plant, pumping station, or pipelines, do not count as acquisitions under section 25. Therefore, the requirement of voter approval does not apply (*Eby v. Board of Water and Light of the City of Lansing*, 1983).

## SECTION 26

**Cities and villages, loan of credit.** Except as otherwise provided in this constitution, no city or village shall have the power to loan its credit for any private purpose or, except as provided by law, for any public purpose.

Section 26 is new to the Michigan Constitution. It limits the ability of cities and villages to loan their credit. No credit may be loaned for any private purpose. Credit may be loaned for a public purpose if allowed by the constitution or by state law.

The definition of what constitutes "credit" or a "loan of credit" has been difficult for Michigan courts. At bottom, the credit of a municipality is its power to levy general taxes. When a city pledges all or part of that power, it pledges its credit and incurs an obligation (*Request for Advisory Opinion on Constitutionality of 1986 PA 281*, 1988). The loan of credit comes into play when a city issues bonds. General obligation bonds, for which the credit of the state is pledged for payment, are loans of credit (*Schureman v. State Highway Commission*, 1966). Self-liquidating, special obligation, and revenue bonds are excluded from the constitutional definition of a loan of credit (*Allan v. Wayne County*, 1972). Special obligation bonds are retired from tax revenues earmarked for that purpose. Revenue bonds are retired from the proceeds of the operation of the public structure or enterprise supporting their issuance (*Schuremen v. State Highway Commission*, 1966). To determine whether or not a given bond issue constitutes a loan of credit, Michigan courts ask whether the given bond issue is more like a general obligation, special obligation, or revenue bond. If a given bond issue most closely resembles a general obligation bond, then it is a loan of credit (*Request for Advisory Opinion on Constitutionality of 1986 PA 281*, 1988).

Section 26 is an exception to the general rule of Article IX, section 18, which governs the lending of the credit of the state (*City of Gaylord v. Gaylord City Clerk*, 1966). In order for a loan of credit to conform to the requirements of the section 26 exception, the loan of credit must be both: (1) authorized by law and (2) for a public purpose (*Request for Advisory Opinion on Constitutionality of 1986 PA 281*, 1988).

For Michigan courts, authorized by law means that the municipal action has been sanctioned by either the state constitution or a state statute (*Request for Advisory Opinion on Constitutionality of 1986 PA 281*, 1988). The question of a public purpose is more difficult, but generally Michigan courts are reluctant to second-guess the wisdom of the legislature on a public purpose determination (*Request for Advisory Opinion on Constitutionality of 1986 PA 281*, 1988). As the Michigan Supreme Court put it in *City of Gaylord v. Gaylord City Clerk* (1966), "generally, a public purpose has for its object the promotion of the public health, safety, morals, general welfare, security, prosperity, and the contentment of all the inhabitants within the municipal corporation." Under this view, Michigan courts have found all of the following diverse activities to serve a public purpose: the promotion of the sale of Michigan apples, payment of dues by a city to the Michigan Municipal League, the construction of a port marina, the issuance of bonds to finance the construction of privately owned industrial buildings, the construction of a sports arena, and the public finance of gubernatorial elections (*Request for Advisory Opinion on Constitutionality of 1986 PA 281*, 1988).

Payments made to a private party, for example payments to a police officer and attorneys to bring nuisance abatement suits, can also constitute a public purpose (*Horton v. City of Kalamazoo*, 1978).

## SECTION 27

**Metropolitan governments and authorities.** Notwithstanding any other provision of this constitution the legislature may establish in metropolitan areas additional forms of government or authorities with powers, duties and jurisdictions as the legislature shall provide. Wherever possible, such additional forms of government or authorities shall be designed to perform multipurpose functions rather than a single function.

Article VIII, section 31 of the Constitution of 1908 allowed the state legislature to incorporate any combination of cities, villages, and townships into metropolitan districts. These districts could be empowered to perform functions such as acquiring, owning, and operating parks, public utilities, and transportation facilities. Section 27 revises the 1908 Constitution to give the legislature greater flexibility in the creation of metropolitan districts. The last sentence of this section introduces a new proviso: Metropolitan districts should be designed to perform multiple functions whenever possible.

The Michigan legislature has provided for a number of metropolitan governments and authorities.[5] The 1908 version of section 27 only specifically allowed the legislature to create metropolitan districts by combining cities, villages, or townships. Despite this reference to cities, villages, and townships, the legislature still possesses the power to incorporate counties into metropolitan districts to develop and operate parks (*Huron-Clinton Metropolitan Authority v. Boards of Supervisors of Wayne, Washtenaw, Livingston, Oakland and Macomb Counties*, 1942).

## SECTION 28

**Governmental functions and powers; joint administration, costs and credits, transfers.** The legislature by general law shall authorize two or more counties, townships, cities, villages or districts, or any combination thereof among other things to: enter into contractual undertakings or agreements with one another or with the state or with any combination thereof for the joint administration of any of the functions or powers which each would have the power to perform separately; share the costs and responsibilities of functions and services with one another or with the state or

---

[5] For charter water authorities, see M.C.L.A. section 121.1 et seq. For Huron-Clinton Metropolitan Authority, see M.C.L.A. section 119.51 et seq. For metropolitan districts, see M.C.L.A. section 119.1 et seq. For bonds, see M.C.L.A. section 141.401 For joint water and sewer disposal systems, see M.C.L.A. section 123.331 et seq. For metropolitan authorities, see M.C.L.A. section 124.401.

with any combination thereof which each would have the power to perform separately; transfer function or responsibilities to one another or any combination thereof upon the consent of each unit involved; cooperate with one another and with state government; lend their credit to one another or any combination thereof as provided by law in connection with any authorized publicly owned undertaking.

Any other provision of this constitution notwithstanding, an officer or employee of the state or any such unit of government or subdivision or agency thereof, except members of the legislature, may serve on or with any governmental body established for the purposes set forth in this section and shall not be required to relinquish his office or employment by reason of such service.

Section 28 is new to the constitution. The framers designed this section to encourage the solution of metropolitan problems through existing units of government, rather than create a fourth layer of local government (*Address to the People*). Under this section, the state legislature may authorize two or more units of local government to enter into cooperative agreements with each other. These cooperative agreements may provide for the joint administration of functions or services and the sharing of costs and responsibilities. Any cooperative agreement must cover a government function or project that all parties to the agreement have the power to perform separately.

The second paragraph of section 28 covers the local officials who are involved in these cooperative agreements. The Michigan Constitution usually prohibits government officials from holding multiple offices. This paragraph carves out an exception to this policy for any state employee or official, excluding members of the state legislature. Members of the state legislature are prohibited from holding any other office by Article IV, section 8 of this constitution.

The Michigan legislature has provided for numerous cooperative agreements, the most important of which is the Urban Cooperation Act of 1967 (M.C.L.A. sections 124.501 et seq.).

Because of the clear language of section 28, a county commissioner may serve as both county commissioner and a member of a cooperative enterprise such as the Detroit/Wayne County Port Authority (*Attorney General Opinion No. 6440*, 1987). Under section 28, local units of government may not delegate the legislative function to a zoning authority. However, local units of government may allow a zoning authority to handle the administrative aspects of zoning, provided that all the units of local government involved are subject to the same zoning enabling act (*Attorney General Opinion No. 5312*, 1978).

## SECTION 29

**Highways, streets, alleys, public places; control, use by public utilities.** No person, partnership, association or corporation, public or private, operating a public

> utility shall have the right to the use of highways, streets, alleys or other public places of any county, township, city or village for wires, poles, pipes, tracks, conduits or other utility facilities without the consent of the duly constituted authority of the county, township, city or village; or to transact local business therein without first obtaining a franchise from the township, city or village. Except as otherwise provided in this constitution the right of all counties, townships, cities and villages to the reasonable control of their highways, streets, alleys and public places is hereby reserved to such local units of government.

Article VIII, section 28 of the Constitution of 1908 required operators of public utilities to secure the consent of the appropriate unit of local government before using highways, streets, alleys, or other public places for conveyances such as pipelines or wires. Section 29 of this article of the 1963 Constitution revises the old language and adds counties to the list of local governments. Section 29 also affirms the right of units of local government to control their highways, streets, alleys, and public places unless an exception is made elsewhere in the constitution.

Section 29 must be considered with section 16 of this article, which gives the legislature primary authority over roads in Michigan. In 1931 in the McNitt Act (M.C.L.A. sections 247.1 et seq.), the legislature abolished the system of township roads and turned responsibility for the laying out, construction, improvement, and maintenance of roads to the county roads commissions. However, Michigan courts have concluded that section 16 and the McNitt Act do not negate all township control over roads. Public utilities and others must still secure the consent of a township before the erection of poles, pipes, wires, conduits, and the like on a township's right-of-way alongside county roads (*Union Township v. City of Mount Pleasant*, 1968). However, townships' consent cannot be refused arbitrarily or unreasonably (*Union Township v. City of Mount Pleasant*, 1968). Courts regard the granting or denying of consent a discretionary, legislative act. Therefore, a court will not issue a writ of mandamus to compel a township to grant consent provided that the township's decision was not arbitrary or unreasonable (*City of South Haven v. South Haven Charter Township*, 1994).

Again, even in light of section 16 and the McNitt Act, townships still retain reasonable control over roads within their boundaries. Reasonable control means that regulation of roads within a township must not be unreasonable and cannot be inconsistent with any regulation passed by the state (*Fenton Gravel Co., Inc. v. Village of Fenton*, 1963; *People v. McGraw*, 1915). Courts determine whether a local regulation constitutes reasonable control on a case-by-case basis. Factors that courts consider in determining whether a given municipal action is reasonable include peculiar local conditions, fiscal considerations, safety factors, and the extent to which a regulation is consistent with state law (*City of Trenton v. County Board of Road Commissioners of the County of Wayne*, 1982).

The definition of a public utility for the purposes of section 29 differs from the definition of a public utility in section 25. Cable television counts as a public utility under section 29, while it does not under section 25. This reading of section 29 means that a cable television operator must obtain a franchise before doing business in a municipality. However, a section 29 franchise (unlike a section 25 franchise) need not be revocable at the will of the municipality and does not require a three-fifths vote of the people. A panel of the Michigan court of appeals in *Charter Township of Meridian v. Roberts* (1982) reasoned that section 29 does not contain the same limiting language as section 25. Moreover, section 29 should be read along with section 34 of this article, which requires that the powers of counties, townships, cities, and villages be liberally construed. The court of appeals also believed that this interpretation of section 29 is consistent with the public policy considerations outlined by the Michigan Supreme Court in *White v. City of Ann Arbor* (1979). In *White*, the Michigan Supreme Court was fearful that expanding the list of section 25 public utilities would discourage entrepreneurs from making large and risky investments in various business enterprisesin cities.

## SECTION 30

**Franchises and licenses, duration.** No franchise or license shall be granted by any township, city or village for a period longer than 30 years.

Section 30 simply revises the language of the 1908 Constitution by substituting the words "township, city or village" for "municipality of this state."

The language of section 30 is regarded as a limitation on, rather than a grant of, municipal power (*City of Niles v. Michigan Gas and Electric Co.*, 1935).

## SECTION 31

**Vacation or alteration of roads, streets, alleys, public places.** The legislature shall not vacate or alter any road, street, alley or public place under the jurisdiction of any county, township, city or village.

Since 1850, Michigan constitutions have limited the ability of the state legislature to interfere with any road or street laid out by local authorities. The contemporary version of section 31 revises the language of the 1908 Constitution.

The control of the state legislature over state roads is unquestioned and unaffected by this section (*Davies v. Board of Supervisors of Saginaw County*, 1891). State trunk roads within city limits are considered state roads, not streets for the purpose of this section (*Allen v. Rogers*, 1929).

## SECTION 32

**Budgets, public hearing.** Any county, township, city, village or school district empowered by the legislature or by this constitution to prepare budgets of estimated expenditures and revenues shall adopt such budgets only after a public hearing in a manner prescribed by law.

Section 32 is new to the constitution. It requires any unit of local government or school district that is authorized under the constitution or state law to prepare a budget and adopt that budget only after a public hearing. The state legislature prescribes the way in which the public hearing must be conducted (M.C.L.A. sections 141.411 to 141.415).

Section 32 is designed to give affected citizens a meaningful opportunity to be heard on a proposed budget before its adoption. The requirements of section 32 and its associated statutes mean that the proposed budget must be available to the public before the public hearing on the budget, not at the public hearing (*Attorney General Opinion No. 6152*, 1983).

## SECTION 33

**Removal of elected officers.** Any elected officer of a political subdivision may be removed from office in the manner and for the causes provided by law.

Michigan constitutions have provided for the removal of elected officers of local government since 1835. Section 33 simply revises the language of Article IX, section 8 of the Constitution of 1908. Under section 33, the state legislature defines the reasons for removing an elected local official from office and the procedures by which this is accomplished. The legislature has implemented section 33 in a series of statutes.[6]

Section 33 is one of a number of sections of the Michigan Constitution dealing with the removal from public office.[7] Removals under section 33, as well as removals under other sections of the Michigan Constitution, must be done with careful consideration to issues of separation of powers (*Buback v. Governor*, 1968).

The words "political subdivision" in this section refer to counties, cities, villages, townships, and school districts (*Attorney General Opinion No. 5395*, 1978).

---

[6] For removal of city officers by the governor, see M.C.L.A. section 168.327. For removal of county officers, see M.C.L.A. sections 168.207, 168.238, and 168.268. For removal of township officers, see M.C.L.A. section 168.341. For removal of village officers, see M.C.L.A. section 168.383.

[7] See Article IV, section 16 (legislative expulsion of a member); Article VI, section 25 (the removal of judges); Article V, section 10 ( the power of the governor to remove elected or appointed state officers, except legislative or judicial); Article XI, section 5 (the civil service).

A reduction in the duties of an office does not count as a removal from office for the purposes of section 33 (*Wayne County Prosecuting Attorney v. Wayne County Board of Commissioners,* 1972).

## SECTION 34

**Construction of constitution and law concerning counties, townships, cities, villages.** The provisions of this constitution and law concerning counties, townships, cities and villages shall be liberally construed in their favor. Powers granted to counties and townships by this constitution and by law shall include those fairly implied and not prohibited by this constitution.

Section 34 is new to the constitution. This section directs courts interpreting constitutional provisions or statutes relating to local government to construe the law in favor of the unit of local government. Under common law, courts narrowly construed the powers delegated to local government (*Harding v. Bader,* 1889). Section 34 replaces the common law approach with a constitutional approach more favorable to local government (*Square Lake Hills Condominium Association v. Bloomfield Township,* 1991).

Section 34 is not an independent grant of constitutional power to units of local government. It is instead a framework for the analysis of powers granted to local government under other provisions of the constitution and in statutes (*Square Lake Hills Condominium Association v. Bloomfield Township,* 1991).

# Article VIII

*Education*

## SECTION 1

**Encouragement of education.** Religion, morality and knowledge being necessary to good government and the happiness of mankind, schools and the means of education shall forever be encouraged.

The language of section 1 is drawn from the Northwest Ordinance of 1787. Neither the Constitution of 1835 or the Constitution of 1850 contained a similar declaration of principle. The language of section 1 was placed into the constitution in 1908 and was carried over to the 1963 Constitution unchanged.

Section 1 serves two purposes. First, this section is used to underscore the importance of education in modern society. Although education in not considered a fundamental right (*East Jackson Public Schools v. State of Michigan*, 1984), Section 1 helps to provide evidence that the state interest in education is "longstanding" and "of the highest importance"[8] (*Sheridan Road Baptist Church v. State of Michigan*, 1986). For Michigan courts, the antiquity of this section shows a settled state purpose of providing and fostering education (*Snyder v. Charlotte Public Schools*, 1985). Second, section 1, along with the Michigan Constitution's separate article on education, demonstrates that education is a key attribute of government responsibility (*Governor v. State Treasurer*, 1972).

[8] See Article 1, section 2 for the effects of fundamental rights on equal protection analysis.

Moreover, section 1 (together with section 2 of this article) means that control for the state's public school system is a matter for the state legislature and state law, even though schools throughout Michigan are administered by local agencies (*Jones v. Grand Ledge Public Schools*, 1957).

## SECTION 2

**Free public elementary and secondary schools; discrimination.** The legislature shall maintain and support a system of free public elementary and secondary schools as defined be law. Every school district shall provide for the education of its pupils without discrimination as to religion, creed, race, color or national origin.

Michigan has required the maintenance of public schools since 1835. The 1835 Constitution required the legislature to provide for a system of common schools open for at least three months of the year. The 1850 Constitution contained two provisions on public education. Once again free schools were to be open for at least three months a year, but a new provision required that all instruction be in English. More attention was paid to funding the schools: Funding would come from the state's primary school fund and taxes levied for the support of schools. The 1908 Constitution lengthened the school year to five months and included language on the distribution of funds from the primary school fund. Section 2 represents a revision of the 1908 Constitution. The "primary" schools of 1908 are now "elementary and secondary" schools. The statutory-type language on school funding was omitted and the legislature was entrusted to provide for school funding. The last sentence of the first paragraph of section 2 was added in 1963 in order to underscore Michigan's position on nondiscrimination in education.

The phrase "free public elementary and secondary schools" clearly means without cost or charge. In interpreting which school services must be available free, the Michigan Supreme Court has borrowed from the Idaho Supreme Court's reading of a similar provision in the Idaho Constitution.[9] Under this approach, necessary elements of any school activity or integral fundamental parts of elementary and secondary education must be available free of charge (*Bond v. Ann Arbor School District*, 1970). Therefore, textbooks must be available free of charge (*Bond v. Ann Arbor School District*, 1970) but extracurricular activities need not be (*Attorney General v. East Jackson Public Schools*, 1985). The constitutional requirement of a free public elementary education does not mean that, in the absence of state rules or regulations specifying the length of the

[9] The Idaho case is *Paulson v. Minidoka County School District No. 331*, 93 Idaho 469, 463 P2d 935 (1970).

school day, local school boards may not shorten the school day due to lack of funds (*Welling v. Livonia Board of Education*, 1969).

As the United States Supreme Court noted in *Milliken v. Bradley* (1974), the Michigan Constitution and Michigan law have required unitary schools for over one hundred years. A unitary school system is one that does not discriminate by race, religion, creed, color, or national origin.

> **Nonpublic schools, prohibited aid.** No public monies or property shall be appropriated or paid or any public credit utilized, by the legislature or any other political subdivision or agency of the state directly or indirectly to aid or maintain any private, denominational or other nonpublic, pre-elementary, elementary or secondary school. No payment, credit, tax benefit, exemption or deductions, tuition voucher, subsidy, grant or loan of public monies or property shall be provided, directly or indirectly, to support the attendance of any student or the employment of any person at any such nonpublic school or at any location or institution where instruction is offered in whole or in part to such nonpublic school students. The legislature may provide for the transportation of students to and from any school. Amendment ratified Nov. 3, 1970. Effective Dec. 19, 1970.

This second paragraph of Section 2 was proposed by initiative petition. It prohibits the use of any public resources to support nonpublic schools. The amendment does allow the legislature to provide transportation for students to and from any school, be it public or private.

This amendment was added to the constitution as a citizen response to a state law and an interpretation of that law by the Michigan Supreme Court. The state legislature began to consider the issue of aid to private schools in 1968 with the creation of a joint committee to study the matter. The governor created a Commission on Educational Reform in 1969 to review the matter further. In 1970, the state legislature passed PA 100, which authorized state subsidies to salaries of lay teachers in nonpublic schools who taught secular subjects. This state assistance for nonpublic schools was termed "parochiaid." The Michigan Supreme Court indicated in *Advisory Opinion re Constitutional of 1970 PA 100* that this act was constitutional despite concerns about separation of church and state.[10] Following this decision, citizens began circulating initiative petitions to create a state constitutional prohibition against parochiaid. Critics of the proposal thought that adoption of the amendment might jeopardize programs providing auxiliary services to nonpublic schools such as police or fire protection or school lunch programs. Proponents countered with the argument that the proposed amendment would simply outlaw parochiaid. In the words of Justice

[10] See Article 1, section 4.

Williams, "as far as the voter was concerned... Proposal C was an anti-parochiaid amendment—no public monies to run parochial schools—and beyond that all else was complete and utter confusion" (*Traverse City School District v. Attorney General*, 1971).

Given citizen confusion over the meaning of Proposal C, along with concerns about freedom of religion and separation of church and state, Michigan courts have struggled with the five prohibitions in this amendment. Courts have attempted to solve this problem by drawing a distinction between services simply incidental to the educational process and services that are essential to the educational process. Generally, courts have held that while this amendment clearly prohibits parochiaid, it does not prohibit the provision of "incidental" services to nonpublic schools (*Traverse City School District v. Attorney General*, 1971). Incidental services can include "shared time" instruction, health and nursing services, street crossing guards, drivers' education, and programs for the handicapped. The courts have reasoned that these services are general health and welfare measures that only have an incidental relation to the instruction of private school children. However, the provision of school supplies and textbooks are not simply incidental to education, instead they are essential aids that constitute a primary feature of the educational process. This type of aid is clearly prohibited by this section of the constitution (*Advisory Opinion re Constitutionality of 1974 PA 242*, 1975).

## SECTION 3

**State board of education; duties.** Leadership and general supervision over all public education, including adult education and instructional programs in state institutions, except as to institutions of higher education granting baccalaureate degrees, is vested in a state board of education. It shall serve as the general planning and coordinating body for all public education, including higher education, and shall advise the legislature as to the financial requirements in connection therewith.

**Superintendent of public instruction; appointment, powers, duties.** The state board of education shall appoint a superintendent of public instruction whose term of office shall be determined by the board. He shall be the chairman of the board without the right to vote, and shall be responsible for the execution of its policies. He shall be the principal executive officer of a state department of education which shall have powers and duties provided by law.

**State board of education; members, nomination, election term.** The state board of education shall consist of eight members who shall be nominated by party conventions and elected at large for terms of eight years as prescribed by law. The governor shall fill any vacancy by appointment for the unexpired term. The governor shall be ex-officio a member of the state board of education without the right to vote.

**Boards of institutions of higher education, limitation.** The power of the boards of institutions of higher education provided in this constitution to supervise their respective institutions and control and direct the expenditure of the institutions' funds shall not be limited by this section.

Section 3 describes the leadership of the state's system of public education. Michigan's first constitution created the office of superintendent of public instruction. The superintendent was appointed by the governor with the advice and consent of both houses of the legislature. The superintendent held office for two years, and the legislature was directed to prescribe the duties of the office. The 1850 Constitution provided for direct election of the superintendent for a two-year term, and the 1908 Constitution retained this method of selection. The framers of the 1963 Constitution developed a new approach to the supervision of public education. The *Address to the People* indicates that this section is designed to embody two fundamental principles: the concern of all people in educational processes as a safeguard of democracy and the need for greater public participation in the operation of educational institutions. The provisions of section 3 also create a mechanism whereby information from all levels of public education can be coordinated by a state board.

Section 3 creates an eight-member state board of education to supervise all public instruction except institutions of higher education granting baccalaureate degrees. The *Address to the People* noted that as of 1962, Michigan was one of only three states that did not have a state board of education. The board is responsible for general planning and coordination of public education. Candidates for the state board are nominated by the political parties at their conventions and are elected at statewide elections as provided by the legislature. The elements of section 3, providing for the nomination and election of state board of education members, have been declared unconstitutional by a panel of the Sixth Circuit of the United States Court of Appeals (*Goldman-Frankie v. Austin*, 1984). The federal appellate court reasoned that requirement of nomination at a party convention was unconstitutional under the equal protection clause of the federal Constitution because it unfairly disadvantaged independent candidates.

A board member serves an eight-year term. Section 9 of the constitution's Schedule and Temporary Provisions created a system of staggered terms for the state board so that only two seats at a time are up for election. Vacancies in the board are filled by the governor. The governor is also an ex-officio member of the state board but does not possess a vote. The state board of education appoints the superintendent of public instruction, who serves as chairperson (without vote) of the board of education and is charged with executing its policies. The superintendent is also the principal executive officer of the state department of education.

The final paragraph of section 3 discusses the relationship between its provisions and the powers of governing boards of state institutions of higher education. Section 3 does not serve to limit the power of the governing boards to supervise and control their respective institutions. Sections 4 and 5 of this article cover governing boards of Michigan colleges and universities.

Section 3 grants the state board of education leadership and general supervision over all public education in Michigan (*Grand Rapids School Employees Benefit Association v. Board of Education of the City of Grand Rapids*, 1980).[11] This constitutional provision does not give the state board of education supervisory power over private educational institutions (*Attorney General Opinion No. 5296*, 1978). However, the word "leadership" in the first paragraph of section 3 does not mean or imply the power to control or dominate other boards and institutions, such as the governing boards of Michigan's public universities (*Regents of the University of Michigan v. State*, 1974).

While section 3 grants general supervisory power over public education to the state board of education, the state may delegate its authority to local school boards. However, these school boards possess only those powers that have been expressly granted, or implied to be necessary, by the state (*Snyder v. Charlotte Public Schools*, 1985). Removal of members of boards of education of local school districts is not governed by section 3, but instead under Article VII, section 33 (*Attorney General Opinion No. 5395*, 1978).

Under section 3, the state board of education is an advisory body to Michigan public universities. Michigan courts are mindful of the special status of public colleges and universities granted by sections 4 and 5 of this article. The state legislature may require universities to inform the state board of education of proposed programs and their costs so that the board can fulfill its duty to advise state government. However, the board cannot exercise veto power over any of the programs proposed by the universities. The board may choose to make an unfavorable recommendation of a university's program to the legislature, but the board cannot prevent the university from going directly to the legislature with its proposals and requests (*Regents of the University of Michigan v. State*, 1973).

---

[11] The State Board of Education is also addressed by state statutes. See M.C.L.A. Sec. 388.1001 et seq.

## SECTION 4

**Higher education institutions; appropriations, accounting, public sessions of boards.** The legislature shall appropriate moneys to maintain the University of Michigan, Michigan State University, Wayne State University, Eastern Michigan University, Michigan College of Science and Technology, Central Michigan University, Northern Michigan University, Western Michigan University, Ferris Institute, Grand Valley State College, and by whatever names such institutions may hereafter be known, and other institutions of higher education established by law. The legislature shall be given an annual accounting of all income and expenditures by each of these educational institutions. Formal sessions of governing boards of such institutions shall be open to the public.

Section 4 must be read with sections 2 and 5 of this article. Section 4 represents a revision of Article XI, section 10 of the Constitution of 1908. The 1908 Constitution required the legislature to maintain the state university, college of mines, agricultural college, state normal college, and other state educational institutions that might be established by law. Now the legislature maintains the named institutions and other institutions of higher education established by law. These institutions of higher education must provide the legislature with an annual accounting of income and expenditures. The *Address to the People* notes that such annual accounting had been a practice by the institutions. The constitution also requires that the formal sessions of the governing boards of the institutions be open to the public.

Since the legislature by constitutional command appropriates funds for the maintenance of state colleges and universities, all state colleges and universities are regarded as state agencies (*Regents of the University of Michigan v. Employment Relations Commission*, 1973) located within the executive branch of state government (*Regents of the University of Michigan v. Brooks*, 1923). In *Booth Newspapers, Inc. v. Board of Regents of the University of Michigan* (1993), the Michigan Supreme Court held that the Michigan Open Meetings Act applied to searches for state university presidents because Michigan's public colleges and universities are state agencies. Moreover, state colleges and universities are public employers of even nonacademic personnel. Therefore, state colleges and universities are subject to Article IV, section 48 of this constitution, which authorizes the legislature to enact laws to govern the resolution of disputes concerning public employees (*University of Michigan v. Labor Mediation Board*, 1969).

Under section 4, the Michigan state legislature has occasionally made conditional appropriations to public colleges and universities. Conditional appropriations are grants of funds with provisions that the money be used for specific purposes. The University of Michigan, Michigan State, and Wayne State have argued that such conditional appropriations interfere with the grant of autonomy in section 5 of this article. The Michigan Supreme Court has held that while the legislature cannot interfere with the management and control of these institutions, the legislature within those limitations may appropriate funds for a specific purpose. If the university accepts those funds, the university must use those funds for that purpose (*Regents of the University of Michigan v. Labor Mediation Board*, 1975).

## SECTION 5

**University of Michigan, Michigan State University, Wayne State University; controlling boards.** The regents of the University of Michigan and their successors in office shall constitute a body corporate known as the Regents of the University of Michigan; the trustees of Michigan State University and their successors in office shall constitute a body corporate known as the Board of Trustees of Michigan State University; the governors of Wayne State University and their successors in office shall constitute a body corporate known as the Board of Governors of Wayne State University. Each board shall have general supervision of its institution and the control and direction of all expenditures from the institution's funds. Each board shall, as often as necessary, elect a president of the institution under its supervision. He shall be the principal executive officer of the institution, be ex-officio a member of the board without the right to vote and preside at meetings of the board. The board of each institution shall consist of eight members who shall hold office for terms of eight years and who shall be elected as provided by law. The governor shall fill board vacancies by appointment. Each appointee shall hold office until a successor has been nominated and elected as provided by law.

The Constitution of 1850 inaugurated the election of regents to govern the University of Michigan. These eight regents were chosen at a statewide election, and they served eight-year, staggered terms. The regents were given the responsibilities of selecting the president of the university, providing general supervision of the university, and controlling all expenditures from the university interest fund. The Constitution of 1908 maintained this system of regents for the University of Michigan and granted constitutional status to the board of trustees of Michigan State University. The Michigan State board of trustees differed slightly from the University of Michigan's board of regents. There were only six trustees, and they served six-year, staggered terms. Wayne State University achieved constitutional status via an amendment to the constitution in 1959. Wayne State University was supervised by a six-person board of governors. Like the board of Michigan State, the governors served six-year, staggered terms.

Section 5 is a revision of the Constitution of 1908 as amended. All governing boards of the three constitutional universities consist of eight members, elected at statewide elections, who serve staggered eight-year terms. Each board has the same responsibilities. The boards select the university president, supervise the university, and control expenditures of funds.

Section 5 is designed to place entire control and management of the universities' property and affairs in the hands of the governing board and provide for autonomy in the educational sphere (*Regents of the University of Michigan v. Employment Relations Commission*, 1973). The framers of section 5 and its predecessors sought to remove the universities from political influence. Therefore, the universities are governed by boards accountable directly to the people of Michigan. The members of these governing boards serve long terms of office in order to insulate them from political pressures and afford them the opportunity to investigate the needs of the university, to deliberate carefully, and to look after its interests (*Regents of the University of Michigan v. State of Michigan*, 1988).

The constitutional autonomy granted the three named universities in section 5 concerns primarily educational and financial matters. This autonomy does not exempt these institutions from the reach of state law or allow them to thwart the public policy of the state (*Regents of the University of Michigan v. Employment Relations Commission*, 1973). Therefore, state statutes such as the Open Meetings Act (*Booth Newspapers, Inc. v. Board of Regents of the University of Michigan*, 1993), the Public Employees Relations Act (*Regents of the University of Michigan v. Employment Relations Commission*, 1973), workers compensation (*Peters v. Michigan State College*, 1948), and waivers of governmental immunity (*Branum v. University of Michigan Regents*, 1966) all govern these section 5 universities.

## SECTION 6

**Other institutions of higher education, controlling boards.** Other institutions of higher education established by law having authority to grant baccalaureate degrees shall be governed by a board of control which shall be a body corporate. The board shall have general supervision of the institution and control and direction of all expenditures from the institution's funds. It shall, as often as necessary, elect a president of the institution under its supervision. He shall be the principal executive officer of the institution and be ex-officio a member of the board without the right to vote. The board may elect one of its members or may designate the president, to preside at board meetings. Each board of control shall consist of eight members who shall hold office for terms of eight years, not more than two of which shall expire in the same year, and who shall be appointed by the governor by and with the advice and consent of the senate. Vacancies shall be filled in like manner.

Section 6 is new to the state constitution, and it governs all the state baccalaureate-granting colleges and universities not covered under section 5. Each of these colleges and universities is governed by a board of control, appointed by the governor by and with the advice and consent of the senate. The board appoints the college or university president who sits on the board of control without vote. Board members serve eight-year terms of office with terms of office staggered, such that only two seats are open for gubernatorial appointment every two years.

Boards of control of these colleges and universities are constitutional corporations (*Board of Control of Eastern Michigan University v. Labor Mediation Board,* 1971) located within the executive branch of government (*Attorney General Opinion No. 6130,* 1983). The governing boards of section 6 colleges and universities possess the same constitutional powers and rights regarding the general supervision of their institutions and expenditure of funds as the universities covered by section 5 of this article (*Marquette County v. Board of Control of Northern Michigan University,* 1981; *Board of Control of Eastern Michigan University v. Labor Mediation Board,* 1971). The state cannot control the actions of these governing boards, and the state cannot add to or take away from the property of the college or university without the consent of the governing board (*Attorney General Opinion No. 5494,* 1979).

Since boards of control of these colleges and universities are located within the executive branch of government, board members are executive officers. Therefore, a probate judge cannot serve as a member of a board of control without offending principles of separation of powers in government (*Attorney General Opinion No. 6130,* 1983).[12]

## SECTION 7

**Community and junior colleges; state board, members, terms, vacancies.** The legislature shall provide by law for the establishment and financial support of public community and junior colleges which shall be supervised and controlled by locally elected boards. The legislature shall provide by law for a state board for public community and junior colleges which shall advise the state board of education concerning general supervision and planning for such colleges and requests for annual appropriations for their support. The board shall consist of eight members who shall hold office for terms of eight years, not more than two of which shall expire in the same year, and who shall be appointed by the state board of education. Vacancies shall be filled in like manner. The superintendent of public instruction shall be ex-officio a member of this board without the right to vote.

This new section of the constitution requires the legislature to create and support community and junior colleges. The legislature fulfilled this constitutional responsibility in the Community College Act of 1966 (M.C.L.A. Sections

[12] Separation of powers is covered in Article III, section 2.

380.1601 et seq.). Community colleges are supervised and controlled by locally elected boards. The legislature also is empowered to create a state level board on community and junior colleges, whose purpose is to advise the state board of education on supervision, appropriations, and planning. This state board consists of eight members who are appointed by the state board of education. The state board members serve eight-year terms. The terms of office are staggered, such that there are only two vacancies on the board every two years.

Since section 7 grants the board of a community college the power to supervise and control a community college, the board has the power to set tuition rates at the college in an amount higher than that contained in a schedule prescribed by the legislature (*Kowalski v. Board of Trustees of Macomb County Community College*, 1976).

Section 7 vests control and supervision of community colleges in locally elected boards. Therefore, the boards cannot delegate this power to a community college president or any other administrator (*Attorney General Opinion No. 5843*, 1981).

## SECTION 8

**Services for handicapped persons.** Institutions, programs and services for the care, treatment, education or rehabilitation of those inhabitants who are physically, mentally or otherwise seriously handicapped shall always be fostered and supported.

The Constitutions of 1850 and 1908 contained provisions that read: "Institutions for the benefit of those inhabitants who are deaf, dumb, blind or insane shall always by fostered and supported." The Constitution of 1963 recognizes changes in the fields of physical and mental rehabilitation and no longer limits state support to those confined in institutions. As the Michigan Supreme Court noted in *City of Livonia v. Department of Social Services* (1985), the revisions to the Constitution of 1908 recognize that the old language was not only too restrictive in scope but also outmoded by recent developments in the fields of physical and mental rehabilitation. The Michigan legislature has implemented the provisions of section 8 in a series of statutes, the most important of which are the Michigan Handicappers' Civil Rights Act (M.C.L.A. Section 37.1101 et seq.) and the Mental Health Code (M.C.L.A. Section 330.1708 et seq.).

Since the constitution requires the state to foster and support various programs and services for the handicapped, courts usually find the operation of state mental health facilities and similar services fall within the state's immunity for the purposes of government tort liability (*Perry v. Kalamazoo State Hospital*, 1978).

## SECTION 9

**Public libraries, fines.** The legislature shall provide by law for the establishment and support of public libraries which shall be available to all residents of the state under regulations adopted by the governing bodies thereof. All fines assessed and collected in the several counties, townships and cities for any breach of the penal laws shall be exclusively applied to the support of such public libraries, and county law libraries as provided by law.

Michigan began a system of public libraries in each township in 1835. These early libraries were funded by fees paid by persons to avoid military service and by fines assessed in counties for the breach of criminal laws. The Constitutions of 1850 and 1908 continued the system of funding via fines. Section 9 revises the language of 1908. New language allows local library boards to develop rules and procedures for the use of the library.[13]

A panel of the Michigan Court of Appeals declared unconstitutional a state statute that levied an additional "cost" of 10 percent for violation of designated penal laws and earmarked the revenue generated for a law enforcement officers training fund. The court reasoned that the "cost" was in reality a supplemental fine, and section 9 requires all such fines to be applied exclusively to the public libraries (*People v. Barber*, 1968).

Since the state constitution requires the state to establish and maintain public libraries, courts treat libraries as quasi-municipal corporations. A quasi-municipal corporation is a government agency authorized by constitution or statute to operate for and about the business of the state. Because of this status, libraries can sue and be sued (*Jackson District Library v. Jackson County*, 1985).

All residents of Michigan have the right to use public library facilities. This right includes the right to enter the library and read books there and borrow books subject to reasonable regulations (*Attorney General Opinion No. 5739*, 1980). Reasonable regulations may include borrowing fees for state residents not residing within the geographic boundaries of the local library unit. In order for the borrowing fees to be considered reasonable, the fees must be proportionate to the costs, direct and indirect, of issuing a library card, facilitating the return of loaned books, and the attendant costs of administration (*Attorney General Opinion No. 6188*, 1983).

[13] State statutes also govern public libraries. See M.C.L.A. Section 397.11 et seq.

# Article IX

## *Finance and Taxation*

### SECTION 1

**Taxes for state expenses.** The legislature shall impose taxes sufficient with other resources to pay the expenses of state government.

Section 1 requires the state government to generate enough money through taxes (when combined with other resources of the state) to pay for state government. This section finds its origins in Article XIV, section 1 of the Constitution of 1850. The 1963 version is a simply a revision of the 1908 language.

A tax is an enforced proportioned burden, charge, or contribution from persons and property, levied by the state, by virtue of its sovereignty, for the support of government in discharge of its various functions and duties for all public needs (*Cooper, Wells & Company v. St. Joseph*, 1925). Taxes are also described as extractions or involuntary contributions of money, the collection of which is sanctioned by law and enforceable by the courts. Government assessments and fees share these characteristics of taxes. However, there is a critical difference between taxes and assessments or fees. Revenues from taxes, unlike revenues from assessments and fees, must be put to a primarily public purpose for the benefit of all. Assessments and fees primarily benefit individuals or groups, although a side effect of an assessment or fee may contribute to the public welfare (*Dukesherer Farms, Inc. v. Director of the Department of Agriculture*, 1979).

The power to tax has been described as the strongest and most pervading of all government powers. In Michigan, the power to tax is limited only by the federal and state constitutions (*Attorney General Opinion No. 6331*, 1986). However, the state may impose a tax only if it is expressly authorized by law. Courts will not infer the authority to tax (*In re Dodge Brothers*, 1928). The sources of tax revenue and the apportionment of taxes require legislative action (*Request for Advisory Opinion on Constitutionality of 1986 PA 281*, 1988).

The power to tax is vested exclusively in the legislature pursuant to section 1. Legislature, in developing a system of taxation, is not restricted to imposing those taxes enumerated in the constitution. (*Bailey v. Muskegon County Board of Commissioners*, 1983).

## SECTION 2

**Power of taxation, relinquishment.** The power of taxation shall never be surrendered, suspended or contracted away.

This section guarantees that the state will always possess the power to tax. The basic language of section 2 first made its appearance in Article X, section 3 of the Constitution of 1908. This section underscores the fact that the power to tax is an inherent power of the state and that that power may only be exercised for public purposes.

Section 2 is inapplicable to assessments and fees because assessments are not taxes.[14] The legislature, therefore, may delegate the power to set assessments and fees to other government bodies (*Dukesherer Farms, Inc. v. Director of the Department of Agriculture*, 1979).

Section 2 must be read in light of Article IV, section 48, which permits the legislature to provide for the resolution of disputes concerning public employees. Article IV, section 48 gives the legislature the power to provide for compulsory arbitration of police and fire department labor disputes. Orders of arbitration panels may include increases in employee compensation and benefits. These increases may, in turn, require that a city raise more revenue and increase taxes. However, Michigan courts do not see the system of compulsory arbitration as an unconstitutional surrender of the power to tax to an arbitration panel (*Dearborn Fire Fighters Union Local No. 412, I.A.F.F. v. City of Dearborn*, 1975).

## SECTION 3

**Property taxation; uniformity; assessments; limitations; classes; approval of legislature.** The legislature shall provide for the uniform general ad valorem taxation

[14] See Section 1 of this Article.

of real and tangible personal property not exempt by law except for taxes levied for school operating purposes. The legislature shall provide for the determination of true cash value of such property; the proportion of true cash value at which such property shall be uniformly assessed, which shall not, after January 1, 1966, exceed 50 percent; and for a system of equalization of assessments. For taxes levied in 1995 and each year thereafter, the legislature shall provide that the taxable value of each parcel of property adjusted for additions and losses, shall not increase each year by more than the increase in the immediate preceding year in the general price level, as defined in section 33 of this article, or 5 percent, whichever is less until the ownership of the parcel of property is transferred. When ownership of the property is transferred as defined by law, the parcel shall be assessed at the applicable proportion of current true cash value. The legislature may provide for alternative means of taxation of designated real and tangible personal property in lieu of general ad valorem taxation. Every tax other than the general ad valorem property tax shall be uniform upon the class or classes on which it operates. A law that increases the statutory limits in effect as of February 1, 1994 on the maximum amount of ad valorem property taxes that may be levied for school district operating purposes requires the approval of 3/4 of the members elected to and serving in the Senate and in the House of Representatives. Amendment approved March 15, 1994. Effective April 30, 1995.

Section 3 sets up a system of personal property taxes. The legislature is required to provide for uniform ad valorem taxes of real and tangible property not exempted by law from such taxation. An exception is made for property taxes levied for schools. An ad valorem tax is a tax based on the value of the item being taxed. Real property here refers to land and things fixed to the land, such as dwellings. Other tangible personal property can include such things as automobiles or the inventory of a business. Since an ad valorem tax depends on the value of the item being taxed, the legislature is required to provide for a mechanism to determine the true cash value of the item and for a system of equalization of assessments. Property taxes must be uniformly assessed. Property taxes are calculated on a basis of no higher than 50 percent of the true cash value. Section 3 also allows the legislature to provide for alternative means (i.e., other than ad valorem taxation) of taxing real and tangible personal property. Taxes other than ad valorem taxes must be uniform. Section 3 also gives the legislature the freedom to exempt property from taxation.

Section 3 underwent major revision in 1994 as part of a major effort to reform the system of school finance in Michigan.[15] Local property taxes are at the heart of funding for the public schools. This system leads to great disparities from school district to school district in the amount of per-pupil spending. At the same time, there is a general feeling that Michigan property taxes are too high. One part of the 1994 amendment to section 3 caps how fast property

---

[15] See also sections 5, 8, 10, and 11 of this Article.

assessments can grow. An assessment cannot increase from year to year by more than 5 percent or by the percentage increase in the consumer price index, whichever is less. The other part of the amendment requires a supermajority vote of both houses of the state legislature in order to increase the statutory limits in effect on February 1, 1994, on the amount of property taxes that may be levied for school operating purposes.

Michigan constitutions have provided for ad valorem taxation of personal and corporate property since 1850. Article XIV, sections 10 through 13 of the Constitution of 1850 provided for a uniform system of ad valorem property taxes based upon true cash value. The 1908 Constitution continued these general themes.

According to the *Address to the People,* the important constitutional objective in section 3 is uniformity of assessment. As indicated in the *Address,* section 3 has a number of features that contribute to the uniformity of assessment. All property is assessed at 50 percent of cash value, regardless of the jurisdiction levying the tax. Since the legislature by statute must fix the standard of value, the legislature can amend the statute to reflect changes in price structures. This system is designed to help eliminate inequities that have resulted from the inability of assessors to keep up with changes in the dollar value of real property.

The *Address to the People* explains that the provision for alternative means of taxing property is necessary to maintain such taxes as the automobile weight tax or the severance tax on oil and gas.

Section 3 and the General Property Tax Act (M.C.L.A. 211.27[1]) define true cash value. True cash value of property is essentially the price that could be obtained for the property at a private sale between a willing seller and a willing buyer (*Washtenaw County v. State Tax Commission,* 1985). True cash value is also synonymous with fair market value (*C.A.F. Investment Co. v. State Tax Commission,* 1974). The General Property Tax Act sets out in broad terms the factors to be considered in determining the true cash value of real property. These factors include location, zoning, existing uses, quality of soil, and present economic income of structures. The General Property Tax Act does not specify the assessment process to be used in determining true cash value. In the absence of a required assessment process, Michigan courts have approved or disapproved specific valuation methods for determining true cash value (*Meadowlanes Limited Dividend Housing Association v. City of Holland,* 1991; *Antisdale v. City of Galesburg,* 1984).

Michigan courts accept three traditional methods of determining true cash value: (1) the cost-less-depreciation approach; (2) the sales-comparison approach; and (3) the capitalization-of-income approach. Under the cost approach, true cash value is derived by adding the estimated land value to an estimate of the current cost of reproducing or replacing improvements and then deducting the loss in value from the depreciation of the structure. The sales-comparison approach indicates true cash value by analyzing recent sales of similar properties, comparing them with the subject property, and adjusting the sales price of the comparable properties to reflect the differences in the two properties. The income-capitalization approach measures the present value of the future benefits of property ownership by estimating the property's income stream and resale value, and then developing a capitalization rate that is used to convert the estimated future benefits into a present lump-sum value (*Meadowlanes Limited Dividend Housing Association v. City of Holland*, 1991). For the purposes of assessing taxes under section 3, the assessment must be based on the value of the real property alone and cannot include considerations, such as creative financing, that may increase the price of the property (*Washtenaw County v. State Tax Commission*, 1985).

The process of equalization required by section 3 is also specified in the General Property Tax Act. Under that process, local assessors assess property at 50 percent of its true cash value. County boards of commissioners perform countywide equalization. These commissioners examine assessment rolls and ascertain whether the real and personal property in the various cities and townships has been equally and uniformly assessed at 50 percent of true cash value. The state tax commission then meets to equalize the aggregate assessed value of each class of property in each of Michigan's 83 counties (*Town & Country Dodge, Inc. v. Michigan Department of Treasury*, 1985).

The uniformity requirement of section 3 and its predecessor in the 1908 Constitution require that taxation be done by one and the same unvarying standard. Uniformity of taxation requires not only uniformity in the rate of taxation but also uniformity in the mode of assessment. Uniformity of taxation implies equality of the tax burden. The uniformity must be coextensive with the territory to which it applies. A state tax must be uniform across the state; a county, town, or city tax must be uniform throughout the extent of the territory to which it applies (*Huron-Clinton Metropolitan Authority v. Boards of Supervisors of Five Counties*, 1943).

For Michigan courts, the requirements of the equal protection clause and the uniformity of taxation clause of section 3 are identical.[16] The controlling principle for each clause is one of equal treatment for similarly situated taxpayers. Neither the equal protection clause or the uniformity of taxation clause removes from the legislature the power to make classifications. However, the classification of objects for taxation purposes must be based upon natural distinguishing characteristics and must have a reasonable relationship to the objective of the tax (*Armco Steel Corporation v. State of Michigan*, 1984). The Michigan Supreme Court has struck down a state statute providing for variable millage rates within school districts (M.C.L.A. 211.252) as violative of the uniformity of taxation requirement of section 3 (*The School District of the City of East Grand Rapids,*

[16] See Article 1, section 2, particularly the section on rational basis analysis.

*Kent County v. Kent County Tax Allocation Board,* 1982). In so doing, the supreme court overruled an earlier decision sustaining variable millage rates (*Thoman v. Lansing,* 1946).

## SECTION 4

**Exemption of religious or educational nonprofit organizations.** Property owned and occupied by nonprofit religious or educational organizations and used exclusively for religious or educational purposes, as defined by law, shall be exempt from real and personal property taxes.

Section 4 exempts nonprofit religious and education organizations from real and personal property taxes. As the *Address to the People* noted, until the 1963 Constitution, such exemptions were granted only by state statute. Placing the exemptions in the constitutions makes it more difficult to alter the law to allow for taxation of these organizations. As the attorney general noted, unless an exemption is rooted in the constitution, the legislature may limit or withdraw the exemption (*Attorney General Opinion No. 6697,* 1991).

The General Property Tax Act (M.C.L.A. 211.7) implements section 4 by spelling out the tax exemptions. Since exemptions from taxation effect the unequal removal of the burden generally placed on all landowners to share in support of the government, any exemption must be narrowly construed in favor of the taxing unit (*Michigan Baptist Homes & Development Company v. City of Ann Arbor,* 1976).

Michigan courts read section 4 as reinforcing rather than changing or modifying statutory tax exemptions for the specified nonprofit corporations (*St. Paul Lutheran Church v. City of Riverview,* 1987). Language from the debates at the constitutional convention indicates that the sponsors of section 4 did not intend it to take away power from the legislature to define exemptions or prevent abuses. Rather, the intent of the framers was to validate existing statutory law (*American Youth Foundation v. Township of Benona,* 1967).

## SECTION 5

**Assessment of property of public service businesses.** The legislature shall provide for the assessment by the state of the property of those public service businesses assessed by the state at the date this constitution becomes effective, and of other property as designated by the legislature, and for the imposition and collection of taxes thereon. Property assessed by the state shall be assessed at the same proportion of its true cash value as the legislature shall specify for property subject to general ad valorem taxation. The rate of taxation on such property shall be the average general rate levied upon other commercial, industrial, and utility property in this state under the general ad valorem tax law, or, if the legislature provides, the rate of tax applicable to the property of each business enterprise assessed by the state shall be the average rate of ad valorem taxation levied upon other commercial, industrial, and utility property in all counties in which any of such property is situated. Amendment approved March 15, 1994. Effective April 30, 1994.

The Constitution of 1850 in Article XIV, section 10 allowed for state taxation of corporations and corporate property. The 1908 Constitution continued to allow for the taxation of corporations and corporate property. This constitution specified the kinds of businesses subject to taxation, including telephone and telegraph companies and railroads. Section 5 is new to the constitution, and it directs the legislature to provide for the state assessment and collection of property taxes of the property of certain utilities. The 1994 amendment to section 5 added the adjectives "commercial, industrial, and utility" to the noun property.[17]

Commercial, industrial, and utility properties are assessed on the basis of true cash value and at the same rate as levied on property subject to the general ad valorem tax described in section 3 of this article. Under section 5, there are two possible rates of taxation for business property. One possibility bases the tax rate on a statewide average. The legislature can set the rate of taxation at the average rate levied on other property in the state under the general ad valorem property tax law. The other possibility bases the tax rate on county-by-county averages. The legislature can set the rate of taxation as the average rate levied upon other property in the counties in which the business property is located. Michigan public utility taxes are covered in M.C.L.A. 207.1 et seq. Railroad taxes are covered under M.C.L.A. 201.7 et seq. and M.C.L.A. 465.1.

As noted above, Michigan statutes implement the provisions of section 5. In this statute, the legislature has defined "true cash value." Michigan courts recognize five possible methods of determining the true cash value of business properties covered by section 5: The first method is based on the current selling price of the property or similar properties at private sale. The second method is the adjusted reproduction cost method, and the third method is capitalization of income. The fourth method bases the value of the property on depreciated net cost or "book value." The fifth method involves a comparison of the depreciated cost of reconstructing a similar facility. Which method is most appropriate in an individual case is based on the facts of a particular case and a judgment on what would produce a fair result (*Consumers Power Company v. Big Prairie Township, 1978*).

---

[17] The modifications to section 5 were part of a package of amendments that formed the basis for school finance reform. See also sections 3, 8, 10, and 11 of this Article.

## SECTION 6

**Real and tangible personal property; limitation on general ad valorem taxes; adoption and alteration of separate tax limitations; exceptions to limitations; property tax on school district extending into two or more counties.** Except as otherwise provided in this constitution, the total amount of general ad valorem taxes imposed upon real and tangible personal property for all purposes in any one year shall not exceed 15 mills on each dollar of the assessed valuation of property as finally equalized. Under procedures provided by law, which shall guarantee the right of initiative, separate tax limitation for any county and for the townships and for school districts therein, the aggregate of which shall not exceed 18 mills on each dollar of such valuation, may be adopted and thereafter altered by a vote of a majority of the qualified electors of such county voting thereon, in lieu of the limitation hereinbefore established. These limitations may be increased to an aggregate of not to exceed 50 mills on each dollar of valuation, for a period not to exceed 20 years at any one time, if approved by a majority of the electors, qualified under Section 6 of Article II of this constitution, voting on the question.

The foregoing limitation shall not apply to taxes imposed for the payment of principal and interest on bonds approved by the electors or other evidence of indebtedness approved by the electors or for the payment of assessments or contract obligations in anticipation of which bonds are issued approved by the electors, which taxes may be imposed without limitation as to rate or amount; or, subject to the provisions of sections 25 through 34 of this article, to taxes imposed for any other purposes by any city, village, charter county, charter township, charter authority or other authority, the tax limitations of which are provided by charter or general law.

In any school district which extends into two or more counties, property taxes at the highest rate available in the county which contains the greatest part of the area of the district may be imposed and collected for school purposes throughout the district. Amendment ratified Nov. 7, 1978. Effective Dec. 23, 1978.

Section 6 places limitations on property taxes. Ad valorem taxes of real and tangible personal property are limited to fifteen mills of each dollar of assessed property. There are two exceptions to the fifteen-mill limit. First, under procedures provided by law, which guarantee the right of initiative, voters may choose to aggregate county, township, and school district property taxes. The aggregated tax rate cannot exceed eighteen mils of each dollar, and voters may choose to alter this aggregated rate. Second, voters may choose to raise the property tax limitation up to 50 mills for a period no longer than twenty years at any one time.

The second paragraph of section 6 is known as the "nonapplication provision." This paragraph means the tax rate limitations contained in the section are not applicable to taxes imposed for the payment of principle and interest on voter-approved bonds or for the payment of assessments or contract obligations in anticipation of which bonds are issued. This provision helps guarantee that bond issues of units of local government will have unlimited tax support (*Address to the People*). The limitations also do not apply to taxes imposed for any other purpose by any of the listed units of government where the tax limits are provided by charter or general law. However, the provisions of sections 25 through 34 of Article IX govern this other form of taxation.

The third paragraph of section 6 addresses the situation of school districts that extend into two or more counties and taxes for school purposes. In the case of such a school district, property taxes throughout the district may be set at the highest rate available in the county that contains the largest area of the district. As the *Address to the People* pointed out, this paragraph is intended to answer a problem involving over 60 counties in Michigan.

Section 6 was amended by initiative petition in 1978. This amendment added the words "approved by the electors" to three places in the second paragraph. The amendment also inserted the phrase "subject to the provisions of section 25 through 34 of this article."

Courts use two basic rules to guide the interpretation of section 6: The first rule is that legislation is "clothed" with the presumption of constitutionality and must be sustained if it is within constitutional limits. The second rule is that courts will not declare a statute unconstitutional unless it is plain that it violated some provisions of the constitution and the constitutionality of the act will be supported by all possible presumptions not clearly inconsistent with the language and the subject. Courts are reluctant to second-guess policy determinations made by the legislature. These rules clearly place the burden of proof on the challenger to show that an act of the legislature offends the limitations in section 6 (*Request for Advisory Opinion on Constitutionality of 1986 PA 281*, 1988).

Section 6 places limitations on tax rates but does not govern the allocations of revenues once the fifteen mills or voter-approved additional millage has been imposed. Therefore, a state statute providing for a system of tax increment financing of a development project is constitutional under section 6 (*Request for Advisory Opinion on Constitutionality of 1986 PA 281*, 1988).

Section 6 must be read together with section 16 of this article, which provides for state loans to school districts. Millages levied to pay back section 16 loans do not have to comply with the fifteen mill limit (*Advisory Opinion on Constitutionality re 1973 PA 1 and 2*, 1973).

## SECTION 7

**Income tax.** No income tax graduated as to rate or base shall be imposed by the state or any of its subdivisions.

Section 7 was added to the constitution in 1963. Section 7 makes it clear that no unit of the state government can impose a graduated income tax like the federal income tax. This requirement means that any income tax imposed in

Michigan must be a flat rate tax. The framers of this section were careful to include both the words "rate" and "base." As the *Address to the People* pointed out, the inclusion of the word "base" makes sure that any state income tax could not be calculated on a graduated base, such as federal tax liability. Such impermissible "piggybacking" of the state tax on the basis of federal tax liability would, in effect, give the state tax all the graduations of the federal tax. However, a flat state income tax may be imposed on the basis of income computed for federal tax purposes. The framers of section 7 acknowledged in the *Address to the People* that the legislature could prescribe reasonable exemptions to the flat tax rate.

The Michigan Supreme Court has ruled that the "undoubted" intention behind section 7 is to deny the state the power to enact a graduated federal-type income tax scheme under which tax rates increase as taxable income increases (*Butcher v. Department of Treasury*, 1986). Section 7, however, does not preclude certain types of tax rebates that are income-dependent. An income-graduated property tax credit that employs the income tax to grant the property tax credit does not offend section 7's prohibition against a graduated income tax. The Michigan Supreme Court reasoned that this tax credit is a property tax rebate and not an income tax (*Butcher v. Department of Treasury*, 1986; *Rosenbaum v. Department of Treasury*, 1977). A similar tax credit system to rebate money to taxpayers who pay city income taxes is also permissible (*Kuhn v. Department of Treasury*, 1968). Section 7 also allows the state to classify different kinds of taxpayers into different categories and impose different tax rates on the various categories. Therefore, an income tax that taxes individuals, corporations, and financial institutions at different rates is constitutional (*Kuhn v. Department of Treasury*, 1971).

## SECTION 8

**Sales and use taxes.** Except as provided in this section, the legislature shall not impose a sales tax on retailers at a rate of more than 4% of their gross taxable sales of tangible personal property.

Beginning May 1, 1994, the general sales tax shall be imposed on retailers at an additional rate of 2% of their gross taxable sales of tangible personal property not exempt by law and the use tax at the additional rate of 2%. The proceeds of the sales and use taxes imposed at the additional rate of 2% shall be deposited in the state school aid fund established in section 11 of this article. The allocation of sales tax revenue required or authorized by sections 9 and 10 of this article does not apply to the revenue from the sales tax imposed at the additional 2%.

No sales tax or use tax shall be charged or collected from and after January 1, 1975 on the sale or use of prescription drugs for human use, or on the sale or use of food for human consumption except in the case of prepared food intended for immediate consumption as defined by law. This provision shall not apply to alcoholic beverages.

To compensate units of government other than the state for the loss of revenue resulting from the repeal of the sales tax on food and prescription drugs, each present allocation of sales tax revenue to such units shall be increased by 1/5. Amendment ratified March 15, 1994. Effective April 30, 1994.

Section 8 places a constitutional limitation on sales taxes. Section 8 was amended by the addition of the second paragraph in 1994 as part of the package of constitutional amendments designed to reform the system of public school financing.[18] This second paragraph raises the sales tax by 2 percent and dedicates the revenue raised by this increase to the school aid fund. This dedicated sales tax revenue is designed to help offset the decrease in funds available to schools from the limitations on property taxes created by the 1994 amendments to section 3 of this article.

A sales tax is a tax imposed for the privilege of making sales at retail. Therefore, the legal direct incident of a sales tax falls on the retailer: it is the retailer who pays the tax, not the customer. A sales tax is appropriately recognized as a cost of doing business, just as the price of labor, materials, or overhead are costs of doing business. Therefore, a retailer may reimburse him or herself for the cost of the sales tax by adding the sales tax to the sale price of goods or services (*Sims v. Firestone Tire and Rubber Company*, 1976).

A use tax is a tax levied on tangible personal property purchased outside the state for use, storage, or consumption in Michigan. The purpose of a use tax is to counteract the trend of consumers purchasing tangible property outside Michigan to avoid payment of the Michigan sales tax (*Bailey v. Muskegon County Board of Commissioners*, 1983).

A panel of the Michigan court of appeals has ruled that section 8 unambiguously exempts prescription drugs from both sales and use taxes. Therefore, neither a sales tax or a use tax may be imposed, for example, on a Delaware company's distribution of samples of prescription drugs to licensed physicians in Michigan (*Syntex Laboratories, Inc. v. Michigan Department of Treasury*, 1991).

The Michigan Supreme Court has given the legislature some leeway on the amount of the sales tax despite the clear constitutional limit in section 8. The state supreme court has sustained a sales tax in excess of the constitutional limit on retailers who fail to keep separate records of taxable and nontaxable transactions. The supreme court reasoned that the amount of tax above the constitutional limit should be construed as a penalty rather than an unconstitutional sales tax (*Sims v. Firestone Tire and Rubber Company*, 1976).

---

[18] See also sections 3, 5, 10, and 11 of this Article.

## SECTION 9

**Use of specific taxes on fuels for transportation purposes; authorization of indebtedness and issuance of obligations.** All specific taxes, except general sales and use taxes and regulatory fees, imposed directly or indirectly on fuels sold or used to propel motor vehicles upon highways and to propel aircraft and on registered motor vehicles and aircraft shall, after payment of necessary collection expenses, be used exclusively for transportation purposes as set forth in this section.

Not less than 90 percent of the specific taxes, except general sales and use taxes and regulatory fees, imposed directly or indirectly on fuels sold or used to propel motor vehicles upon highways and on registered motor vehicles shall, after the payment of necessary collection expenses, be used exclusively for the transportation purposes of planning, administering, constructing, reconstructing, financing, and maintaining state, county, city, and village roads, streets, and bridges designed primarily for the use of motor vehicles using tires, and reasonable appurtenances to those state, county, city, and village roads, streets and bridges.

The balance, if any, of the specific taxes, except general sales and use taxes and regulatory fees, imposed directly or indirectly on fuels sold or used to propel motor vehicles upon highways and on registered motor vehicles, after the payment of necessary collection expenses; 100 percent of the specific taxes, except general sales and use taxes and regulatory fees, imposed directly or indirectly on fuels sold or used to propel aircraft and on registered aircraft, after the payment of necessary collection expenses; and not more than 25 percent of the general sales taxes, imposed directly or indirectly on fuels sold to propel motor vehicles upon highways, on the sale of motor vehicles, and on the sale of the parts and accessories of motor vehicles, after the payment of necessary collection expenses; shall be used exclusively for the transportation purposes of comprehensive transportation as defined by law.

The legislature may authorize the incurrence of indebtedness and the issuance of obligations pledging the taxes allocated or authorized to be allocated by this section, which obligations shall not be construed to be evidences of state indebtedness under this constitution. Amendment ratified Nov. 7, 1978. Effective Dec. 23, 1978.

Section 9 earmarks certain taxes for transportation purposes. The funds generated under section 9 are referred to as "restricted funds" because the constitution limits their use (*Michigan Road Builders, et al. v. State Treasurer, 1992*). The Constitution of 1908 was amended by initiative petition in 1938 to earmark taxes on gasoline and like fuels needed to propel motor vehicles and taxes on all motor vehicles registered in Michigan for highway purposes. The current version in section 9 represents a revision of the 1908 Constitution as amended. According to the *Address to the People*, the only significant change is the addition of the words "as defined by law" following the words "highway purposes." The framers included this revision to give the legislature the power to define and limit the meaning of the term "highway purposes." Section 9 underwent major revision in 1978. The 1978 revisions were presented to the people by joint resolution of the legislature. The first change amended the first paragraph to include aircraft in the specific taxes dedicated to transportation purposes by adding the words "and to propel aircraft" and "aircraft." The first-paragraph phrase, "transportation purposes set forth in this section," replaced the phrase "highway purposes as defined by law." The 1978 amendment then added the second, third, and fourth paragraphs.

The 1978 amendments represented a compromise between those who would like to see section 9 money dedicated to road construction and those who wanted to extend the use of these funds for public transportation use (*Michigan Road Builders v. Department of Management and Budget, 1992*). Before the 1978 amendments, the Michigan Supreme Court granted the legislature considerable discretion in defining "highway purposes." In *Advisory Opinion on Constitutionality of 1976 PA 295* (1977), the supreme court held that the legislature could define mass transportation as a highway purpose. The 1978 amendments limited the legislature's discretion in allocating the revenues from gas and license taxes. Under the 1978 amendments, at least 90 percent of these revenues must be used exclusively for general road purposes. The remainder must be used exclusively for other transportation purposes.

The first paragraph of section 9 sets aside certain specific taxes for the transportation purposes set forth in the following paragraphs. Two kinds of specific taxes are dedicated to transportation purposes: Taxes imposed either directly or indirectly on fuels sold or used to propel motor vehicles on highways or to propel aircraft are dedicated for transportation purposes. Taxes on registered motor vehicles and aircraft are also for transportation. Three types of taxes are excluded from the earmarking requirements of section 9: general sales taxes, use taxes, and regulatory fees.[19] Regulatory fees may appear to be taxes but they are not. Regulatory fees are charged in exchange for a particular government service that benefits the party paying the fee in a manner not shared by other members of society. Regulatory fees are paid by choice by those electing to use a government service. The regulatory fee charged is not designed to raise revenue. Instead, a regulatory fee reimburses the government for providing a service (*Attorney General Opinion No. 6496*, 1988).

After covering the costs incurred to collect the specific taxes, the revenue generated by the taxes must be put to the purposes set forth in the remainder of section 9. The disposition of surplus lands purchased with these earmarked funds is also governed by the limitations in this section. Surplus lands purchased with restricted funds may only be sold at fair market value, and the proceeds of the sale of the land must be used for transportation purposes in accordance with section 9 (*Attorney General Opinion No. 6608*, 1990).

---

[19] General sales and use taxes are covered in Article IX, section 8.

The second paragraph states that at least 90 percent of the revenue generated by the specific taxes for motor vehicles must be used exclusively for planning, administering, constructing, reconstructing, financing, and maintaining state, county, city, and village roads, streets, and bridges used primarily for motor vehicles using tires. This paragraph makes sure that the bulk of the money gleaned from the specific taxes will be used to support transportation facilities for cars, motorcycles, and trucks. A panel of the Michigan Court of Appeals has ruled that payments for tort judgments from defective roads may come from section 9 funds. The appeals court reasoned that such payments could be legitimately construed as a cost of administering Michigan's roads (*Michigan Road Builder v. Department of Management and Budget, 1992*). The earmarked funds described in this paragraph may also be expended for "reasonable appurtenances" of roads and bridges. Reasonable appurtenances include features such as: banked curves of roads, traffic lights and signals, mowed and shrubbed parkways between opposing traffic lanes, and hiking trails to promote pedestrian safety near highways (*Attorney General Opinion No. 5733*, 1980). Section 9's restricted funds may not, however, be used for a state study of emissions from private automobiles (*County Road Association of Michigan v. Department of Transportation*, 1979).

The third paragraph allows the rest of the money from the specific taxes on motor vehicles, if any, to go towards funding comprehensive transportation purposes as defined by law, such as public transportation. The state legislature has defined comprehensive transportation purposes in M.C.L.A. Section 247.660c. Certain other taxes are also reserved for comprehensive transportation purposes. All of the specific taxes on registered aircraft and aircraft fuels must be placed towards comprehensive transportation purposes. The state may also choose to use not more than 25 percent of the general sales taxes on motor vehicle fuels, motor vehicle sales, and the sale of motor vehicle parts and accessories for comprehensive transportation purposes. Since general sales taxes are not constitutionally earmarked, the state legislature may use sales tax revenue for any lawful purpose, transportation or otherwise, subject to the 25 percent limit contained in this third paragraph of section 9 (*Attorney General Opinion No. 6344*, 1986).

The fourth paragraph permits the legislature to authorize the incurrence of debt and the issuing of bonds, pledging the earmarked taxes authorized or allocated for repayment of the debt. This debt does not count as evidence of state debt.

## SECTION 10

**Sales tax; distribution to local governments.** Fifteen percent of all taxes imposed on retailers on taxable sales of tangible personal property at a rate of not more than

4% shall be used exclusively for assistance to townships, cities and villages, on a population basis as provided by law. In determining population the legislature may exclude any portion of the total number of persons who are wards, patients or convicts in any tax supported institution. Amendment approved March 15, 1994. Effective April 30, 1994.

The Constitution of 1908, as amended in 1946, dedicated one-eighth of sales tax revenues for the assistance of townships, cities, and villages according to population. The 1963 Constitution revised the 1908 document and removed a reference to a sales tax calculation based on the 1946 base. As explained in the *Address to the People,* this deletion would permit the elimination of a sales tax on food or drugs or other items if the legislature so desired. The 1994 amendment to section 10 increased the amount of sales tax revenues shared with units of local government to 15 percent.[20] The amendment is careful to assure that the 15 percent is calculated on the basis of 4 percent, since section 8 of this article dedicates a portion of the sales tax to the school aid fund.

The purpose behind this section is to help finance local governmental units is proportion to their needs. The framers believed that there should be some direct relationship between population and the expenses incurred by local government. The population count for section 10 purposes should be as accurate as possible without resorting to a state-conducted census. Distribution of section 10 revenues must be based on the population at the time of distribution, not at the time of the collection of the tax (*City of Detroit v. Commissioner of Revenue,* 1951).

Section 10 only requires the distribution of some sales tax revenues to local government. Interest and penalties collected on deficiencies in sales taxes are not a part of revenues available for distribution to localities under section 10 (*Attorney General Opinion No. 6559,* 1989).

## SECTION 11

**State school aid fund; source; distribution; guarantee to local school district.** There shall be established a school aid fund which shall be used exclusively for aid to school districts, higher education and school employees' retirement systems, as provided by law. Sixty percent of all the taxes imposed at a rate of 4% on retailers of taxable sales at retail of tangible personal property, 100% of the proceeds of the sales and use taxes imposed at the additional rate of 2% provided for in section 8 of this article, and other tax revenues provided by law, shall be dedicated to this fund. Payments from this fund shall be made in full on a scheduled basis, as provided by law. Beginning in the 1995–96 state fiscal year and each state fiscal year after 1995–96, the state shall

[20] See also section 3, 5, 8, and 11 of this Article.

guarantee that the total state and local per pupil revenue for school operating purposes for each local school district shall not be less than the 1994–95 total state and local per pupil revenue for school operating purposes for that local school district, as adjusted for consolidations, annexations, or other boundary changes. However, this guarantee does not apply in a year in which the local school district levies a millage rate for school district operating purposes less than it levied in 1994. Amendment approved March 15, 1994. Effective April 30, 1994.

This section creates a school aid fund and dedicates sales tax revenue to it. The Michigan sales tax is currently set at a rate of 6 percent. Sixty percent of all sales tax revenues imposed at 4 percent go to the school aid fund. All of the sales tax revenue imposed at the additional 2 percent goes to the fund. The legislature is also permitted to dedicate other tax revenues to the school aid fund. Section 11 also guarantees that after the 1995–1996 fiscal year, the state will guarantee that the total state and local per-pupil spending will not fall below the 1994–1995 level. This guarantee will not apply if a local school district lowers its school millage rate below the level of 1994.

The *Address to the People* indicates that section 11 is new to the constitution. However, Michigan has a long history of setting aside money for the support of education. Article X, section 2 of the Constitution of 1835 established a perpetual fund for the support of school. Money for the fund was to come from the sale or rent of certain state lands. The 1850 Constitution continued the perpetual fund and added to the fund proceeds from the sale of land escheated to the state. Article X, section 23 of the Constitution of 1908 (as amended in 1946) dedicated two cents of the sales tax to a special school aid fund, which was distinct from the state's general fund. The legislature could make appropriations from the special fund only for aid to school districts or public school employees' retirement systems.

The 1994 amendments to section 11 were part of a package of amendments put before the people to reform school financing.[21] The revised section 11 set forth the contributions from the raised sales tax to the school aid fund. The amendment also added language guaranteeing level of state and local per-pupil spending.

The Michigan School Aid Act (M.C.L.A. Section 388.1601 et seq.) provides for the administration of funds provided under section 11. The use of the phrase "provided by law" means that the legislature has complete authority for the implementation of section 11. The legislature, therefore, has the power to determine the qualifications for receiving state school aid by school districts (*Attorney General Opinion No. 6419*, 1987).

The state legislature may use money from the school aid fund to reimburse school districts for the transportation of pupils to schools. The legislature may

[21] See also sections 3, 5, 8, and 10 of this Article.

allow school districts to choose the most efficient and economical means of transportation. The legislature may also reimburse school districts for the cost of transportation of pupils to nonpublic schools without offending either section 11 or Article I, section 4 of this constitution (*Alexander v. Bartlett*, 1968).

Section 11 only requires the distribution of some sales tax revenues to the school aid fund. Interest and penalties collected on deficiencies in sales taxes are not a part of revenues available for allocation to the school aid fund under section 11 (*Attorney General Opinion No. 6559*, 1989).

## SECTION 12

**Evidence of state indebtedness.** No evidence of state indebtedness shall be issued except for debts authorized pursuant to this constitution.

This section is designed to limit the capacity of the legislature to borrow money and issue evidence of debt. Article XIV, section 7 of the Constitution of 1850 introduced language limiting evidence of debt to debts authorized by the constitution. The 1908 Constitution continued this limitation. The current language of section 12 is simply an improvement of the phrasing of the 1908 provision.

The state of Michigan incurs debt any time the state borrows money. The usual vehicle for state borrowing is the issuing of bonds. Sections 14, 15, and 16 of Article IX cover the specifics of various kinds of state borrowing.

Certain kinds of bonds do not count as evidence of state debt for the purposes of section 12. Self-liquidating revenue bonds do not constitute state debt because the state makes no pledge of general tax revenues to repay the bonds. The state also will not make up any deficiency if there is a default in payment (*Advisory Opinion on Constitutionality of 1975 PA 301*; *Young v. Ann Arbor*, 1934). Bonds that are considered "analogous" to self-liquidating revenue bonds are also not evidence of state indebtedness (*State Highway Commissioner v. Detroit Controller*, 1951). One such "analogous" bond is the special obligation bond (*Schureman v. State Highway Commission*, 1966). However, the Michigan Supreme Court is reluctant to extend exceptions to the constitutional limitations of section 12 and place other novel revenue schemes in the same category as self-liquidating revenue bonds or special obligation bonds (*Advisory Opinion re Constitutionality of 1973 PA 1 and 2, 1973*).

## SECTION 13

**Public bodies, borrowing power.** Public bodies corporate shall have power to borrow money and to issue their securities evidencing debt, subject to this constitution and law.

Section 13 is a new provision of the constitution designed to allow public bodies to issue bonds. The 1908 Constitution allowed various public corporate bodies to issue bonds. Counties (Article VIII, section 10), drainage districts (Article VIII, section 15a), cities (Article VIII, section 20), and cities and villages acquiring or operating public utilities (Article VIII, section 24) were all allowed to issue bonds. The 1963 Constitution deletes these individual references in favor of a general grant of power to public corporate bodies. The borrowing power of public corporate bodies is limited by the state constitution and state statutes governing the various public bodies (*Fizer v. Onekama Consolidated Schools*, 1978).

## SECTION 14

**State borrowing; short term.** To meet obligations incurred pursuant to appropriation for any fiscal year, the legislature may by law authorize the state to issue its full faith and credit notes in which case it shall pledge undedicated revenues to be received within the same fiscal year for the repayment thereof. Such indebtedness in any fiscal year shall not exceed 15 percent of undedicated revenues receivedcby the state during the preceding fiscal year and such debts shall be repaid at the time the revenues so pledged are received, but not later than the end of the same fiscal year.

Section 14 deals with short-term borrowing by the state. The Constitution of 1850 allowed the state to incur debts to meet deficits in revenue and to repel invasion, suppress insurrection, or defend the state in times of war. The 1850 Constitution limited the state's capacity to incur debt to meet deficits of up to $50,000 per year. The 1908 Constitution maintained limitations on state borrowing but increased the maximum amount that the state could borrow; the state could incur debt no greater than $250,000 to meet revenue shortfalls and $50 million dollars for the improvement of highways.

Section 14 is a new approach to deal with short-term borrowing designed to give the state greater flexibility in meeting cash crises within the general fund. Under section 14, the state is allowed to borrow an amount not exceeding 15 percent of the state's undedicated revenues from the previous fiscal year. The legislature must authorize the state to borrow money. Any short-term borrowing must be in anticipation of revenues to be received in the same fiscal year. The amount borrowed must be paid in full at the time the revenues are received.

The *Address to the People* explained the reasons for the provisions of section 14. The old dollar amount from the 1908 Constitution was seen as simply unrealistic. Also, the financial flexibility created by section 14 should eliminate the need for the state to "borrow" from creditors by making late payments on debts. The requirement that the amount borrowed be paid in full when pledged revenues are received is designed to prevent the state from borrowing up to its limit and then renewing the loan year to year. There have been no interpretations of this section.

## SECTION 15

**Long-term borrowing by state.** The state may borrow money for specific purposes in amounts as may be provided by acts of the legislature adopted by a vote of two-thirds of the members elected to and serving in each house, and approved by a majority of the electors voting thereon at any general election. The question submitted to the electors shall state the amount to be borrowed, the specific purpose to which the funds shall be devoted, and the method of repayment.

Section 15 addresses long-term borrowing by the state. The state may borrow money under the conditions specified in section 15. A two-thirds majority of both houses of the legislature must approve the bond issue and submit the issue to the people for approval. The bond issue question submitted to the people must state the amount borrowed, the specific purpose for which the money is intended, and the way in which the money will be repaid. These three elements constitute the substantive question on which the people vote. The bond issue submitted to the people must be approved by a majority vote of voters voting on the bond issue question.

Article XIV, section 3 and 4 of the Constitution of 1850 allowed the state to incur certain limited debts for deficits and to repel invasions, suppress rebellions, and defend the state. Article X of the Constitution of 1908 strictly limited the ability of the state to authorize long-term borrowing. Michigan could borrow only to meet deficits in revenue up to a total amount of $250,000. The state could also borrow to repel invasion, suppress insurrection, or defend the state or the United States. Any additional borrowing required a constitutional amendment. The Constitution of 1908 was amended nine times to borrow additional money for purposes as diverse as veterans' bonuses (following both World Wars and the Korean Conflict) and the construction and equipment of hospitals and training schools. Section 15 is a new provision of the constitution. It is designed to eliminate "cluttering up" the constitution with amendments to authorize particular debts. Section 15 continues to make sure that the people must approve borrowing by setting forth procedures for the approval of long-term borrowing (*Advisory Opinion on Constitutionality of 1982 PA 47*, 1983).

The legislature may change the particulars of bond legislation, such as the interest rate at which money will be repaid, so long as the three substantive elements of the bond question remain unchanged (*Advisory Opinion on Constitutionality of 1982 PA 47*, 1983).

## SECTION 16

**State loans to school districts.** The state, in addition to any other borrowing power, may borrow from time to time such amounts as shall be required, pledge its full faith and credit and issues its notes or bonds therefor, for the purpose of making loans to school districts as provided in this section.

If the minimum amount which would otherwise be necessary for a district to levy in any year to pay principal and interest on its qualified bonds, including any necessary allowances for estimated tax delinquencies, exceeds 13 mills on each dollar of its assessed valuation as finally equalized, or such lower millage as the legislature may prescribe, then the school district may elect to borrow all or any part of the excess from the state. In that event the state shall lend the excess amount to the school district for the payment of principal and interest. If for any reason any school district will be or is unable to pay the principal and interest on its qualified bonds when due, then the school district shall borrow and the state shall lend to it an amount sufficient to enable the school district to make the payment.

The term "qualified bonds" means general obligation bonds of school districts issued for capital expenditures, including refunding bonds, issued prior to May 4, 1955, or issued thereafter and qualified as provided by law pursuant to Section 27 or Section 28 of Article X of the Constitution of 1908 or pursuant to this section.

After a school district has received loans from the state, each year thereafter it shall levy for debt service, exclusive of levies for nonqualified bonds, not less than 13 mills or such lower millage as the legislature may prescribe, until the amount loaned has been repaid, and any tax collections therefrom in any year over and above the minimum requirements for principal and interest on qualified bonds shall be used toward the repayment of state loans. In any year when such levy would produce an amount in excess of the requirements and the amount due to the state, the levy may be reduced by the amount of the excess.

Subject to the foregoing provisions, the legislature shall have the power to prescribe and to limit the procedure, terms and conditions for the qualification of bonds, for obtaining and making state loans, and for the repayment of loans.

The power to tax for the payment of principal and interest on bonds hereafter issued which are the general obligation of any school district, including refunding bonds, and for the repayment of any state loans made to school districts, shall be without limitation as to rate or amount.

All rights acquired under Sections 27 and 28 of Article X of the Constitution of 1908, by holders of bonds heretofore issued, and all obligations assumed by the state or any school district under these sections, shall remain unimpaired.

Section 16 covers state school bond financing. A 1955 amendment to the Constitution of 1908 (Article X, section 27) allowed the state to issue bonds for the purpose of making loans to school districts for school construction and improvement. This amendment expired on July 1, 1962. A subsequent amendment (Article X, section 28) ratified in 1960 also allowed for state loans to school districts after the expiration of Article X, section 27 of the Constitution of 1908. Section 16 is a revision of Article X, section 28 of the 1908 Constitution. This section continues to allow the state to issue bonds to make loans to school districts.

Under the terms of Section 16, the state is empowered to issue bonds and pledge the full faith and credit of the state in order to make loans to school districts.

These loans are designed to help school districts pay the principal and interest on general obligation bonds issued by the school districts for capital expenditures. The state legislature is given the general authority to make laws governing the qualification of bonds and the method for obtaining, making, and repaying state loans.[22]

Under the terms of this section and its predecessors (Article X, sections 27 and 28 of the Constitution of 1908), school districts are allowed to issue bonds for capital expenditures. These are the "qualified bonds" described in the third paragraph and governed by the provisions of section 16.

School districts may choose to borrow money to pay principal and interest on qualified bonds when the cost of paying for the bonds reaches a certain level. The third paragraph of section 16 allows a school district to borrow state money if the cost of payment of principal and interest exceeds thirteen mills of the district's equalized, assessed value. The legislature may lower this threshold amount if it so chooses. School districts must borrow from the state if the district cannot, for any reason, pay the principal and interest on its bonds when the payment comes due.

School districts must repay money loaned by the state. School districts must levy a millage to repay the state. Section 16 sets the amount of this millage at thirteen mills, although the legislature is given the power to prescribe a lower millage rate for the repayment of the debt. Any tax revenues received by the school district, over and above what is needed to pay for the qualified bonds, must be used towards repayment of the state loan. The sixth paragraph of section 16 helps make sure bonds and loans are paid by guaranteeing that the power to tax to repay bonds and loans is unlimited.

Section 16 must be read as an exception to the tax limitations contained in Article IX, section 6. The sixth paragraph of section 16 is seen as a clear indication that millages levied to pay back state loans are not covered by the fifteen-mill limitation in section 6. The pay back provision also creates an exception to the usual requirement that school districts receive voter approval before issuing bonds. While school districts cannot borrow money and issue bonds without a vote of the people, school districts may borrow money and issue bonds for repaying section 16 loans (*Advisory Opinion on Constitutionality re Constitutionality of 1973 PA 1 and 2*, 1973; *Attorney General Opinion No. 5652*, 1980).

Section 16's loan program may be used only for funding capital expenditures. It cannot be used to grant loans to school districts to meet shortfalls in operating expenses (*Advisory Opinion on Constitutionality re Constitutionality of 1973 PA 1 and 2*, 1973).

---

[22] Numerous Michigan statutes govern the loan program of section 16. In general, loans to school districts are covered in M.C.L.A. sections 388.931, 388.951, and 388.981. School loan bonds are treated in M.C.L.A. section 388.921.

The definition of "qualified bonds" in section 16 is clarified in M.C.L.A. 388.953. Qualified bonds are general obligation bonds of school districts issued for capital expenditures. General obligation bonds are full faith and credit obligations supported by the power to tax for the repayment of the principal and interest on the bonds (*Attorney General Opinion No. 6587*, 1989).

## SECTION 17

**Payments from state treasury.** No money shall be paid out of the state treasury except in pursuance of appropriations made by law.

The language of section 17 made its first appearance in Article XIV, section 5 of the Constitution of 1850. It has remained unchanged since then.

An appropriation is a legislative enactment. Section 17, along with Article IV, section 31, form the constitutional basis for the legislature's power to appropriate money (*Police Officer's Association of Michigan v. County of Oakland*, 1984). Both these sections require that legislative judgments be exercised in advance of the expenditure of state funds (*Wayne County Circuit Judges v. Wayne County*, 1971). These sections also prevent the legislature from delegating the authority to appropriate to the state budget director, a state senate, or house appropriations committee (*Attorney General Opinion No. 6603*, 1989).

Monetary judgments awarded by the Michigan Court of Claims under the Court of Claims Act (M.C.L.A. 600.6458) are not regarded by the Michigan Supreme Court as appropriations and do not interfere with the appropriations process under section 17 or Article IV, section 31 (*City of Adrian v. State of Michigan*, 1984).[23]

## SECTION 18

**State credit.** The credit of the state shall not be granted to, nor in aid of any person, association or corporation, public or private, except as authorized in this constitution.

This section shall not be construed to prohibit the investment of public funds until needed for current requirements or the investment of funds accumulated to provide retirement or pension benefits for public officials and employees, as provided by law.

The Constitution of 1950 first introduced limitations on the granting of state credit. The framers of the 1963 Constitution made two major changes to the 1908 version of the limitation. In the first paragraph, the framers added the

---

[23] See section 22 of this Article for the function of and constitutional basis for the Court of Claims.

words "as authorized in this constitution." This addition was needed to harmonize section 18 with Article IX, section 16, which allows for loans to school districts. The second paragraph of this section is new to the constitution. This paragraph allows for the investment of idle funds of the state and its political subdivisions. As the *Address to the People* explained, attorneys for public bodies were reluctant to authorize investments except in federal securities. This new paragraph allows for the legislature to authorize investments under appropriate safeguards.

This section of the constitution is designed to make certain that the state, which itself cannot borrow, except as authorized, does not accumulate unauthorized debts by endorsing or guaranteeing the obligations of others (*Advisory Opinion on Constitutionality of 1966 PA 346*, 1968). Section 18 is violated when the state creates an obligation legally enforceable against it for the benefitof another (*Petrus v. Dickinson County Board of Commissioners*, 1990; *Sprik v. Regents of the University of Michigan*, 1972). The prohibitions in section 18 apply not only to the state government but also to local governments as political subdivisions of the state and to other instrumentalities of the state (*Oakland County Drain Commissioner v. City of Royal Oak*, 1943).

Section 18's prohibition against the loan of state credit must be read together with Article VII, section 26, which provides for special limitations on the loan of credit by cities and villages. In reviewing state action in light of either of these sections, Michigan courts follow two basic rules: First, courts will grant all legislation a presumption of constitutionality. Second, courts will not declare legislation unconstitutional unless it is plain that the legislation violated the constitution and the constitutionality of the legislation will be supported by all possible presumptions not clearly inconsistent with the language and the subject matter (*Advisory Opinion on Constitutionality of 1986 PA 281*, 1988).

In order to determine whether an enactment is constitutional under section 18, Michigan courts first ascertain whether a loan of credit has been granted. There are two kinds of state financial transactions that do not qualify as a loan of credit. First, certain kinds of bonds do not qualify as loans of credit. Self-liquidating, special obligation, or revenue bonds are excluded from the constitutional definition of a loan of credit. Second, if the government acquires or transfers something of value in return for value, there is no loan of credit under the constitution (*Advisory Opinion on Constitutionality of 1986 PA 281*, 1988; *Alan v. Wayne County*, 1972). For example, a county could provide funds to a private, nonprofit hospital, if the hospital provides services to the county that aid in the performance of a governmental function (*Attorney General Opinion No. 6431*, 1987). On the other hand, a county could not simply give loans to a private business (*Attorney General Opinion No. 6398*, 1986). How much value the government must receive to avoid section 18 problems is tested under a lenient standard. Michigan courts assume that government officials exercise proper judgment in the determination of consideration received for value transferred. That judgment will be respected unless there is a clear and demonstrable abuse of discretion (*Attorney General Opinion No. 5842*, 1981).

## SECTION 19

**Subscription to or interest in stock by state prohibited; exceptions.** The state shall not subscribe to, nor be interested in the stock of any company, association or corporation, except that funds accumulated to provide retirement or pension benefits for public officials and employees may be invested as provided by law; and endowment funds created for charitable or educational purposes may be invested as provided by law governing the investment of funds held in trust by trustees and other state funds or money may be invested in accounts of a bank, savings and loan association, or credit union organized under the laws of this state or federal law, as provided by law. Amendment ratified Nov. 7, 1978. Effective Dec. 23, 1978.

The Constitution of 1850 prohibited the state from investing in the stock of any company, association, or corporation. The 1908 Constitution continued this prohibition. The prohibition was designed to help prevent state ownership of private business. The framers of the 1963 Constitution amended the 1908 language to allow for investment of retirement funds and pension benefits (as permitted under section 18 of this article) and endowment funds for charitable or educational purposes. The 1978 amendment to section 19 added the language "and other state funds or money...as provided by law." This new language allows state money to be invested in accounts in banks, savings and loan associations, or credit unions.

While the language of section 19 refers to the state specifically, the entire section has been understood to apply to other units of government, such as municipalities (*Attorney General Opinion No. 6395*, 1986). The state and municipalities may only invest funds accumulated to provide for retirement and pension benefits as provided by law. M.C.L.A. section 331.79 is the statute that governs legal investments. A trust fund created by a city to preserve the principal of a bequest for the expansion of its park and playground system cannot be invested in stock without offending section 19 (*Attorney General Opinion No. 6395*, 1986).

The phrase that allows that endowment funds "may be invested as provided by law governing the investment of funds held in trust by trustees" means that endowment funds must be held and managed pursuant to existing laws governing the investment of trust funds. Trust funds are governed by M.C.L.A. 700.813. This requirement means that trustees must meet the "prudent man" standard in managing trust assets (*Attorney General Opinion No. 5807*, 1980).

## SECTION 20

**Deposit of state money in certain financial institutions; requirements.** No state money shall be deposited in banks, savings and loan associations, or credit unions, other than those organized under the law of this state or federal law. No state money shall be deposited in any bank, savings and loan association, or credit union, in excess of 50 percent of the net worth of the bank, savings and loan association, or credit union, Any bank, savings and loan association, or credit union, receiving deposits of state money shall show the amount of state money so deposited as a separate item in all published statements. Amendment ratified Nov. 7, 1978. Effective Dec. 23, 1978.

Section 20 restricts the state to depositing state money in only those banks, savings and loan associations, or credit unions organized under federal or state law. The state also may not deposit money in excess of 50 percent of the net worth of the financial institution. The Constitution of 1908 introduced these limitations on the deposit of state money. The 1978 amendments added savings and loan associations and credit unions as financial institutions covered by this section. The 1978 amendments made two other language changes: The words "law of this state or federal law" replaced "national or state banking law" and "net worth of the" replaced "capital and surplus of such."

Numerous state statutes govern the deposit of state moneys. M.C.L.A. section 21.141 governs surplus funds of the state; 389.142 addresses funds of community colleges; 380.622 and 380.1221–1223 concern the funds of intermediate and local school districts; and 129.11 is devoted to counties, townships, school districts, cities, and villages.

Section 20 was introduced in 1908 in order to render the moneys belonging to the state absolutely secure. The provision requiring published statements of the amount of state money held in a bank "secures a wholesome publicity" that allows interested officials and the people themselves to know in what amounts the moneys of the state are deposited in the several depositories (*Attorney General Opinion No. 6163*, 1983). According to the attorney general, the clear language and intent of Section 20 means financial institutions that receive state money must disclose the amounts held in a conspicuous fashion in order to secure funds against the improvident selection of depositories, to prohibit the deposit of state money in excess of the financial resources of the institution, and to inform the public as to where state funds are on deposit. State funds may not be deposited in financial institutions that refuse to meet the disclosure requirements of Section 20 (*Attorney General Opinion No. 6163*, 1983).

Tuition collected by state colleges and universities and appropriation to state colleges and universities are considered state money for the purposes of section 20 (*Attorney General Opinion No. 4786*, 1973). Moneys of the Michigan Employment Security Commission (MESC), designated for administration, and the contingent fund also count as state funds. MESC funds designated to the employment compensation fund are not state moneys because the state has no beneficial interest in these funds (*Attorney General Opinion No. 6163,* 1983).

## SECTION 21

**Accounting for public moneys.** The legislature shall provide by law for the annual accounting for all public moneys, state and local, and may provide by law for interim accounting.

The legislature shall provide by law for the maintenance of uniform accounting systems by units of local government and the auditing of county accounts by competent state authority and other units of government as provided by law.

Section 21 requires that the legislature provide for at least an annual accounting of public money. The second paragraph requires the legislature to maintain uniform accounting systems of units of local government and to audit county accounts and any other government accounts as the legislature sees fit. The legislature has provided for a uniform system of accounting with the Uniform Budget and Accounting Act (M.C.L.A. 141.421). The current version of section 21 revises the language of Article X, section 18 of the Constitution of 1908.

Section 21 requires a specific grant of power in order to perform public audits. No government agency can audit another government agency without a specific grant of power from the legislature (*County Road Commission of Michigan v. State Highway Commission,* 1976).

## SECTION 22

**Examination and adjustment of claims against state.** Procedures for the examination and adjustment of claims against the state shall be provided by law.

Article VIII, section 4 of the Constitution of 1850 created a board of auditors to examine and adjust all claims against the state. The 1908 document continued the use of this procedure. The Constitution of 1963 was revised to allow the legislature to determine the mechanism for the examination and adjustment of claims against the state. The Michigan legislature has created the Court of Claims (M.C.L.A. section 600.6401 et seq.) to provide this function.

The power of the Court of Claims is limited by the doctrine of government immunity (*Genesee County Road Commission v. Michigan State Highway Commission,* 1978).

## SECTION 23

**Financial records; statement of revenues and expenditures.** All financial records, accountings, audit reports and other reports of public moneys shall be public records and open to inspection. A statement of all revenues and expenditures of public moneys shall be published and distributed annually, as provided by law.

Michigan has a long and proud tradition of open government. Article 12, section 4 of the Constitution of 1835 required the annual publication of the receipts and expenditures of public money. The Constitutions of 1850 and 1908 maintained this requirement. The Constitution of 1908 also added a new section requiring public accounting of all financial transactions of state officials, county officials, and public boards and institutions. Section 23 continues to guarantee the public ready access to all state financial records, accountings, and other reports of public money. The legislature is also required to provide for the annual publication and distribution of revenues and expenditures.

The "manifest purpose" of section 23 is to allow the public to keep its finger on the pulse of government spending (*Booth Newspapers, Inc. v. Board of Regents of the University of Michigan*, 1993; *Grayson v. Board of Accountancy*, 1970).

A panel of the Michigan Court of Appeals has interpreted the meaning of the phrase "financial records" in light of the manifest purpose of section 23. Financial records include "summaries, balance sheets and other such compilations which map out and correlate a myriad of financial transactions into a meaningful account." Section 23 does not give the public the right to inspect every receipt or every writing that evidences a receipt or an expenditure (*Grayson v. Board of Accountancy*, 1970).

## SECTION 24

**Public pension plans and retirement systems, obligation.** The accrued financial benefits of each pension plan and retirement system of the state and its political subdivisions shall be a contractual obligation thereof which shall not be diminished or impaired thereby.

Financial benefits arising on account of service rendered in each fiscal year shall be funded during that year and such funding shall not be used for financing unfunded accrued liabilities.

Section 24 creates a clear contractual obligation to ensure the full payment of financial benefits in the pension and retirement system. (*Shelby Township Police and Fire Retirement Board v. Charter Township of Shelby*, 1991). In Section 24, "accrued financial benefits" means the right to receive certain pension payments on the basis of the length of service performed (*Kosa v. State Treasurer*, 1980).

The paramount concern of the framers of section 24 was to insure the proper maintenance and the actuarial integrity of the state pension system. The framers rejected pension funding methods that did not account for unfunded accrued liabilities, which would result in the taxpayers' children bearing the burden of a failed pension system. "Unfunded accrued liabilities" are the estimated amounts needed according to actuarial projections to fulfill presently existing pension obligations (*Shelby Township Police and Fire Retirement Board v. Charter Township of Shelby*, 1991).

## SECTION 25

**Voter approval of increased local taxes; prohibitions; emergency conditions; repayment of bonded indebtedness guaranteed; implementation of section.** Property taxes and other local taxes and state taxation and spending may not be increased above the limitations specified herein without direct voter approval. The state is prohibited from requiring any new or expanded activities by local governments without full state financing, from reducing the proportion of state spending in the form of aid to local governments, or from shifting the tax burden to local government. A provision for emergency conditions is established and the repayment of voter approved bond indebtedness is guaranteed. Implementation of this section is specified in Sections 26 through 34, inclusive, of this Article. Enactment ratified Nov. 7, 1978. Effective Dec. 23, 1978.

Sections 25 through 34 of this article are known collectively as the "Headlee Amendment" to the constitution. The amendment was named after its major proponent, Richard Headlee. The Headlee Amendment was Michigan's contribution to the nationwide taxpayer revolt of the late 1970s that sought to curb what was perceived to be excessive government spending and to lower state and local taxes (*Durant v. State of Michigan*, 1985).

Section 25 requires voter approval for increases in property taxes and other local taxes, and in state taxation and spending, above the limits specified in sections 26 through 34. The direct voter approval requirement in sections 25 and 31 is satisfied by a majority of vote of the qualified voters in the unit of local government seeking the increase in the tax (*Commuter Tax Association of Metropolitan Detroit v. City of Detroit*, 1981). The state legislature may not require new or expanded activities from local governments without full financing of the activities by the state. The state must not reduce spending by reducing aid to local government, and the state cannot shift tax burdens to local government.

Section 25 is construed as an introductory paragraph to the Headlee Amendment, which indicates that substantive implementation comes in sections 26 to 34. The introductory sentences of section 25 do not have the substantive effect of creating specific rights and duties (*Waterford School District v. State Board of Education*, 1983).

## SECTION 26

**Limitation on taxes; revenue limit; refunding or transferring excess revenues; exceptions to revenue limitation; adjustment of state revenue and spending**

**limits.** There is hereby established a limit on the total amount of taxes which may be imposed by the legislature in any fiscal year on the taxpayers of this state. This limit shall not be changed without approval of the majority of the qualified electors voting thereon, as provided for in Article 12 of the Constitution. Effective with fiscal year 1979–80, and for each fiscal year thereafter, the legislature shall not impose taxes of any kind which, together with all other revenues of the state, federal aid excluded, exceed the revenue limit established in this section. The revenue limit shall be equal to the product of the ratio of Total State Revenues in fiscal year 1978–79 divided by the Personal Income in Michigan in calendar year 1977 multiplied by the Personal Income of Michigan in either the prior calendar year or the average of Personal Income of Michigan in the previous three calendar years, whichever is greater.

For any fiscal year in the event that Total State Revenues exceed the revenue limit established in this section by 1% or more, the excess revenues shall be refunded pro rata based on the liability reported on the Michigan income tax and single business tax (or its successor tax or taxes) annual returns filed following the close of such fiscal year. If the excess is less than 1%, this excess may be transferred to the State Budget Stabilization Fund.

The revenue limitation established in this section shall not apply to taxes imposed for the payment of principal and interest on bonds, approved by the voters and authorized under Section 15 of this Article, and loans to school districts authorized under Section 16 of this Article.

If responsibility for funding a program or programs is transferred from one level of government to another, as a consequence of constitutional amendment, the state revenue and spending limits may be adjusted to accommodate such change, provided that the total revenue authorized for collection by both state and local governments does not exceed that amount which would have been authorized without such change. Enactment ratified Nov. 7, 1978. Eff. Dec. 23, 1978.

Section 26 establishes a constitutional limit on the total amount of taxes that may be imposed by the legislature in any given year. The revenue limit created by section 26 does not apply to taxes imposed to pay back the principal and interest on bonds approved by the people and authorized under Article IX, sections 15 and 16. This section also provides for a refund or transfer of excess revenue.

The tax limitations in section 26 are derived from the total state revenues in fiscal year 1978–1979 and the personal income of Michigan in calendar year 1977. Total state revenues are divided by the personal income to give a ratio of revenues to income. The tax limit for a given fiscal year is found by multiplying this ratio by either the personal income for the prior calendar year or the average of the personal income for the previous three years, whichever is greater.

If total state revenues exceed the revenues set by section 26 by 1 percent or more, the state must make refunds in income tax or the single business tax. If the excess revenue is less than 1 percent, the state may choose to transfer the excess to the State Budget Stabilization Fund.

The limits created by section 26 may be altered only through constitutional amendment, following the procedures set forth in Article XII.

The limits in section 26 apply only to taxes, which are involuntary extractions.[24] A utility surcharge program to help poor persons pay their utility bills is not governed by section 26 for two reasons: First, such surcharges do not fit the definition of a tax. Second, the surcharges are not mandatory fundraisers because they are the product of a voluntary contract between a utility provider and the government (*Consumers Power Commission v. A.B.A.T.E.*, 1994).

## SECTION 27

**Exceeding revenue limit; conditions.** The revenue limit of Section 26 of this Article may be exceeded only if all of the following conditions are met: (1) The governor requests the legislature to declare an emergency; (2) the request is specific as to the nature of the emergency, the dollar amount of the emergency, and the method by which the emergency will be funded; and (3) the legislature thereafter declares an emergency in accordance with the specific of the governor's request by a two-thirds vote of the members elected to and serving in each house. The emergency must be declared in accordance with this section prior to incurring any of the expenses which constitute the emergency request. The revenue limit may be exceeded only during the fiscal year for which the emergency is declared. In no event shall any part of the amount representing a refund under Section 26 of this Article be the subject of an emergency request. Enactment ratified Nov. 7, 1978. Effective Dec. 23, 1978.

Section 27 allows the state to exceed the revenue limits in section 26 in the case of an emergency. The revenue limits may be exceeded only if three conditions are met: First, the governor must ask the legislature to declare an emergency. Second, the governor must tell the legislature the specific nature of the emergency, the dollar amount needed, and the method by which the emergency will be funded. Third, the legislature must declare an emergency in accord with the governor's request. A two-thirds vote of both houses of the legislaturebis needed to declare the emergency. There have been no interpretations of this section.

## SECTION 28

**Limitation on expenses of state government.** No expenses of state government shall be incurred in any fiscal year which exceed the sum of the revenue limit

[24] See the definitions of a tax in Article IX, section 1.

established in Sections 26 and 27 of this Article plus federal aid and any surplus from a previous fiscal year. Enactment ratified Nov. 7, 1978. Effective Dec. 23, 1978.

Section 28 limits the expenses that the state government can incur in a given fiscal year. State government expenses are limited to the sum of: (1) the revenue limit in sections 26 and 27; plus (2) the amount of federal aid to the state; and plus (3) any surplus left over from a previous fiscal year. There have been no interpretations of this section.

## SECTION 29

**State financing of activities or services required of local government by state law.** The state is hereby prohibited from reducing the state financed proportion of the necessary costs of any existing activity or service required by units of Local Government by state law. A new activity or service or an increase in the level of any activity or service beyond that required by existing law shall not be required by the legislature or any state agency of units of Local Government, unless a state appropriation is made and disbursed to pay the unit of Local Government for any necessary increased costs. The provision of this section shall not apply to costs incurred pursuant to Article VI, Section 18. Enactment ratified Nov. 7, 1978. Effective Dec. 23, 1978.

Section 29 is designed to forestall any attempt by the state legislature to shift responsibility for services to local government, once state government revenues were limited by section 27 of the Headlee Amendment. The phrase "state law" in this section refers only to state statutes and state agency rules, not to state constitutional requirements. The Michigan Supreme Court reasoned that the phrase "required by the legislature or any state agency" in the second sentence of this section must be read together with the words "state law" in the first sentence. Moreover, the supreme court found that the constitution itself makes distinctions between the constitution and other forms of state law. Therefore, state constitutional requirements, such as the requirement of a free public education in Article VIII, section 2, are not covered by section 29 (*Durant v. State of Michigan*, 1986). Section 29 does not apply to optional services or activities undertaken by a unit of local government (*Livingston County v. Department of Natural Resources*, 1988). Similarly, section 29 does not apply to a state law that allows a unit of local government to perform an activity or service but does not require it (*Kramer v. City of Dearborn Heights*, 1992). Requirements of local government based largely on federal law are also not covered by section 29 (*Birmingham and Lamphere School Districts v. Superintendent of Public Instruction*, 1982).

"Necessary costs" of a required service or activity are generally those costs that are essential to the completion of the intended purpose of the state-mandated activity (*Waterford School District v. State Board of Education*, 1983).

The legislature has crystallized the definition of "necessary costs" in the statute implementing the Headlee Amendment, specifically M.C.L.A. 21.233(6).

The method of calculation of the amount of state appropriations needed to satisfy section 29 has been the source of considerable debate. The Michigan Supreme Court believes that voters intended neither to freeze legislative discretion nor to permit state government full discretion in the allocation of state support for mandated activities or services. The Michigan Supreme Court has found that a "statewide to local district funding ratio" secures a minimum funding guarantee while simplifying calculations and avoiding "inequitable anomalies." The statewide-to-local funding ratio calculation works as follows: The process begins with the initial calculation of the proportion of statewide funding for a particular mandated activity to the total necessary costs of providing that activity. Second, the necessary costs to each local unit of government in the funding year are calculated. Third, the proportion of state financed funding for the activity in the base year is compared to the proportion of funding provided to the district in the year at issue. The end result of this process should result in the state affording each unit of local government performing a required activity the same proportion of funding the state provided on a statewide basis in the year that the Headlee Amendment was ratified (*Gaertner v. Buena Vista School District*, 1993).

The reference to Article IV, section 18 is a reference to the constitutional provision on judicial salaries. Since Article IV, section 18 is not self-executing, statutes and rules enacted under that section are exempt from coverage under Section 29 (*Durant v. State of Michigan*, 1986).

## SECTION 30

**Reduction of state spending paid to units of local government.** The proportion of total state spending paid to all units of Local Government, taken as a group, shall not be reduced below that proportion in effect in fiscal year 1978–79. Enactment ratified Nov. 7, 1978. Effective Dec. 23, 1978.

The phrase "taken as a group" means that the overall percentage allotment of the state budget for local units of government must remain at 1978 levels (*Durant v. State of Michigan*, 1986).

## SECTION 31

**Levying tax or increasing rate of existing tax; maximum tax rate on new base; increase in assessed valuation of property; exceptions to limitations.** Units of Local Government are hereby prohibited from levying any tax not authorized by law or charter when this section is ratified or from increasing the rate of an existing tax above that rate authorized by law or charter when this section is ratified, without the approval of a majority of the qualified electors of that unit of Local Government voting thereon. If the definition of the base of an existing tax is broadened, the maximum authorized rate of taxation in the new base in each unit of Local Government shall be reduced to yield the same estimated gross revenues as on the prior base. If the assessed valuation of property as finally equalized, excluding the value of new construction and improvements, increased by a larger percentage than the increase in the General Price Level from the previous year, the maximum authorized rate applied thereto in each unit of Local Government shall be reduced to yield the same gross revenue from existing property, adjusted for changes in the General Price Level, as could have been collected at the existing authorized rate on the prior assessed value.

The limitations of this section shall not apply to taxes imposed for the payment of principal and interest on bonds or other evidence of indebtedness or for the payment of assessments of contract obligations in anticipation of which bonds are issued which were authorized prior to the effective date of this amendment. Enactment ratified Nov. 7, 1978. Effective Dec. 23, 1978.

Section 31 requires a vote of the people before a unit of local government can institute a new tax or raise the rate of a tax authorized by law at the time of the ratification of the Headlee Amendment. Section 31 also rolls back millage rates when property values rise beyond the inflation rate as measured by the Consumer Price index (*Durant v. State of Michigan,* 1986).

Tax levies not authorized by December 23, 1978, must be subject to a vote and approved by a majority of voters. The same is true of a proposal to raise the rate of an existing tax authorization (*Taxpayers United for the Michigan Constitution v. City of Detroit,* 1992). Section 31 does not require a vote of the people in order to permit a local unit of government to increase taxes if the local unit of government already has the authority, by law or by charter, to levy the increase (*Smith v. Township of Scio,* 1988; *Bailey v. Muskegon County Board of Commissioners,* 1983). The Michigan Court of Appeals believes that this approach to section 31 is dictated by the plain language of section 31 and sound public policy. The court of appeals reasons that if the "maximum rate authorized by law" was lowered every time a municipality decided to reduce its millage rate, the purpose of the Headlee Amendment would be chilled, since government officials would hesitate to impose a lower tax for fear that the lower rate would establish a new ceiling and, if the economy turned downward, municipal services could not be maintained (*Smith v. Township of Scio,* 1988).

## SECTION 32

**Suit to enforce sections 25 to 31.** Any taxpayer of the state shall have standing to bring suit on the Michigan State Court of Appeals to enforce the provisions of Sections 25 through 31, inclusive, of this Article and, if the suit is sustained, shall receive from the applicable unit of government his costs incurred in maintaining such suit. Enactment ratified Nov. 7, 1978. Effective Dec. 23, 1978.

This section allows taxpayers to go to court to enforce the provisions of the Headlee Amendment. The Revised Judicature Act (M.C.L.A. section 600.308a) addresses taxpayers' suits under the Headlee Amendment.

"Standing" is the legal term used to denote a party's interest in the outcome of litigation. A stake in the outcome of a case assures sincere and vigorous advocacy. Under Michigan common law, taxpayers did not have standing to sue to vindicate a public wrong or enforce a public right. The Headlee Amendment and the Revised Judicature Act relax this traditional common law bar and specifically confer upon taxpayers the right to sue to enforce the amendment (*Waterford School District v. State Board of Education*, 1980).

A one-year statute of limitations in the Revised Judicature Act for bringing suits under section 32 does not impermissibly infringe on rights guaranteed under the Headlee Amendment or place an undue burden on the exercise of those rights (*Taxpayers Allied for Constitutional Taxation v. Wayne County*, 1994).

## SECTION 33

**Definitions applicable to sections 25 to 32.** Definitions. The definitions of this section shall apply to Section 25 through 32 of Article IX, inclusive.

"Total State Revenues" includes all general and special revenues, excluding federal aid, as defined in the budget message of the governor for fiscal year 1978–79. Total State Revenues shall exclude the amount of any credits based on actual tax liabilities or the imputed tax components of rental payments, but shall include the amount of any credits not related to actual tax liabilities. "Personal Income of Michigan" is the total income received by persons in Michigan from all sources, as defined and officially reported by the United States Department of Commerce or its successor agency. "Local Government" means any political subdivision of the state, including, but not restricted to, school districts, cities, villages, townships, charter townships, counties, charter counties, authorities created by the state, and authorities created by other units of local government. "General Price Level" means the Consumer Price Index for the United States as defined and officially reported by the United States Department of Labor or its successor agency. Enactment ratified Nov. 7, 1978. Effective Dec. 23, 1978.

Section 33 simply provides definitions to govern the interpretation of the various provisions of the Headlee Amendment. There have been no interpretations of the section.

## SECTION 34

**Implementation of sections 25 to 33.** The Legislature shall implement the provisions of Sections 25 through 33, inclusive, of this Article. Enactment ratified, Nov. 7, 1978. Effective Dec. 23, 1978.

The 1994 amendments to section 35 increased the size of the trust fund and changed the ways in which money from the fund may be distributed. Each year, until the natural resources trust fund reaches a principal of $400 million, $10 million of revenues that would have gone into the fund must be deposited into an endowment for state parks. When the natural resources trust fund reaches $400 million, no more than half of the revenues that would have gone into the trust fund must be deposited into the endowment for state parks. The principal of the natural resources trust fund is capped at $400 million. When the trust fund reaches that cap, all of the revenues that would have gone into the fund must be deposited in the state park endowment. The principal of the state park endowment is capped at $800 million. When that cap is reached, all revenues above the cap destined for the endowment must be spent as provided by law.

Section 35 contains some limits on the way in which money is paid out of the fund. The legislature may provide that no more than one-third of the revenues received in a year may be expended during the following year. At least one-quarter of the total expenditures in any given year must be used to acquire land or rights in land. Not more than one-quarter of the total expenditures in any year may be used for the development of public recreational facilities.

The trust fund is administered by a board created by the legislature. The board is a part of the department of natural resources. The board is entitled to make recommendations on which projects should be funded with trust fund money. The board submits its recommendations to the governor, who in turn submits the recommendations to the legislature.

Section 35 requires the legislature to pass laws to implement the provisions contained in the section. The legislature has fulfilled this constitutional responsibility by passing the Michigan Natural Resources Trust Fund Act of 1985 (M.C.L.A. section 318.501 et seq.).

Section 35 must be read in harmony with Article IX, section 9, which earmarks certain revenues for transportation purposes. The dedication of revenues from oil and gas leases to the trust fund must be regarded as an exception to the restrictions that might otherwise apply to revenue generated by leasing property purchased with funds restricted to transportation purposes (*Attorney General Opinion No. 6608*, 1990).

## SECTION 36

**Tax on tobacco products; dedication of proceeds.** Six percent of the proceeds of the tax on tobacco products shall be dedicated to improving the quality of health care of the residents of this state. Amendment approved, March 15, 1994. Effective April 30, 1995.

Section 36 was added to the constitution in 1994. This section simply earmarks 6 percent of the revenues gleaned from the tax on tobacco to the improvement of health care. There have been no interpretations of this section.

## SECTION 36[1]

**Michigan state parks endowment fund.** There is hereby established the Michigan state parks endowment fund. The endowment fund shall consist of revenues as provided in section 35 of this article, and as provided by law. The endowment fund may also receive private contributions of money or other things of value. All money in the Genevieve Gillette state parks endowment fund shall be transferred to the endowment fund.

The accumulated principal of the endowment fund shall not exceed $800,000,000.00, which amount shall be annually adjusted pursuant to the rate of inflation beginning when the endowment fund reaches $800,000,000.00. This annually adjusted figure is the accumulated principal limit of the endowment fund.

Money available for expenditure from the endowment fund as provided in this section shall be expended for operations, maintenance, and capital improvements at Michigan state parks.

Money in the endowment fund shall be expended as follows:

(1) Until the endowment fund reaches an accumulated principal of $800,000,000.00, each state fiscal year the legislature may appropriate not more than $5,000,000.00 of the money in the endowment fund as this $5,000,000.00 amount is annually adjusted puruant to the rate of inflation.

(2) Once the accumulated principal in the endowment fund reaches $800,000,000.00, only the interest earnings of the endowment fund in excess of the amount necessary to maintain the endowment fund's accumulated principal limit may be made available for expenditure.

Unexpended appropriations of the endowment fund from any state fiscal year as authorized by this section may be carried forward or may be appropriated as determined by the legislature for purposes of this section.

The legislature shall provide by law for implementation of this section. Amendment approved Nov. 8, 1994. Effective Dec. 24, 1994.

This new amendment to the constitution was added to help prevent the state legislature from raiding funds dedicated to acquisition and maintenance of park land. This section is meant to work with section 35 of this article, which sets forth the general program for raising money for park land and describes the kinds of purposes for which endowment money may be spent.

Section 36[1] creates an endowment fund for state parks, which is capped at $800 million as adjusted each year for inflation. Until the fund reaches its cap, the legislature is limited to spending $5 million, as adjusted for inflation, from the fund each year. After the cap is reached, the legislature may not touch the accumulated principal of the fund. Instead, the legislature is restricted to spending only interest and earnings from the endowment fund.

The legislature is required to implement the provisions of Section 36[1], and it has fulfilled this responsibility in M.C.L.A. 318.311a. This statute uses the Detroit consumer price index to calculate the rate of inflation.

# Article X

*Property*

## SECTION 1

**Disabilities of coverture abolished; separate property of wife; dower.** The disabilities of coverture as to property are abolished. The real and personal estate of every woman acquired before marriage and all real and personal property to which she may afterward become entitled shall be and remain the estate and property of such woman, and shall not be liable for the debts, obligations or engagements of her husband, and may be dealt with and disposed of by her as if she were unmarried. Dower may be relinquished or conveyed as provided by law.

Section 1 is designed to guarantee the property rights of married women. Under this section, the real and personal property of every married woman—property acquired before and during marriage—remain the property of the woman. This property cannot be used to pay for the debts and obligations of her husband. Section 1 traces its origins to Article XVI, section 5 of the Constitution of 1850, which first guaranteed the real and personal property rights of married women.

Coverture refers to an ancient common law concept that the husband and wife are one person, and that one person is the husband. A married woman was unable to contract or convey property without her husband's consent; she was unable to sue or be sued without his consent. After marriage, a husband acquired complete dominion over his wife's property. The husband's power extended to complete rights to the possession, use, and income of the wife's property. In 1866 in *Tong v. Marvin*, the Michigan Supreme Court described some of the disabilities that attached to coverture. Under the concept of coverture, the husband: (1) had control of the wife's person and the right to appropriate her earnings to his own use; (2) became the owner of all of the wife's property, including that acquired before marriage; (3) could dispose of her lands or property for his own use; (4) became vested with her estate of inheritance; and (5) had the better right to control and have custody of the children in case of separation. Contemporary Michigan courts have described the situation of the wife as a "bare legal existence" or a "complete legal black out" (*Morgan v. Cincinnati Insurance Company*, 1981).

Section 1 eliminates these legal disabilities associated with coverture and gives a married woman control over her separate estate (*Citizens Commercial & Savings Bank v. Raleigh*, 1987). Delegates to the constitutional convention offered three general classes of reasons for placing section 1 in the 1963 Constitution: (1) support for the property rights of married women would avoid antagonizing a majority of the electorate, who happen to be female; (2) section 1 would help protect married women and their children from economic hardship; and (3) section 1 would also read the married woman's property act into the constitution (*City Finance Company v. Kloostra*, 1973). Michigan courts see this provision as a contribution to advance the equal protection of the laws for women. While section 1 enhances the ability of a married woman to get credit, it does not permit a married woman to avoid the liability that normally arises from the undertaking of a joint obligation with her husband (*Citizens Commercial & Savings Bank v. Raleigh*, 1987).

The last sentence of section 1 refers to another common law concept—dower rights. This is the right of a widow to the use during her natural life of one-third of the lands of her deceased husband (*Attorney General Opinion No. 6564*, 1989). The Michigan legislature has codified dower rights in M.C.L.A. 558.1.

## SECTION 2

**Eminent domain; compensation.** Private property shall not be taken for public use without just compensation therefor being first made or secured in a manner prescribed by law. Compensation shall be determined in proceedings in a court of record.

This section limits and governs the use of the state's power of eminent domain. Michigan's constitutional protection for private property began in 1835. Article I, section 19 of the Constitution of 1835 prohibited the taking of private property for public use without just compensation. The 1850 Constitution added to this simple prohibition by requiring that just compensation be made or secured according to state law before the taking of the property. The 1850 document also added two additional protections for private property. Article XVIII, section 2 allowed a jury of twelve local landholders or a panel of court-appointed commissioners to determine the necessity of taking the property and the just compensation for it. In section 14 of the same article, the 1850 Constitution provided for a mechanism of opening private roads to the public. Here, a jury of landowners would determine the necessity of opening the private road and the required compensation. The compensation for the opening of the road, along with the expenses for the proceedings, had to be borne by the persons benefiting from the opening of the road. The Constitution of 1908 included the 1850 innovations (Article XIII, section 1, 2, and 3) and added a provision allowing the regents of the University of Michigan to exercise the power of eminent domain under procedures prescribed by the legislature (Article XIII, section 4). A 1927 amendment governed the exercise of eminent domain by municipalities (Article XIII, section 5).

The Constitution of 1963 revises the language of section 1 of Article XIII of the Constitution of 1908 and deletes the remaining provisions. The *Address to the People* indicates that the framers believed that this language is sufficient to protect private property. The legislature has the power to prescribe procedures for the exercise of eminent domain. The sentence requiring compensation proceedings to take place in a court of record is designed to give people the right to know that their property rights will be determined by a court rather than a board or bureau. However, this revision does not change the meaning of just compensation (*City of Muskegon v. Slater*, 1967). It simply requires that proceedings for the determination of compensation take place in a court of record following procedures appropriate to a court of record (*Oakland County v. Schoenrock*, 1971).

The power of eminent domain is inherent in state sovereignty (*In re Petition of City of Detroit for Condemnation of Lands for Airport*, 1944). The state's power of eminent domain exists independently of federal and state constitutional provisions. Federal and state constitutions do not confer the power on the government; instead, constitutional provisions, such as section 2, regulate it and limit its use (*Shizas v. City of Detroit*, 1952).

The usual method for the exercise of the power of eminent domain is the condemnation of private property. The state cannot take title to the condemned property until two conditions are met: First, there must be a determination that the property be taken for a public purpose. Next, compensation must be made or secured by placing the money in the state treasury. Only after these conditions are met, may the state take title to the property (*Anderson Trust Company v. American Life Insurance Company*, 1942).

Section 2 of this article means that eminent domain cannot be invoked except to further a public use or purpose. Condemnation for private use cannot be authorized, whatever the incidental public benefit, and condemnation for a public purpose cannot be forbidden whatever the incidental private gain (*Poletown Neighborhood Council v. City of Detroit*, 1981).

Michigan courts generally defer to the judgment of the legislature in the determination of what constitutes a public use or purpose. A court will not disturb a legislative determination that property is needed for a public use or purpose unless that determination is palpable and manifestly arbitrary and incorrect (*Gregory Marina, Inc. v. Detroit*, 1966). Michigan courts follow the United States Supreme Court's reasoning in *Berman v. Parker* (1954): when the legislature speaks, the public interest has been declared in terms well-nigh conclusive (*Poletown Neighborhood Council v. City of Detroit*, 1981).

The Michigan legislature by statute (M.C.L.A. 213.23 et seq.) has delegated to public corporations and state agencies the power to take private property for public purposes within the scope of their powers. This statute is given liberal construction when applied to Michigan counties, townships, cities, and villages as required by Article VII, section 34 of this constitution. However, the Michigan Supreme Court has found there is insufficient public purpose involved in a municipality's condemnation of private property for the purpose of providing access onto private property by a city-franchised cable television operator (*City of Lansing v. Edward Rose Realty*, 1993).

A taking of private property can occur without the state taking actual title to land. A taking can occur when there is serious injury to property that results in a diminution of value (*Hart v. City of Detroit*, 1982). A taking may also occur when there is partial destruction of property (*Board of Education, City of Detroit v. Clarke*, 1979) or when private property is pressed into the public service (*Tamulion v. Michigan State Waterways Commission*, 1973). Courts follow no set formula in determining when a taking has occurred. Courts will examine the form, intensity, and deliberateness to determine whether or not there has been a taking (*In re Virginia Park*, 1982). If a taking has occurred, just compensation is due. Where there has been a partial taking, just compensation is measured by the amount by which the value of the remainder of the property has been diminished (*Michigan State Highway Commissioner v. Minckler*, 1975).

A city may not by deliberate acts reduce the value of private property and thereby deprive the owner of just compensation. Cities cannot engage in actions such as lax police protection, reduction in refuse collection or street cleaning, or intense building department inspection in order to bring down the value of property (*In re Urban Renewal, Elmwood Park Project*, 1965). Such actions constitute a taking of property and require just compensation.

Just compensation is the amount of money needed to put an injured party in the same position he or she would have been in had the property not been taken. Just compensation should neither enrich the individual at the public's expense nor the public at an individual's expense (*Board of Education of the City of Detroit v. Clark*, 1979). Interest on a deferred payment of an award in a condemnation proceeding is considered an element of just compensation (*In re Petition of State Highway Commissioner*, 1937).

## SECTION 3

**Homestead and personalty, exemption from process.** A homestead in the amount of not less than $3,500 and personal property of every resident of this state in the amount of not less than $750, as defined by law, shall be exempt from forced sale on execution or other processes of any court. Such exemptions shall not extend to any lien thereon excluded from exemption by law.

Few sections of the Michigan Constitution have caused Michigan courts and constitutional delegates to wax poetic as the homestead exemption provided by section 3. Section 3 exempts certain property from forced sale for the payment of debts. The constitution provides the minimum amounts of the exemptions and empowers the legislature to define the homestead and the personal property. The Michigan legislature has implemented the provisions of section 3 in two statutes: Exempted personal property is covered by M.C.L.A. Section 600.6023 et seq., and the homestead is covered by M.C.L.A. 700.688.

The Constitution of 1850 introduced provisions exempting a homestead and a certain amount of personal property from forced sale for the payment of debts. As the Michigan Supreme Court noted, the homestead exemption's purpose is to preserve a home for the family, even at the sacrifice of the just demands of creditors (*Kleinert v. Lefkowitz*, 1935). The homestead exemption was added to the 1850 Constitution to perpetuate the homestead exemption law of 1848, which was enacted to protect people from the kinds of extreme financial hardship that resulted from the Panic of 1837. The Michigan Supreme Court described the effect of the 1837 panic:

> The fancy values of landed property melted like snow in the April sun; immense quantities of commodities, stored up without any regard to the real wants of the country, lost in a day fully one-third of their value; the figures on all kinds of value-paper became a bitter mockery with every hour; bankruptcies came in avalanches; one manufactury after another stopped and the number of those who could find neither bread nor work increased by thousands and tens of thousands. (*Kleinert v. Lefkowitz*, 1935)

One speaker at the 1850 convention framed the purpose of the homestead exemption in the following way:

> The homestead exemption was founded upon principles of the soundest policy—those looking to the general welfare, as well as to the individual citizen; and the obvious intent of the act to secure to every householder or head of a family home,—a place of residence—which he may improve and make comfortable, and where the family may be sheltered when the hand of adversity presses hard upon them. The measure is so accordant with the real spirit of progress, so just in itself, so wisely expedient in all exigencies to which families are liable ... so consonant with the popular sentiment and the principles of true Christian morality, that no power on earth can

> prevent its universal adoption, and they shall sit every man under his vine and fig tree. It is the high duty of the State to throw around every homestead, every fireside, every hearth stone, the shield of its protection.[25]

The 1908 Constitution continued the two classes of exemptions and increased the dollar amount of exempted property. The 1963 revisions to the exemption provisions eliminate much statutory-type language and again increases the dollar amount of the allowable exemptions.

The constitutional and statutory provisions on the homestead exemption are construed by courts with "extreme liberality" in behalf of the owners. Michigan courts believe that this construction of the provisions is necessary in order not to impair or nullify these important safeguards of the home. Homesteaders are protected in the full enjoyment of the homestead, and incidental income, such as room rentals, are appurtenant to the homestead (*Bartold v. Lewandowska*, 1943).

While the homestead exemption benefits individuals, Michigan courts and legislators also believe that it serves important public interests. Preservation of the home is seen as essential to the preservation of freedom. As Senator Thomas H. Benton noted,

> Tenantry is unfavorable to freedom. It lays the foundation for separate orders in society, annihilates the love of country, and weakens the spirit of independence. The tenant has, in fact, no country, no hearth, no domestic altar, no household god. The freeholder, on the contrary, is the natural supporter of free government, and it should be the policy of republics to multiply their freeholders, as it is the policy of monarchies to multiple their tenants."[26]

## SECTION 4

> **Escheats.** Procedures relating to escheats and to the custody and disposition of escheated property shall be prescribed by law.

Escheated property is property that reverts to the state when no person is qualified to inherit the property. Section 4 requires the legislature to pass laws regulating the custody and disposition of escheats. The Michigan legislature has addressed the issue of escheated property in M.C.L.A. 567.11 et seq.

The Constitution of 1908, as amended in 1955, allowed the board of state auditors to act as a board of escheats. There have been no interpretations of this section.

---

[25] Convention Debates, 1850, p. 569.

[26] The Michigan Supreme Court quoted this excerpt from the Colorado decision of *McPhee v. O'Rourke*, 10 Col. 301, in *Kleinert v. Lefkowitz*, 1935.

## SECTION 5

**State lands.** The legislature shall have general supervisory jurisdiction over all state owned lands useful for forest preserves, game areas and recreational purposes; shall require annual reports as to such lands from all departments having supervision or control thereof; and shall by general law provide for the sale, lease or other disposition of such lands.

The legislature by an act adopted by two-thirds of the members elected to and serving in each house may designate any part of such lands as a state land reserve. No lands in the state land reserve may be removed from the reserve, sold, leased or otherwise disposed of except by an act of the legislature.

Section 5 is new to the constitution. As the *Address to the People* points out, this section is designed to recognize the public interest in state-owned lands and give the legislature general supervisory power over such state lands.

The legislature may designate any part of state lands as a state land reserve by a two-thirds majority of both houses of the state legislature. No land in the state land reserve can be sold or leased or otherwise disposed of without approval by an act of the legislature.

Various state statutes deal with state lands: State lands in general are addressed by M.C.L.A. sections 211.355a et seq. and 320.21 et seq.; state parks are treated in M.C.L.A. section 318.3 et seq.; forest reserves are covered by M.C.L.A. section 320.101 et seq.; and hunting grounds are covered by M.C.L.A. section 317.271 et seq. There have been no interpretations of this section.

## SECTION 6

**Resident aliens, property rights.** Aliens who are residents of this state shall enjoy the same rights and privileges in property as citizens of this state.

Michigan has had a long history of protecting the rights of aliens who reside in the state. The Constitution of 1850, in Article XVIII, section 13, protected property of aliens who are or who become bona fide residents of Michigan. This provision was designed to encourage immigration to Michigan. The 1908 Constitution continued these sentiments.

For the most part, Michigan courts rely on the equal protection clause of the Fourteenth Amendment to the federal Constitution in evaluating the rights and privileges of resident aliens. Any state classification based upon alienage is subject to strict judicial scrutiny under federal equal protection guarantees. Michigan courts rely on the federal model even when urged to consider the independent effect of section 6 (*Souri v. Department of Social Services*, 1987).

# Article XI

## *Public Officers and Employment*

### SECTION 1

**Oath of public officers.** All officers, legislative, executive and judicial, before entering upon the duties of their respective offices, shall take and subscribe the following oath or affirmation: I do solemnly swear (or affirm) that I will support the Constitution of the United States and the constitution of this state, and that I will faithfully discharge the duties of the office of ______ according to the best of my ability. No other oath, affirmation, or any religious test shall be required as a qualification for any office or public trust.

Every Michigan Constitution has required an oath of office for public officers. Section 1 represents an improvement of language from the oath of the Constitution of 1908.

For the purposes of the Michigan Constitution and state statutes,

> an oath is an external pledge or assertation made in verification of statements made, or to be made, coupled with an appeal to a sacred or venerated object, in evidence of the serious and reverent state of mind of the party, or with an invocation to a supreme being to witness the words of the party, or to visit him with punishment if they be false. (*June v. School District No. 11*, 1938)

Michigan's requirement of an oath of office applies broadly to all state officers, even to low level executive officers such as school officers (*People ex rel. Simmons v. Anderson*, 1917).

The final sentence of section 1 prohibits the state from requiring an additional oath, affirmation, or religious test as a prerequisite for public office. The purpose of this sentence is to abolish any political or religious requirements for holding public office. Other qualifications for public office, such as a residency requirement or the requirement that prosecuting attorneys be members of the state bar, do not qualify as "tests" within the meaning of Section 1 (*Attorney General, ex rel. Selby v. MacDonald*, 1911).

## SECTION 2

**Terms of office of state and county officers.** The terms of office of elective state officers, members of the legislature and justices and judges of courts of record shall begin at twelve o'clock noon on the first day of January next succeeding their election, except as otherwise provided in this constitution. The terms of office of county officers shall begin on the first day of January next succeeding their election, except as otherwise provided by law.

The Constitution of 1850 introduced provisions defining the terms of office of state and county officials. The 1963 Constitution improves the language of the 1908 document and includes a specification of the time of day at which a term of office commences. There have been no interpretations of this section.

## SECTION 3

**Extra compensation.** Neither the legislature nor any political subdivision of this state shall grant or authorize extra compensation to any public officer, agent or contractor after the service has been rendered or the contract entered into.

Section 3 traces its origins to the Constitution of 1850. As one panel of the Michigan Court of Appeals put it, section 3 expresses the strong public policy of the state against granting any additional payment to any public officer, agent, or contractor once a service has been rendered or a contract negotiated and signed (*Blue Water Excavating Company, Inc. v. State Highway Commissioner*, 1966). Section 3 was modified significantly by the framers of the 1963 Constitution. The Constitutions of 1850 and 1908 extended the prohibition against retroactive payments to state employees as well as public officers, agents, or contractors. By eliminating employees from the coverage of section 3, state workers may be given retroactive payments (*Attorney General Opinion No. 6643*, 1990).

The Michigan Supreme Court considered the meaning of extra compensation under the 1908 Constitution in *Attorney General v. Detroit Board of Education* (1923). Here, the court held that the 1908 equivalent of section 3 did not prohibit the board of education, by mutual agreement with teachers, from canceling teachers' contracts midway through a school year and entering into new contracts for the remainder of the year at a higher rate. Two other kinds of pay increases also do not offend the extra compensation proscription of section 3. A pay increase is valid if: (1) an increase in compensation is paid prospectively, and not retroactively, pursuant to an agreement or (2) the pay increase is part of an incremental salary contract, entered into prior to the performance of services, providing for additional compensation at set intervals during the contractual period (*Attorney General Opinion No. 5731*, 1980).

## SECTION 4

**Custodian of public moneys; eligibility to office, accounting.** No person having custody or control of public moneys shall be a member of the legislature, or be eligible to any office of trust or profit under this state, until he shall have made an accounting, as provided by law, of all sums for which he may be liable.

The Constitution of 1850 was the first Michigan Constitution to contain a provision such as section 4. This section prohibits a person controlling public money from holding a seat in the legislature or another office until that person has made an accounting of the public funds for which he or she is responsible. The legislature specifies by statute the procedure for accounting for public money. Article IX, sections 21 and 23 governing accounting of public moneys require that all financial records be open for public inspection. There have been no interpretations of this section.

## SECTION 5

**Classified state civil service; scope; exempted positions; appointment and terms of members of state civil service commission; state personnel director; duties of commission; collective bargaining for state police troopers and sergeants; appointments, promotions, demotions, or removals; increases or reductions in compensation; creating or abolishing positions; recommending compensation for unclassified service; appropriation; reports of expenditures; annual audit; payment for personal services; violation; injunctive or mandamus proceedings.** The classified state civil service shall consist of all positions in the state service except those filled by popular election, heads of principal departments, members of boards and commissions, the principal executive officer of boards and commissions heading principal departments, employees of courts of record, employees of the legislature, employees of the state institutions of higher education, all persons in the armed forces of the state, eight exempt positions in the office of the governor, and within each principal department, when requested by the department head, two other exempt positions, one of which shall be policy-making. The civil service commission may exempt three additional positions of a policy-making nature within each principal department.

The civil service commission shall be non-salaried and shall consist of four persons, not more than two of whom shall be members of the same political party, appointed by the governor for terms of eight years, no two of which shall expire in the same year.

The administration of the commission's powers shall be vested in a state personnel director who shall be a member of the classified service and who shall be responsible to and selected by the commission after open competitive examination.

The commission shall classify all positions in the classified service according to their respective duties and responsibilities, fix rates of compensation for all classes of positions, approve or disapprove disbursements for all personal services, determine by competitive examination and performance exclusively on the basis of merit, efficiency and fitness the qualifications of all candidates for positions in the classified service, make rules and regulations covering all personnel transactions, and regulate all conditions of employment in the classified service.

State Police Troopers and Sergeants shall, through their elected representative designated by 50% of such troopers and sergeants, have the right to bargain collectively with their employer concerning conditions of their employment, compensation, hours, working conditions, retirement, pensions, and other aspects of employment except promotions which will be determined by competitive examination and performance on the basis of merit, efficiency and fitness; and they shall have the right 30 days after commencement of such bargaining to submit any unresolved disputes to binding arbitration for the resolution thereof the same as now provided by law for Public Police and Fire Departments.

No person shall be appointed to or promoted in the classified service who has not been certified by the commission as qualified for such appointment or promotion. No appointments, promotions, demotions or removals in the classified service shall be made for religious, racial or partisan considerations.

Increases in rates of compensation authorized by the commission may be effective only at the start of a fiscal year and shall require prior notice to the governor, who shall transmit such increases to the legislature as part of his budget. The legislature may, by a majority vote of the members elected to and serving in each house, waive the notice and permit increases in rates of compensation to be effective at a time other than the start of a fiscal year. Within 60 calendar days following such transmission, the legislature may by a two-thirds vote of the members elected to and serving in each house, reject or reduce increases in the rates of compensation authorized by the commission. Any reduction ordered by the legislature shall apply uniformly to all classes of employees affected by the increases and shall not adjust pay differentials already established by the civil service commission. The legislature may not reduce rates of compensation below those in effect at the time of the transmission of increases authorized by the commission.

The appointing authorities may create or abolish positions for reasons of administrative efficiency without the approval of the commission. Positions shall not be created nor abolished except for reasons of administrative efficiency. Any employee considering himself aggrieved by the abolition or creation of a position shall have a right of appeal to the commission through established grievance procedures.

The civil service commission shall recommend to the governor and to the legislature rates of compensation for all appointed positions within the executive department not a part of the classified service.

To enable the commission to exercise its power, the legislature shall appropriate to the commission for the ensuing fiscal year a sum not less than one percent of the aggregate payroll of the classified service for the preceding fiscal year, as certified by the commission. Within six months after the conclusion of each fiscal year the commission shall return to the state treasury all moneys unexpended for that fiscal year.

The commission shall furnish reports of expenditures, at least annually, to the governor and the legislature and shall be subject to annual audit as provided by law.

No payment for personal services shall be made or authorized until the provisions of this constitution pertaining to civil service have been complied with in every particular. Violation of any of the provisions hereof may be restrained or observance compelled by injunctive or mandamus proceeding brought by any citizen of the state.

As the framers of the 1963 Constitution pointed out in the *Address to the People,* section 5 of this article continues "Michigan's national leadership among the states in public personnel practice." Section 5 governs the state's civil service system. This section is generally designed to limit political patronage by instituting a merit system (*Council 11, American Federation of State, County and Municipal Employees, AFL-CIO v. Michigan Civil Service Commission,* 1978) and encourage a career of service to state government.

Michigan instituted a constitutionally based state civil service system through a 1940 amendment to the Constitution of 1908, which became section 22 of Article VI. Michigan's earliest experience with a civil service system came in 1936 in response to the recommendations of a civil service study commission, which was appointed by Governor Frank D. Fitzgerald. The study commission condemned the "spoils" system and recommended the creation of a nonpartisan, merit-based system. A civil service act was passed by the state legislature, but so many exemptions were authorized by the legislature, that the number of classified positions in the civil service fell to just over 50 percent.[27] Popular disgust with the legislature's effort led to the constitutionalization of the civil service system. The 1940 amendment established a state civil service that included most state government employees. Only certain positions were exempt from the civil service: positions filled by popular election; heads of departments; members of boards and commissions; employees of courts of record, the legislature, or institutions of higher education; and persons in the armed forces of the state. A bipartisan, nonsalaried civil service commission was empowered to classify all positions in the state civil service and fix rates of compensation, as well as to administer, through a state personnel director, the civil service merit system. Candidates for office were to be evaluated on the basis of merit, efficiency, and fitness determined through competitive examination. The civil service was also responsible for making rules and regulations covering conditions of employment and personnel transactions. Section 22 specifically proscribed any removals or demotions in the state civil service for partisan, racial, or religious considerations.

The 1963 Constitution continues the basic framework of the 1940 amendment. Again, almost all state employees are covered by the civil service system. The specific employees exempt from the civil service system are listed in the first paragraph. The 1963 Constitution adds some new exempted positions: The office of the governor has eight exempted positions, and there may be three additional exempt policy-making positions within each principal department. These additional exemptions help strengthen the governor's control of the executive branch. The other exemptions, for employees of the other two branches of government and state colleges and universities of higher education, are designed to preserve the independence of these institutions. Persons in the armed forces are exempted because they are not part of the civil service There has been some controversy over the definition of "boards and commissions" in the list of exemptions. For the purposes of the exemptions of section 5, a board or commission may be one person or a group of persons. There is no requirement of collective action in the definition of a board or commission (*Michigan Civil Service Commission v. Michigan Department of Labor*, 1986).

The second paragraph specifies that the civil service commission shall have four members, no more than two of whom can be from the same political party. Commissioners are appointed by the governor, and they serve for eight-year terms. The terms of office for the commissioners are staggered to provide continuity in office. Commissioners do not receive a salary for their work.

The third paragraph covers the state personnel director who is charged with the administration of the powers of the civil service commission. The state personnel

---

[27] See Litchfield, "Another Chapter in Michigan Civil Service Reform," 25 *American Political Science Review* 76 (1941).

director must be a member of the classified civil service and be selected by the civil service commission after an open, competitive examination. While the state personnel director has important administrative authority, the final authority over the system is vested in the civil service commission (*Hardy v. State Personnel Director*, 1974).

The fourth paragraph describes the responsibilities of the civil service commission. As in the 1940 amendment, the civil service commission determines the qualifications of candidates for the civil service on the basis of merit, efficiency, and fitness through competitive examination and performance evaluation. Language from 1940 prohibiting removals or demotions for racial, religious, or partisan reasons has been moved to its own paragraph.

The commission has plenary authority to regulate matters such as: job specification, compensation, grievance procedures, discipline, collective bargaining, and job performance. The commission's "sphere of authority" covers on-the-job or job-related behavior, but the civil service commission's power does not extend to the authority to regulate or prohibit off-duty political activity by members of the classified civil service. As one court put it: "It is the purpose of the commission to keep politics out of the classified civil service, not to keep classified employees out of politics" (*Council 11, American Federation of State, County and Municipal Employees, AFL-CIO v. Michigan Civil Service Commission*, 1978).

The commission has plenary authority—limited only by constitutional concerns for due process—to determine procedures for the processing of grievances in the civil service system. Moreover, since the commission has constitutionally derived authority, the state legislature is without power to regulate the internal procedures of the civil service commission (*Viculin v. Department of Civil Service*, 1971).

The fifth paragraph was added in 1978 by initiative petition to allow state police troopers and sergeants to engage in collective bargaining. The state police troopers and sergeants elect a bargaining representative, who then bargains with the state over such matters as: conditions of employment, compensation, hours, working conditions, and retirement. However, promotions are not a subject of collective bargaining. Promotions must be determined by competitive examination and performance based on merit, efficiency, and fitness. This paragraph also provides for binding arbitration for the resolutions of disputes that may arise during collective bargaining.

The sixth paragraph reiterates the merit-based nature of the classified civil service: Only qualified individuals may be appointed to or promoted in the civil service. As in 1940, there is a constitutional proscription against personnel decisions based on race, religious, or partisan considerations.

The seventh paragraph of section 5 sets forth the procedures used for increases in compensation. The civil service commission authorizes compensation increases. The recommended increases can only take effect at the start of the fiscal year. The commission gives notice to the governor of its compensation increases. The governor then incorporates these figures into the budget, and the budget is sent to the state legislature. The legislature has a number of choices with respect to the compensation increases contained in the governor's budget. The legislature may, by simple majority vote, waive the notice required and allow increases to take effect at a time other than the start of the fiscal year. The legislature may also reject or reduce the increases in compensation authorized by the commission. Any rejection of reduction requires a two-thirds vote of members serving in each house of the legislature. The legislature must also act within 60 days of its receipt of the budget transmission. If the legislature chooses to reduce the authorized pay increases, it must abide by three rules: First, any reduction must apply uniformly to all classes of employees. Second, the legislature cannot adjust the pay differentials among the various classes of civil service employees that have already been established by the commission. Third, the legislature cannot reduce compensation rates below those already in effect at the time of the budget transmission.

The seventh paragraph allows appointing authorities to create or abolish positions without the approval of the civil service commission. The only allowable reason for such action is administrative efficiency. A civil service employee who feels harmed by the creation or abolition of a position can appeal the decision to the civil service commission through established grievance procedures.

The eighth paragraph deals with compensation for all appointed positions within the executive branch. While the commission cannot authorize compensation increases for nonclassified positions, the commission is entitled to make recommendations to the governor regarding these positions.

The ninth and tenth paragraphs provide for funds for the operation of the civil service commission and require any accounting for the expenditure of the funds. The legislature must appropriate to the commission each fiscal year an amount no less than 1 percent of the total payroll of the classified civil service. The commission must return to the state treasury any unexpended funds within six months of the close of the fiscal year.

The last paragraph of section 5 prohibits any payment for personnel until all the constitutional requirements governing the civil service have been met. Citizens are empowered to go to court to seek judicial enforcement of the constitutional requirements governing the civil service.

## SECTION 6

**Merit systems for local governments.** By ordinance or resolution of its governing body which shall not take effect until approved by a majority of the electors voting thereon, unless otherwise provided by charter, each county, township, city, village, school district and other governmental unit or authority may establish, modify or discontinue a merit system for its employees other than teachers under contract or tenure.

The state civil service commission may on request furnish technical services to any such unit on a reimbursement basis.

Section 6 is new to the constitution. This section allows political subdivisions in Michigan to establish, modify, or discontinue a civil service merit system if a majority of voters voting on the question approve the action. Teachers under contract or tenure are exempted from section 6. This section also allows political subdivisions to request and receive technical assistance from the state civil service commission. The state civil service commission may request that the political subdivision pay for the services it renders.

The Michigan Supreme Court reads section 6 as a provision that simply allows for the establishment, modification, or discontinuance of civil service merit systems in the various political subdivisions of the state without prior approval from the state legislature. The requirement of a vote of the electorate is designed to block local officials from unilaterally changing merit systems and, at the same time, to protect local employees from political purges. Section 6 is not seen as limiting the power of the state legislature under Article IV, section 48 of this constitution to pass laws governing the resolution of disputes involving public employees. Legislation passed pursuant to Article IV, section 48 (The Public Employment Relations Act, M.C.L.A. Section 423.201 et seq.) prevails over local civil service systems. Therefore, a collective bargaining agreement that has the effect of modifying a local civil service system is valid without an affirmative vote of the electorate (*Local 1383 of the International Association of Fire Fighters v. City of Warren and Police and Fire Civil Service Commission for the City of Warren*, 1981).

Section 6 does not prevent the state legislature from passing any laws relating to local civil service. This section simply allows units of local government to structure a civil service system. Once a local civil service system is in place, it is independent of state legislative control. The legislature may pass laws governing local civil service systems not organized under section 6 (*Council 23 A.F.S.C.M.E. v. Wayne County Civil Service Commission*, 1971).

## SECTION 7

**Impeachment of civil officers.** The house of representatives shall have the sole power of impeaching civil officers for corrupt conduct in office or for crimes or misdemeanors, but a majority of the members elected thereto and serving therein shall be necessary to direct an impeachment.

When an impeachment is directed, the house of representatives shall elect three of its members to prosecute the impeachment.

Every impeachment shall be tried by the senate immediately after the final adjournment of the legislature. The senators shall take an oath or affirmation truly and impartially to try and determine the impeachment according to the evidence. When the governor or lieutenant governor is tried, the chief justice of the supreme court shall preside.

No person shall be convicted without the concurrence of two-thirds of the senators elected and serving. Judgment in case of conviction shall not extend further than removal from office, but the person convicted shall be liable to punishment according to law.

No judicial officer shall exercise any of the functions of his office after an impeachment is directed until he is acquitted.

This section describes the impeachment process for civil officers. Each Michigan Constitution has provided for impeachment, with the general format unchanged since 1835.

Officials may be impeached for corrupt conduct in office or for crimes or misdemeanors. The state house of representatives has the sole power of impeachment with majority vote of the members elected to and serving in the house required for impeachment. Impeachment does not remove the accused official from office. A bill of impeachment is akin to an indictment by a grand jury. Just as a trial must follow the indictment, so also must impeachment: A trial of the accused official takes place in the state senate following impeachment.

The house of representatives elects three of its members to prosecute the impeachment before the state senate. This procedure was introduced in the Constitution of 1850. The state senators, who act as jurors, take an oath of affirmation to try the impeachment according to the evidence. Usually, the presiding officer of the senate presides over the impeachment trial. However, if the governor or lieutenant governor is on trial, then the chief justice of the state supreme court presides over the impeachment.

A two-thirds vote of senators elected to and serving in the senate is required for conviction. A conviction simply removes the accused official from office. Although the state senate cannot impose any other penalty, the convicted official is still liable to the legal process for any crimes committed in office and may be punished for them. The determination of guilt and the penalty for the misconduct is determined in a regular court of law using regular procedures.

Judicial officers cannot exercise any functions of the office after an impeachment is directed by the house of representatives. A judicial officer may resume the duties of office only after he or she has been acquitted by the senate. This provision is designed to preserve the integrity of the judiciary. The Constitution of 1850 introduced this innovation. There have been no interpretations of this section.

# Article XII

## *Amendment and Revision*

### SECTION 1

**Amendment by legislative proposal and vote of electors.** Amendments to this constitution may be proposed in the senate or house of representatives. Proposed amendments agreed to by two-thirds of the members elected to and serving in each house on a vote with the names and vote of those voting entered in the respective journals shall be submitted, not less than 60 days thereafter, to the electors at the next general election or special election as the legislature shall direct. If a majority of electors voting on a proposed amendment approve the same, it shall become part of the constitution at the end of 45 days after the date of the election at which it was approved.

Section 1 sets forth the first of two ways in which Michigan's Constitution may be amended: through the state legislature, with subsequent submission to the people for ratification. Each Michigan constitution has provided for constitutional amendments through the state legislature. The Constitution of 1835 required two rounds of legislative action before a proposed amendment could be submitted to the people. In the first round, the proposed amendment had to be approved by a simple majority of both houses of the state legislature. The proposed amendment was then submitted to the next elected legislature, which then had to approve the proposed amendment by a two-thirds vote. If a proposed amendment passed both rounds of legislative action, the amendment was submitted to the people. A simple majority of voters qualified to vote for the state legislature was sufficient to secure ratification. The Constitution of 1850 eliminated the first round of legislative action, requiring only a two-thirds vote of the legislature and ratification by a majority of the people. The Constitutions of 1908 and 1963 preserved the 1850 framework.

Under section 1, the state legislature first proposes amendments to the constitution; the people then must ratify the proposed amendments. The process of constitutional amendment may begin in either house of the legislature. Proposed amendments to the constitution must pass both houses of the legislature by a two-thirds majority after a roll call vote. After no less than 60 days pass after approval in the legislature, the proposed amendment must be submitted to the people for consideration at the next general election or a special election called by the legislature. A majority of voters voting on the question of the amendment must approve the amendment for it to become law. The amendment takes effect 45 days after the election at which it was approved.

The secretary of state is the state official charged by the constitution and associated statutes with the implementation of technical elements of constitutional amendment by both legislative proposal and popular initiative. M.C.L.A. sections 168.707 to 168.709 govern the implementation of section 1. The secretary of state has broad discretion in crafting ballot designations so long as the designation is impartial and fair. This discretion remains intact even in the case of constitutional amendments submitted to the people by joint resolution of the legislature. This secretary of state may prepare a ballot designation that differs from the text of the joint resolution passed by the legislature (*Graham v. Miller*, 1957).

The purpose of the 45-day delay before a constitutional amendment becomes effective is designed to enable the public to become acquainted with the new provision after it has been approved. Nothing in the constitution prevents the postponement of the effective date beyond the required 45 days. However, the postponed effective date must have been submitted to the people for their consideration when they voted on the constitutional amendment (*Attorney General Opinion No. 5533*, 1979).

## SECTION 2

**Amendment by petition and vote of electors.** Amendments may be proposed to this constitution by petition of the registered electors of this state. Every petition shall include the full text of the proposed amendment, and be signed by registered electors of the state equal in number to at least 10 percent of the total vote cast for all candidates for governor at the last preceding election at which a governor was elected.

Such petitions shall be filed with the person authorized by law to receive the same at least 120 days before the election at which the proposed amendment is to be voted upon. Any such petition shall be in the form, and shall be signed and circulated in such manner, as prescribed by law. The person authorized by law to receive such petition shall upon its receipt determine, as provided by law, the validity and sufficiency of the signatures on the petition, and make an official announcement thereof at least 60 days prior to the election at which the proposed amendment is to be voted upon.

Any amendment proposed by such petition shall be submitted, not less than 120 days after it was filed, to the electors at the next general election. Such a proposed amendment, existing provisions of the constitution which would be altered or abrogated thereby, and the question as it shall appear on the ballot shall be published in full as provided by law. Copies of such publication shall be posted in each polling place and furnished to news media as provided by law.

The ballot to be used in such election shall contain a statement of the purpose of the proposed amendment, expressed in not more than 100 words, exclusive of caption. Such statement of purpose and caption shall be prepared by the person authorized by law, and shall consist of a true and impartial statement of the purpose of the amendment in such language as shall create no prejudice for or against the proposed amendment.

If the proposed amendment is approved by a majority of the electors voting on the question, it shall become part of the constitution, and shall abrogate or amend existing provisions of the constitution at the end of 45 days after the date of the election at which it was approved. If two or more amendments approved by the electors at the same election conflict, that amendment receiving the highest affirmative vote shall prevail.

Section 2 provides a second mode of constitutional amendment, namely amendment initiated by the people through petitions.

Registered voters of Michigan may petition for constitutional amendment. The petition must contain the full text of the proposed amendment and be signed by at least 10 percent of the total vote cast for governor at the last election in which a governor was chosen. The state legislature is given the power to fill in the details governing the form and manner of circulating the petitions. The legislature also designates the person authorized to receive the petitions. M.C.L.A. section 168.471 et seq. governs the petition process and designates the secretary of state as the person in charge of the receipt of the petitions. The secretary of state then determines whether or not there are enough valid signatures on the petition. If the number of signatures is sufficient, the secretary of state makes an official announcement to this effect at least 60 days before the election at which the amendment is to be voted upon. This deadline is designed to facilitate the electoral process by giving the secretary of state and county clerks enough time to print and distribute ballots and to prepare the voting machinery for election day. The Michigan Supreme Court has refused to let the 60-day deadline thwart the constitutional initiative. The supreme court will not allow opponents of an amendment to "misuse the judicial process" by waiting until the last minute to challenge proposed amendments on technical grounds (*Ferency v. Secretary of State*, 1980).

An amendment proposed by petition must be submitted to the people for a vote not less than 120 days after it was filed. The proposed amendment must be published along with provisions of the existing constitution that will be altered or revoked by amendment. The wording of the ballot question about the amendment must also be published, provided to the news media, and posted at each polling place.

The secretary of state is charged with developing for inclusion on the ballot a short statement of the purpose of the proposed amendment. The statement cannot be more than 100 words long. The statement must be an accurate and impartial representation of purpose of the amendment so that voters are not prejudiced for or against the amendment.

A proposed amendment must be approved by a majority of voters voting on the amendment. If two or more amendments approved by the voters at the same elections conflict, then the amendment receiving the higher number of votes prevails.

Provisions for constitutional amendment by petition were added to the 1908 Constitution in 1913 as a Progressive Era reform. The 1963 revision eliminates statutory-type language and leaves the details of implementation to the legislature. The 1963 Constitution also adds the section that covers the case when two approved amendments conflict with each other.

Michigan courts profess a reluctance to strike down amendments proposed by the constitutional initiative for technical reasons (*City of Jackson v. Commissioner of Revenue*, 1947). Michigan courts will also construe the provisions of section 2 liberally in order to protect the right of the people to propose amendments to their constitution.

Almost any subject is fair game for proposal for inclusion in the constitution through initiative petition. If a subject is typically addressed through a statute rather than a constitutional provision, Michigan courts will allow the constitutional amendment process to go forward—even though the Michigan Constitution allows for the statutory initiative in Article II, section 9 (*City of Jackson v. Commissioner of Revenue*, 1947). A proposed amendment may also include more than one subject (*Graham v. Miller*, 1957).

The words "altered or abrogated" in the second paragraph mean that the proposed constitutional amendment amends or replaces another provision in the constitution (*District of the City of Pontiac v. City of Pontiac*, 1933). Only the constitutional provisions specifically amended or replaced need to be published along with the proposed amendment. It is possible that no provision of the constitution will be altered or abrogated by a proposed amendment, as was the case when the people added a civil service system to the constitution in

1941 (*DeMaggio v. Attorney General,* 1941). Michigan courts have recognized that a proposed constitutional amendment may affect the construction of other sections of the constitution without actually amending or abrogating them. Sections affected in this manner need not be published (*Ferency v. Secretary of State,* 1980; *City of Jackson v. Commissioner of Revenue,* 1947).

The purpose of the 45-day delay before a constitutional amendment becomes effective is designed to enable the public to become acquainted with the new provision after it has been approved. Nothing in the constitution prevents the postponement of the effective date beyond the required 45 days. However, the postponed effective date must have been submitted to the people for their consideration when they voted on the constitutional amendment (*Attorney General Opinion No.* 5533, 1979).

Section 2 is regarded as self-executing; that is, it does not depend on statutory implementation (*Ferency v. Secretary of State,* 1980). Qualified voters of the state may propose constitutional amendments, without curtailments, undue burdens, and interference from the legislature, subject to the procedures and limitations in the constitution (*Hamilton v. Secretary of State,* 1924; *Scott v. Secretary of State,* 1918). Even though section 2 is seen as self-executing, the language of the section clearly authorizes the legislature to provide for the manner of signing and circulating petitions to propose constitutional amendments. The power allows the legislature to pass a law (M.C.L.A. 168.472a) providing that a signature on an initiative petition is stale and void after 180 days (*Consumers Power Company v. Attorney General,* 1986).

## SECTION 3

**General revision of constitution; submission of question, convention of delegates and meeting.** At the general election to be held in the year 1978, and in each 16th year thereafter and at such times as may be provided by law, the question of a general revision of the constitution shall be submitted to the electors of the state. If a majority of the electors voting on the question decide in favor of a convention for such a purpose, at an election to be held not later than six months after the proposal was certified as approved, the electors of each representative district as then organized shall elect one delegate and the electors of each senatorial district as then organized shall elect one delegate at a partisan election. The delegates so elected shall convene at the seat of government on the first Tuesday in October next succeeding such election or at an earlier date if provided by law.

The convention shall choose its own officers, determine the rules of its proceedings and judge the qualifications, election and returns of its members. To fill a vacancy in the office of any delegate, the governor shall appoint a qualified resident of the same district who shall be a member of the same party as the delegate vacating the office. The convention shall have power to appoint such officers, employees and

> assistants as it deems necessary and to fix their compensation; to provide for the printing and distribution of its documents, journals and proceedings; to explain and disseminate information about the proposed constitution and to complete the business of the convention in an orderly manner. Each delegate shall receive for his services compensation provided by law.
>
> No proposed constitution or amendment adopted by such convention shall be submitted to the electors for approval as hereinafter provided unless by the assent of a majority of all the delegates elected to and serving in the convention, with the names and vote of those voting entered in the journal. Any proposed constitution or amendment adopted by such convention shall be submitted to the qualified electors in the manner and at the time provided by such convention not less than 90 days after final adjournment of the convention. Upon the approval of such constitution or amendments by a majority of the qualified electors voting thereon the convention or amendments shall take effect as provided by the convention.

Thomas Jefferson thought that each generation should reconsider its fundamental laws. Michigan has heeded Jefferson's advice. The Constitution of 1835 first provided for a mechanism for calling constitutional conventions. Under the 1835 Constitution, a two-thirds majority of both houses of the legislature could recommend to the voters calling a constitutional convention. A majority vote of people voting in the election was required to approve calling the convention. The legislature was then bound to convene the convention within six months. The 1835 Constitution also required that the number of delegates to the convention could not be less than the number of the members of both houses of the legislature. The Constitution of 1850 made reconsideration of the constitution a regular feature of Michigan politics. The 1850 document introduced the requirement that the people be given the opportunity to consider general constitutional revision every sixteen years. A majority vote of people qualified to vote for members of the legislature voting in the election was needed to call for the convention. If the call for a convention was successful, the legislature was compelled to provide for the election of delegates to the convention at the next session. A new constitution would become effective one year after its adoption. As originally adopted, the Constitution of 1908 followed the 1850 framework with respect to the requirements to call a constitutional convention. The 1908 version also added language setting for the governance of the constitutional convention. The 1908 Constitution defined a quorum, set a $1,000 salary with a mileage allowance for delegates, and empowered the convention to develop its own rules of procedure.

Despite their provisions for putting the question of general constitutional revision before the people, until 1960, all of Michigan's constitutions contained a flaw. Each constitution calculated the majority vote needed to call for a convention by dividing the number of voters approving the convention call by the number of voters voting in the election. There is a well-known phenomenon in elections called "ballot fall-off." Ballot fall-off occurs when voters fail to vote for offices and proposals that appear towards the end of a lengthy ticket. It is not uncommon for a voter to vote for major offices, such as president, governor, or senator, and neglect choosing a candidate for a judgeship or voting on ballot proposals. Ballot proposals appear at the very end of the ballot. Because of ballot fall-off, Michigan could secure the majority needed to call a constitutional convention in the 1950s. The Gateway Amendments of 1960 revised the way in which the majority was counted. Under the Gateway Amendments, the majority needed to call for a constitutional convention was defined as the majority of voters voting on the question of a convention. Approval of the Gateway Amendments allowed for the convening of the Constitutional Convention of 1961–1962.[28]

Section 3 requires that every sixteen years the people shall be presented with an opportunity for general constitutional revision. If a majority of voters voting on the question of revision agree, then Michigan must convene a constitutional convention.

Once called, a constitutional convention has supreme power. No branch of government can control its deliberations or actions. The constitution sets forth a limited role for the legislature in constitutional amendment. The legislature may submit a single amendment as in section 1 of this article. The legislature also submits to the people the question of general constitutional revisions every sixteen years. Finally, the legislature provides for the election of delegates to a constitutional convention should the people approve one (*Carton v. Secretary of State*, 1908).

The convention has full control over its officers and its business. In describing the autonomy of the convention, Michigan courts have quoted from Robert Livingston speaking at the New York Constitutional Convention of 1821: "The people are here themselves. They are present in their delegates. No restriction limits our proceedings—we are standing on the foundation of society" (*Carton v. Secretary of State*, 1908).

## SECTION 4

**Severability.** If any section, subsection or part of Article 2, Section 10, Article 4, Section 54 or Article 5, Section 30 is for any reason held to be invalid or unconstitutional, the remaining section, subsections or parts of those sections shall not be affected but will remain in full force and effect. Amendment approved November 3, 1992. Effective December 19, 1992

[28] For a discussion of the politics of the Gateway Amendments, see the constitutional history at the beginning of this book.

In 1992, Michigan voters ratified constitutional amendments providing for term limits for members of the Congress (Article II, section 10), members of the state legislature (Article IV, section 54), and the governor and other executive officers (Article V, section 30). This addition to the constitution preserves as much of those amendments as possible if any element of them is declared unconstitutional (see the constitutional commentary for each of these sections).

# Schedule and Temporary Provisions

As explained in its preamble, the Schedule and Temporary Provisions were written to provide for the transition from the old constitution to the new constitution. The Schedule and Temporary Provisions are no longer needed. They are printed for historical interest only.

To insure the orderly transition from the constitution of 1908 to this constitution the following schedule and temporary provisions are set forth for such period as are thereby required.

## SECTION 1

**Recommendations by attorney general for changes in laws.** The attorney general shall recommend to the legislature as soon as practicable such changes as may be necessary to adapt existing laws to this constitution.

## SECTION 2

**Existing public and private rights, continuance.** All writs, actions, suits, proceedings, civil or criminal liabilities, prosecutions, judgments, sentences, orders, decrees, appeals, causes of action, contracts, claims, demands, titles and rights existing on the effective date of this constitution shall continue unaffected except as modified in accordance with the provisions of this constitution.

## SECTION 3

**Officers, continuance in office.** Except as otherwise provided in this constitution, all officers filling any office by election or appointment shall continue to exercise their powers and duties until their offices have been abolished or their successors selected and qualified in accordance with this constitution or the laws enacted pursuant thereto.

No provision of this constitution, or of law or of executive order authorized by this constitution shall shorten the term of any person elected to state office at a statewide election on or prior to the date on which this constitution is submitted to a vote. In the event the duties of any such officers shall not have been abolished or incorporated into one or more of the principal departments at the expiration of his term, such officer shall continue to serve until his duties are so incorporated or abolished.

## SECTION 4

**Officers elected in spring of 1963, term.** All officers elected at the same election that this constitution is submitted to the people for adoption shall take office and complete the term to which they were elected under the 1908 Constitution and existing law and continue to serve until their successors are elected and qualified pursuant to this constitution.

## SECTION 5

**State elective executive officers and senators, two-and four-year terms.** Notwithstanding any other provision in this constitution, the governor, the lieutenant governor, the secretary of state, the attorney general and state senators shall be elected at the general election in 1964 to serve for two-year terms beginning on the first day of January next succeeding their election. The first election of such officers for four-year terms under this constitution shall be held at the general election in 1966.

## SECTION 6

**Supreme court, reduction to seven justices.** Notwithstanding the provisions of this constitution that the supreme court shall consist of seven justices it shall consist of eight justices until the time that a vacancy occurs as a result of death, retirement or resignation of a justice. The first such vacancy shall not be filled.

## SECTION 7

**Judges of probate, eligibility for re-election.** Any judge of probate serving on the effective date of this constitution may serve the remainder of the term and be eligible to succeed himself for election regardless of other provisions in this constitution requiring him to be licensed to practice law in this state.

## SECTION 8

**Judicial officers, staggered terms.** The provisions of Article VI providing that terms of judicial office shall not all expire at the same time, shall be implemented by law providing that at the next election for such officers judges shall be elected for terms of varying length, none of which shall be shorter than the regular term provided for the office.

## SECTION 9

**State board of education; first election, terms.** The members of the state board of education provided for in Section 3 of Article VIII of this constitution shall first be elected at the first general election after the effective date of this constitution for the following terms: two shall be elected for two years; two for four years; two for six years, and two for eight years as prescribed by law.

The state board of education provided for in the constitution of 1908 is abolished at twelve o'clock noon January 1 of the year following the first general election under this constitution and the terms of members thereof shall then expire.

## SECTION 10

**Boards controlling higher education institutions and state board of public community and junior colleges, terms.** The provisions of this constitution providing for members of boards of control of institutions of higher education and the state board of public community and junior colleges shall be implemented by law. The law may provide that the term of each member in office on the date of the vote on this constitution may be extended, and may further provide that the initial terms of office of members may be less than eight years.

## SECTION 11

**Michigan State University trustees and Wayne State University governors, terms.** The provision of this constitution increasing the number of members of the Board of Trustees of Michigan State University and of the Board of Governors of

Wayne State University to eight, and of their term of office to eight years, shall be implemented by law. The law may provide that the term of each member in office on the date of the vote on this constitution may be extended one year, and may further provide that the initial terms of office of the addition members may be less than eight years.

## SECTION 12

**Initial allocation of departments by law or executive order.** The initial allocation of department by law pursuant to Section 2 of Article V of this constitution, shall be completed within two years after the effective date of this constitution. If such allocation shall not have been completed within such period, the governor, within one year thereafter, by executive order, shall make the initial allocation.

## SECTION 13

**State contracts, continuance.** Contractual obligation of the state incurred pursuant to the constitution of 1908 shall continue to be obligations of the state.

For the retirement of notes and bonds issued under Section 26 of Article X of the 1908 Constitution, there is hereby appropriated from the general fund each year during their life a sum equal to amount of principal and interest payments due and payable in each year.

## SECTION 14

**Mackinac Bridge Authority; refunding of bonds, transfer of functions to highway department.** The legislature by a vote of two-thirds of the members elected to and serving in each house may provide that the state may borrow money and may pledge its full faith and credit for refunding any bonds issued by the Mackinac Bridge Authority and at the time of refunding the Mackinac Bridge Authority shall be abolished and the operation of the bridge shall be assumed by the state highway department. The legislature may implement this section by law.

## SECTION 15

**Submission of constitution; time, notice.** This constitution shall be submitted to the people for their adoption or rejection at the general election to be held on the first Monday in April, 1963. It shall be the duty of the secretary of state forthwith to give notice of such submission to all other officers required to give or publish any notice in regard to a general election. He shall give notice that this constitution will be duly submitted to the electors at such election. The notice shall be given in the manner required for the election of governor.

## SECTION 16

**Voters, ballots, effective date.** Every registered elector may vote on the adoption of the constitution. The board of election commissioners in each county shall cause to be printed on a ballot separate from the ballot containing the names of the nominees for office, the words: Shall the revised constitution be adopted? ( ) Yes. ( ) No. All votes cast at the election shall be taken, counted, canvassed and returned as provided by law for the election of state officers. If the revised constitution so submitted receives more votes in its favor than were cast against it, it shall be the supreme law of the state on and after the first day of January of the year following its adoption.

*Adopted by the Constitutional Convention of nineteen hundred sixty-one at Constitution Hall in Lansing on the first day of August, nineteen hundred sixty-two.*

*The vote on the Constitution of 1963, as certified by the Board of State Canvassers on June 20, 1963, was 810,860 to 803,436 in favor of its adoption.*

# ■ SELECTED ANNOTATED BIBLIOGRAPHY


## GENERAL HISTORIES

Bald, F. Clever. *Michigan in Four Centuries* (New York: Harper and Row, 1954). Designed for the general reader and illustrated with maps and line drawings, Bald's book is a quick tour of Michigan history from the time of the woolly mammoth to the 1950s. The book contains a chronology, a table of governors, and a good, topical bibliography. The index is a marvelous example of almost compulsive attention to detail.

Campbell, James V. *Outlines of the Political History of Michigan* (Detroit: Schober and Company, 1876). Campbell's book is a hastily generated work written for Michigan's Centennial Committee. The book's best contributions are on early state history, particularly the Ordinance of 1787, the border dispute with Ohio, and the struggle for admission to the Union.

Cooley, Thomas McIntyre. *Michigan: A History of Governments* (Boston: Houghton, Mifflin and Co., 1885). Cooley's volume was part of the American Commonwealth series designed to provide a political, social, and "economical" history of the states. The work traces constitutional history through 1850 with ample insightful editorializing from Michigan's most famous legal scholar.

Dunbar, Willis F. and George S. May. *Michigan: A History of the Wolverine State*, rev. ed. (Grand Rapids, MI: William B. Eerdmans Publishing Co., 1980). This comprehensive state history contains sections on the development of all of Michigan's constitutions. The book is particularly valuable for the political environment of the 1961 Constitutional Convention. Dunbar and May is probably the standard starting point for those interested in Michigan history.

Fuller, George N. *Michigan: A Centennial History of the State and Its People* (Chicago: The Lewis Publishing Company, 1939). Fuller's illustrated work is most valuable for late-nineteenth-century political history, particularly the Constitutions of 1850 and 1908 as well as the failed efforts at constitutional revision in between the two constitutions. Each chapter contains a bibliography, and the book includes an elaborate index.

## GENERAL CONSTITUTIONAL ANALYSIS

Campbell, Henry M. "The Initiative and Referendum," *Michigan Law Review* 10 (1912): 427–36. Campbell's early antipopulist tract gives all the standard arguments against direct democracy. Despite the age of the piece, the criticisms are still very cogent.

Coutts, W. A. "Is a Provision for the Initiative and Referendum Inconsistent with the Constitution of the United States?" *Michigan Law Review* 6 (1908): 305–17. For the most part, Coutts's article is a polemic in favor of populist reform. He does address a novel and important constitutional issue (vintage early twentieth century) for direct democracy: Do the initiative and referendum conflict with the Republican guarantee clause of the federal Constitution? The answer is a resounding no.

Grossman, Barbara. "The Initiative and Referendum Process: The Michigan Experience," *Wayne Law Review* 28 (1981): 77–136. This article is the single best guide to initiative and referendum in Michigan. Grossman clearly explains the constitutional law, legislative implementation, and administrative requirements for the initiative and referendum. The extensive footnotes give the reader much guidance for additional reading on the initiative and referendum in general, in Michigan in particular, and the operation of both processes in other states.

Zalman, Marvin. "The Rise and Fall of the Indeterminate Sentence," *Wayne Law Review* 24 (1977): 44–94. Although a general tour of the development of indeterminate sentences in the United States, Zalman also includes a detailed section on Michigan's experience with this reform. Zalmam carefully describes the Michigan Supreme Court decision, *People v. Cummings,* that caused the 1850 Constitution to be amended to accommodate indeterminate sentences.

## CONSTITUTIONS AND CONSTITUTIONAL CONVENTIONS

Dorr, Harold M., ed. *The Michigan Constitutional Conventions of 1835–36: Debates and Proceedings* (Ann Arbor: The University of Michigan Press, 1940). Dorr's introductory essay on Michigan's first constitutional convention is essential reading for anyone interested in the state's constitutional history. The material from the constitutional convention is well indexed, and the volume contains a table of delegates and all their recorded votes.

Fairlie, John A. "The Michigan Constitutional Convention of 1907–1908," *American Political Science Review* 2 (1908): 443–47. Fairlie provides a brief, journalistic account of this constitutional convention including a portrait of the delegates and highlights of the debates.

Gardner, Washington, comp. *Constitution of the State of Michigan with Side Notes, Annotations and Index* (Lansing, MI: Robert Smith and Company, State Printers and Binders, 1895). Prepared by the Michigan Secretary of State, this volume is not a true annotated constitution but a reprint of the Constitution of 1850 with its amendments to 1894. The book is valuable for its listing of court decisions on each section of the constitution and is the best guide to the interpretation of the 1850 Constitution.

## THE 1963 CONSTITUTION

Reams of material were generated in preparation for the 1961–1962 Michigan Constitutional Convention. Although some works were designed to be permanent bound volumes, much of the material appeared in pamphlet form and hence might be difficult to find.

*A Comparative Analysis of the Michigan Constitution, Volumes I and II* (Detroit: Citizens Research Council of Michigan, Report No. 208, October 1961). This work is an invaluable research guide to the evolution of the Michigan Constitution. Prepared for the 1961–1962 Constitutional Convention, both volumes trace the evolution of the various provisions of the state constitution and compare the provisions with similar provisions in other states and the Model State Constitution prepared by the National Municipal League.

*Con Con: A Special Reading List* (Lansing, MI: The State Library of Michigan, 1961). *Con Con* is an elaborate, annotated bibliography developed for delegates to the 1961–1962 Constitutional Convention. This bibliography includes books, monographs, unpublished Ph.D. dissertations, articles from journals and law reviews, and government documents from other states. Major topics include: legislative reapportionment, civil service in state constitutions, state tax earmarking, the executive branch, the legislature, local government, and the judiciary.

Cramton, Roger C. "The Powers of the Michigan Civil Rights Commission," *Michigan Law Review* 63 (November 1964): 5–58. This is a comprehensive analysis of the civil rights commission added to the 1963 Constitution. The article does a thorough job articulating the intent of the framers of the civil rights commission provision and explaining the powers of the commission.

Friedman, Robert S. *The Michigan Constitutional Convention and Administrative Organization: A Case Study in the Politics of Constitution-Making* (Ann Arbor: University of Michigan, Institute of Public Administration, Michigan Governmental Studies No. 44, 1963). This title is another example of truth-in-advertising: the title describes precisely the contents of the book. The value of the book lies in its description of the political alignments at the convention plus interest group involvement. The book places particular emphasis on the article on the executive branch.

*Michigan Constitutional Issues* (Detroit: Citizens Research Council of Michigan, Report No. 201, June 1960). This slim volume presents both sides of the debate on the various questions likely to surface at the constitutional convention. The book attempts to remain neutral but the reform slant occasionally appears. Despite its brevity, the book is an excellent guide to the major issues that prompted constitutional change.

Nord, Melvin. "The Michigan Constitution of 1963," *Wayne Law Review* 10 (Winter 1964): 309–67. Written by a delegate to the 1961–1962 convention and intended primarily for lawyers, this article compares the new constitution to earlier state constitutions. Nord's article also contains some information on the intent of the framers of the 1963 Constitution and some potential legal problems that may arise in relation to statutes passed under the old 1908 Constitution.

Pealy, Robert H., ed. *The Voter and the Michigan Constitution in 1958* (Ann Arbor: University of Michigan, Bureau of Government, Institute of Public Administration, Michigan Pamphlets No. 27, 1958). This volume of six essays by political scientists explains the deficiencies in the 1908 Constitution and why a new constitution is not only desirable but necessary. Essays cover the arguments for and against constitutional change, the executive branch, the legislative article, the judicial article, and the provisions on local government and finance. Each essay contains a valuable selection of references.

Pollock, James K. *Making Michigan's New Constitution 1961–62* (Ann Arbor: The George Wahr Publishing Company, 1962). Professor Pollack was a prominent Republican delegate to the convention. Here he presents his personal remembrances and analyses of the work of the convention.

Stieber, Carolyn. *Focus on Con-Con* (East Lansing: Michigan State University, College of Business and Public Service, Bureau of Social and Political Research, 1961). Stieber's brief essay outlines the reasons for the 1961–1962 Constitutional Convention, areas of likely constitutional change, and the work of interest groups in amending the 1908 Constitution to facilitate calling a constitutional convention.

Sturm, Albert L. *Constitution-Making in Michigan 1961–62* (Ann Arbor: University of Michigan, Institution of Public Administration, Michigan Governmental Studies No. 43, 1963). Here, Sturm tells everything you could conceivably need to know about the 1961–1962 convention. The first chapter contains a brief history of Michigan constitutional development, and subsequent chapters detail the issues and procedures of the last convention. Appendices include a list of the delegates, convention committees and their membership, the convention budget, and even a floor plan of the seating arrangements at Constitution Hall.

Sturm, Albert L. *Methods of State Constitutional Reform* (Ann Arbor: University of Michigan, Institute of Public Administration, Michigan Governmental Studies No. 28, 1954). Sturm's work is an excellent primer on state constitution-making. The book includes information on the nature of a state constitution, methods of change (such as via legislative proposal, constitutional initiative, and constitutional convention) and the operation of a constitutional convention. The comparative information from the states and Puerto Rico is summarized in clear tables and is particularly valuable.

Sturm, Albert L. and Margaret Whitaker. *Implementing a New Constitution: The Michigan Experience* (Ann Arbor: University of Michigan, Institute of Public Administration, Michigan Governmental Studies, No. 50, 1968). This book is exactly what the title says it is: an analysis of the implementation of the new constitution. The initial chapter contains useful information on the adoption of the new constitution including the campaign for ratification and an analysis of voting patterns. The book's most valuable contribution is its discussion of the reapportionment debate at the convention and its aftermath, including litigation in the state courts and the impact of the United States Supreme Court's decision in *Reynolds v. Sims*.

Wilson, Andrew F. "Citizenship vs. the Power Groups: A Review of the Citizens for Michigan," *Historical Society Chronicle* 21 (1985): 21–29. Wilson's piece highlights the involvement of interest groups, particularly the Citizens for Michigan, in securing the Gateway Amendment and the 1961–1962 Constitutional Convention. The article contains a useful sidebar on the financial crisis of the late 1950s.

## THE MICHIGAN CONSTITUTIONAL CONVENTION STUDIES

In preparation for the 1961–1962 Constitutional Convention, the State of Michigan commissioned a number of studies to guide the deliberations of the delegates. The studies were funded by the Kellogg Foundation. The quality and usefulness of the studies vary with the author but, taken as a whole, they form an excellent guide to issues in state constitutional law. Unfortunately, the studies may be difficult to obtain. Interested readers should try the main branch of the Detroit Public Library, the state library in Lansing, and the research collections of the state universities. The studies are probably noncirculating and may be housed in the rare book collection, as they are at the Wayne State University Law Library. The following studies appear in the collection. The titles of the papers adequately explain their content.

1. Alfred H. Kelly. "The Meaning of Constitutional Government."
2. William J. Pierce and James B. Lowe. "Constitutional Convention Powers."
3. William J. Pierce. "A Prepared Manual of Organization and Procedure for State Constitutional Convention."
4. Sidney Glazer. "Rejected Amendments to the Michigan Constitution 1910–1961."
5. Charles Shull. "The Declaration of Rights in the Michigan Constitution."
6. John P. White. "The Elective Franchise and the Michigan Constitution."
7. Herbert Garfinkel. "The Constitution and the Legislature."
8. Albert L. Sturm and Fred S. Steingold. "The Executive and the Civil Service in the Michigan Constitution."
9. Charles W. Joiner. "The Michigan Constitution and the Judiciary."
10. Louis L. Friedland. "Local Government and the Michigan Constitution."
11. Donald J. Leu. "Elementary and Secondary Education and the Michigan Constitution."
12. Raleigh Barlowe. "Taxation and Fiscal Policy in the Michigan Constitution."

13. Solomon Bienenfeld. "The Michigan Constitution and Eminent Domain."
14. Robert E. Childs. "State Constitutional Provisions on Exemptions."
15. Alfred F. Conrad, Richard W. Ogders, and Timothy F. Scanlon. "Corporations and the Michigan Constitution."
16. "Legislative Apportionment in Michigan."
17. Daniel S. McHargue. "Direct Government in Michigan: Initiative, Referendum, Recall and Revision in the Michigan Constitution."
18. "Miscellaneous Problems"
    a. George S. May. "Boundaries."
    b. Charles W. Joiner and Jon F. DeWitt. "Impeachment and Removal in Michigan."
    c. Charles W. Joiner and Jon F. DeWitt. "Memorandum Concerning Article XVI of the Michigan Constitution." (Article XVI contains the Miscellaneous provisions on the Constitution of 1908.)

## MISCELLANEOUS

Lamb, Karl A., William J. Pierce, and Joseph P. White. *Apportionment and Representative Institutions: The Michigan Experience*. (Washington, D.C.: The Institute for Social Science Research, 1963). The U.S. Supreme Court's decision on legislative apportionment in *Baker v. Carr* (1962) figured prominently at the 1961–62 Constitutional Convention. This work provides a detailed overview of apportionment litigation plus the history of legislative apportionment under Michigan's earlier constitutions. The book also speculates on the impact of the new constitution on representation and politics. There is a valuable introductory comparative section on apportionment in other states.

# ■ TABLE OF CASES

## A

## B

## C

## D

## E



## F



## G



## H

## I



## J

## K



## L



## M

## N

## O

## P

## R



## S

## T



## U

## V



## W



## Y

# INDEX

## About the Author

SUSAN P. FINO is Associate Professor of Political Science at Wayne State University, where she teaches constitutional law and American government. Fino is a specialist in state constitutional law and has written extensively on the subject, including *The Role of State Supreme Courts* (Greenwood, 1987).

www.ingramcontent.com/pod-product-compliance
Ingram Content Group UK Ltd.
Pitfield, Milton Keynes, MK11 3LW, UK
UKHW021135160926
475595UK00020B/76

9 780199 779086